Counseling for Artists, Performers, and Other Creative Individuals

Informed by clinical case studies, scientific research, and relevant theories, *Counseling for Artists, Performers, and Other Creative Individuals* takes an in-depth look at the ways creative traits, the arts-and-entertainment industry, and mental health interact. This hands-on guide examines many of the issues that afflict creative populations, such as performance anxiety, psychiatric disorders, and occupational stress, with a nuanced understanding of the roles that creativity and the arts play in the lives of these individuals. Each chapter provides examples of specific goals and interventions for clinical practice, including additional space for clinicians to write down ideas tailored to their clients' unique needs. This is essential reading for practitioners looking to treat creative clients' psychological difficulties with insight and sensitivity.

Olga E. Gonithellis, MA, LMHC, is a psychotherapist in private practice in New York City, where she specializes in counseling artists, performers, and other creative individuals.

Counseling for Artists, Performers, and Other Creative Individuals

A Guide for Clinicians

Olga E. Gonithellis

NEW YORK AND LONDON

First published 2018
by Routledge
711 Third Avenue, New York, NY 10017

and by Routledge
2 Park Square, Milton Park, Abingdon, Oxon, OX14 4RN

Routledge is an imprint of the Taylor & Francis Group, an informa business

© 2018 Olga E. Gonithellis

The right of Olga E. Gonithellis to be identified as author
of this work has been asserted by her in accordance with
sections 77 and 78 of the Copyright, Designs and Patents Act
1988.

All rights reserved. No part of this book may be reprinted
or reproduced or utilised in any form or by any electronic,
mechanical, or other means, now known or hereafter invented,
including photocopying and recording, or in any information
storage or retrieval system, without permission in writing
from the publishers.

Trademark notice: Product or corporate names may be
trademarks or registered trademarks, and are used only for
identification and explanation without intent to infringe.

Library of Congress Cataloging-in-Publication Data
Names: Gonithellis, Olga E., author.
Title: Counseling for artists, performers, and other creative
   individuals : a guide for clinicians / by Olga E. Gonithellis.
Description: New York, NY : Routledge, 2018. | Includes
   bibliographical references and index.
Identifiers: LCCN 2017058545 (print) | LCCN 2018005293 (ebook) |
   ISBN 9781315173566 (eBook) | ISBN 9781138735330 (hbk) |
   ISBN 9781138735354 (pbk) | ISBN 9781315173566 (ebk)
Subjects: LCSH: Artists—Mental health—Case studies. | Art therapy—
   Case studies. | Group psychotherapy—Case studies.
Classification: LCC RC451.4.A7 (ebook) | LCC RC451.4.A7 G66
   2018 (print) | DDC 616.89/1656—dc23
LC record available at https://lccn.loc.gov/2017058545

ISBN: 978-1-138-73533-0 (hbk)
ISBN: 978-1-138-73535-4 (pbk)
ISBN: 978-1-315-17356-6 (ebk)

Typeset in Bembo
by Apex CoVantage, LLC

Contents

Preface and Acknowledgments		vii
Introduction		1
1	**Low Motivation**	8
2	**Creativity Blocks**	25
3	**Self-Doubts**	42
4	**Personal and Professional Relationships**	57
5	**Trauma and Creativity**	75
6	**Psychiatric Disorders**	90

Part I: Attention Deficit Hyperactivity Disorder 92
Part II: Depression 100
Part III: Bipolar Disorder 110
Part IV: Psychotic Disorders 119

7	**Performance and Audition Anxiety**	133
8	**Artists' and Performers' Bodies**	149

Part I: Eating Disorders 150
Part II: Injuries 161

9	**Stress in the Arts-and-Entertainment World**	175
	Index	193

Preface and Acknowledgments

Back when I first started working as a mental health counselor, I was deeply steeped in the New York City music scene. By day, I'd listen to people's concerns and help them build tools for emotional well-being. By night, I'd be surrounded by musicians in rehearsal studios and spend hours in front of a microphone in recording booths. If there happened to be a weeknight show, I'd sometimes have to run to the venue as soon as a counseling session ended. At first, these two lives felt like they were in competition: I'd have to devote myself either to music or to the field of mental health. However, I slowly began to appreciate the many ways that each set of experiences informed the other: my sessions with clients, many of whom were creative—merely by chance, at first—taught me about the critical role of creativity in clients' lives and the importance of psychological health for accessing and maximizing creative potential. My time in studios and music venues, as well as my personal relationships with other artists, offered me first-hand experience of the stressors—whether inherent to the creative process or environmental—that many creative people face, as well as insight into the unwavering dedication required to achieve creative goals.

At that point, I turned to every source I could to supplement my understanding of the two worlds. In particular, I was interested in literature that offered direction to mental health professionals on how to work with creative clients. To my disappointment, I quickly understood that the available information was limited and scarce. I knew there was a strong need for clinical exploration of the intersection between creativity and mental health, but I couldn't find everything I needed. To organize my thoughts, I started to write down my clinical observations and summaries of useful scientific findings. Years later, as my practice and my fascination with creativity and mental health grew, and the relevance of this topic to my creative clients' needs was confirmed, I managed to morph my initial thoughts into this book, which I hope offers helpful insights into creative clients' psychological needs.

This book could not have turned from idea to published work without the invaluable contribution of many people who inspired, supported, helped, and guided me. First, I want to thank my Routledge editor, Anna Moore, and her editorial assistant Nina Guttapalle for believing in this topic and continuously offering their prompt assistance throughout the process. For assisting me with the overall vision for this book, and for helping me clarify what I wanted to say and the most effective ways to say it, I'd like to thank Marian Sandmaier, Jacob Wainwright Love, and Takis Mousoulis.

I'd like to express my gratitude for the insight and expertise that my colleagues Alexandra Epstein, LMHC, and Dr. Patricia Hunter offered in select chapters of this book. For their big-picture and small-picture suggestions, I'd like to thank Janet Lawrence, Cynthia-Marie Marmo O'Brien, Kathy Thalley, and Mitchell Medina. For helping me find the time to write by maintaining consistent naps and bedtimes, I'd like to thank my daughter, Daphne Sophia, who was a newborn when I started writing this book.

I'm grateful for all the clinicians and researchers who study and write about the mental health needs of creative populations. And most importantly, I'm touched by and deeply appreciative of all my clients who've trusted me with their thoughts and feelings, allowed me to be part of their creative journeys, and inspired me with their unshakable dedication toward their creative pursuits.

Introduction

Mental health practitioners see a variety of clients throughout their careers. Every so often, perhaps more often than they may realize, they'll come across creative clients who struggle to access, utilize, and maximize their creative potential. When this happens, it's important for clinicians to be well versed in *creativity-sensitive treatment*. By this I mean having knowledge of the common mental health concerns held by creative populations and being aware of the psychological challenges associated with creative pursuits. Creativity-sensitive treatment involves supplementing counseling approaches with interventions that consider the close relationship between clients' creativity and their psychological functioning. Through this book, I hope to add to the discussion of what constitutes emotional well-being for creative clients, what threatens it, and how it can be achieved.

Although everyone is creative to some extent, in this book I use the term *creative clients* to describe two groups of people: the first group is composed of those whose professional careers involve the use of creative skills. These might be fine artists, photographers, actors, musicians, graphic designers, writers, singers, lab scientists, dancers, architects, poets, software developers, filmmakers, and others who make a living off of their big or small creative contributions to their field. They exhibit associative, inventive, outside-the-box thinking, and their creative and occupational identities are often intertwined.

The second group consists of people who identify as creative thinkers. This group could overlap with the first, but these creative people aren't necessarily creative by profession. Still, they're interested in generating new ideas and approach daily tasks with a fresh perspective. They value innovation and novelty, and they consider creative qualities to be integral to their sense of self. These are people who use their creative skill sets in their everyday lives.

Though most clients have the potential for creative thought, only a portion of them experience their creativity as a particularly salient trait—one that significantly affects their psychological functioning. For the purposes of this book, creative clients are a distinct population with unique psychological needs associated with their creative skills, interests, and activities.

2 Introduction

Creativity alone doesn't warrant mental health counseling. After all, when optimized, creativity is associated with psychological growth: it leads to self-actualizing behavior, such as authentic self-expression, management of emotions, and effective problem solving. It can reveal people's uniqueness, deepen their range of communication, and foster their search for ideas that lead to progress in art, technology, and the sciences. However, when impaired, creativity fails to serve such functions. Creative clients sometimes struggle to reach their creative potential, they can't access and express thoughts and feelings that unleash their authenticity, or their creativity is so closely linked to psychopathology that the line between them becomes blurred. For different reasons (this book identifies one per chapter), creative people's ability to think and act creatively is hindered by internal (psychological) and external (environmental) obstacles. It is the goal that, upon reading this book, clinicians will become equipped to provide creativity-sensitive treatment by enhancing their understanding of what it's like to treat creative clients and by expanding their knowledge of where the scientific literature stands vis-à-vis the mental health of creative individuals.

One of the traps I've tried to avoid is making vast generalizations about artists, performers, and other creative individuals. Though I draw parallels among creative clients, whom I consider to constitute a distinct demographic group—by virtue of their original, innovative, and insight-filled ways of thinking—I'm mindful that many more differences than similarities exist among creative people, within and across creative fields and professions. Sure, actors, dancers, and musicians might experience similar performance-related pressure: demanding rehearsal schedules, physical and emotional fatigue, cutthroat competitiveness, and so forth. But on an individual level, each person's psychological makeup will bring out differences in the way he or she responds to these stressors.

Similarly, the kind of creativity used by, say, a scientist varies from the one used by a painter: creative scientists tend to follow a heuristic approach to problem solving, so that they land on a single and most useful idea. Painters, in contrast, can let their ideas flow freely, as they transform emotional experiences into tactile ones, without a need to reach an objectively correct outcome. Such distinctions across creative domains matter because they help clinicians understand which types of creativity their clients value the most and which goals they hope to attain.

Finally, creative clients' lifestyles differ drastically across creative professions. Architects and dancers may have to think outside the box, engage in divergent and convergent thought processes, and represent ideas in novel ways, yet architects spend most of their time in offices, collaborate with engineers, and work on deadlines set by clients, whereas dancers rely on physical endurance for expression, perform in front of crowds, and have less employment stability. The book shows how lifestyle differences shape the

Introduction   3

way creative groups use their creative skills and introduce different sets of psychological challenges.

In this book, I try to stay away from conclusive remarks about a causal relationship between creativity and mental illness. Because of the differences among creative people and their domains, and because of pending questions in research about the role that psychopathology plays in creative thinking, there's no clear conclusion as to whether creative traits are tied to psychological disorders. Rather than answer this question, this book investigates this topic's many facets: it looks at how the stress associated with creative and artistic careers exacerbates preexisting psychopathologies; it discusses the neuroscience that explores similarities between cognitive and affective processes involved in creativity and those involved in mental health disorders; it considers how the creative process itself heightens people's emotional difficulties; and it pays attention to the psychologically beneficial effects of creative endeavors, which can ameliorate psychological distress. It explains why emotionally vulnerable people might be drawn to creativity and see it as a vessel for the safe expression of psychological disturbances.

How the Book Is Structured

Earlier, I mentioned that each of this book's nine chapters identifies a reason, or topic, that concerns why people fail to reach their creative potential. The rationale for the division of the book into these particular chapters is based on my observations of the most common psychological concerns that affect creative clients. Each of these topics is discussed in a separate, stand-alone chapter.

Admittedly, the distinctness of each topic is not always cut-and-dried. Common themes, such as the significance of establishing a strong creative identity, the effects of external validation, and the vulnerability associated with self-expression, run throughout many of the book's chapters. As much as possible, I tried to divide the book into independent chapters that reflect the different psychological needs associated with the main topic presented. Some topics, such as creativity blocks in chapter 2, pertain to a wide range of creative individuals irrespective of the creative fields in which they work, whereas others, such as performance and audition anxiety in chapter 7, mostly speak to the experiences of performing artists.

Each chapter attempts to untie the nuanced relationship among the topic discussed, creativity, and mental health. With references to theoretical experts' contributions, relevant findings from evidence-based and scientific literature, and case examples from my clinical experiences,[1] I begin each chapter by describing how creative clients' psychological well-being is affected by the main topic. To the best of my ability, I try to answer the following question: "What's there to know about this topic?" I provide a comprehensive, but

4 Introduction

succinct description of the theoretical background, research findings, and clinical information that illustrate the relevance of each concern in clients' lives.

Then I attempt to answer the following questions: "What's there to do?" and "How can I do it?" As the subtitle of this book, *A Guide for Clinicians*, suggests, I aim to introduce ideas that inform and supplement clinicians' counseling practices. I focus on what clinicians and clients can do together to bring about positive changes in clients' emotional well-being and in their ability to reach creative fulfillment. Each chapter includes a section on "The Clinician's Role," which demonstrates how clinicians can apply the information presented in the beginning of the chapter; a section on "Treatment Goals," which gives clinicians a chance to identify and articulate clients' desired outcomes; and a section on "Suggested Interventions to Achieve Goals," which lists possible treatment interventions that clinicians can use to help their clients. To accentuate the point, I provide illustrative case examples.

The lists of goals and interventions aren't exhaustive. Mental health treatment can involve many approaches—cognitive behavioral therapy, modern psychodynamic therapy, intensive short-term dynamic psychotherapy, internal family-system model therapy, Gestalt therapy, acceptance commitment therapy, and many more—each with its own set of methodologies and tools. This book would be the size of an encyclopedia if it listed every intervention that could possibly be helpful for clients who experience distress with each of the presented topics. Clinicians and their clients are most knowledgeable and able to discern what is and isn't useful. For this reason, blank spaces follow the "Treatment Goals" and "Suggested Interventions to Achieve Goals" sections, to suggest that readers can fill in additional ideas for what might help them make progress, and to encourage them to work collaboratively on finding what works best for every counseling dyad. Though this book strongly advocates for the inclusion of creativity-sensitive treatment when working with artists, performers, and other creative individuals, it's mainly concerned with uncovering particular aspects of creative clients' experiences, and pointing toward helpful treatment tools, rather than replacing the ones that clinicians already have in place.

How to Use This Book

As I mentioned previously, clinicians have their preferred and effective ways to engage clients in mental health treatment, which I strongly encourage them to keep using. The suggested interventions listed in this book aren't meant to replace tried and true approaches; they're meant to supplement them with creativity-sensitive recommendations. For example, mental health professionals who work with depressed clients will most likely have ideas for ways to address clients' negative thoughts, anhedonia, and low self-esteem. To expand the scope of treatment, chapter 6, part II, on depression, draws attention to how ruminating—a cognitive trait of creativity—is associated with the deep reflection that helps creative thinking, and how for many creative clients, unrealized creative potential is itself a source of feelings of depression. Readers are encouraged to incorporate treatment suggestions in ways that enrich their intervention toolbox to enhance their clinical work.

Many of these interventions, such as the ones aimed at helping clients become more self-accepting, are likely useful to most clients, not just creative clients. However, since this book targets the needs of creative people, I've included suggestions for interventions that I've found to be most useful when the mental health concern discussed overlaps with clients' creativity. In contrast, not all the goals and interventions mentioned will be useful for every creative client. For example, some anxious performers might benefit from consulting with a medical professional regarding the use of medication, but most will be able to manage their performance and audition anxiety without it. Similarly, if my list omits interventions that could be clinically instrumental, clinicians can add their ideas in the blank spaces provided. They may find it helpful to make copies of these two sections, distribute them to clients, and work with them directly to identify which suggestions help the most or to complement them with other suitable ideas for treatment.

Finally, a warm and trusting relationship between clients and clinicians will determine the effectiveness of most treatment interventions. The sections on "Suggested Interventions to Achieve Goals" assume that clinicians are ensuring that they've built strong rapport with their clients by demonstrating empathy, openness in communication, authenticity in interactions, benevolence, and a nonjudgmental attitude. Creative clients with a history of trauma, for example, are likely to respond poorly to some of the suggested interventions in the chapter on trauma unless their clinician has helped create a safe environment.

Summary of the Chapters

1. *Low Motivation.* Creative people are thought to be naturally driven by creative pursuits; however, their motivation often falters, resulting in low productivity, unsatisfactory creative fulfillment, and a disrupted sense of creative identity. This chapter explains some of the reasons behind low creative motivation, investigates the role of intrinsic and extrinsic motivation in sustaining creative drive, and discusses ways to enhance the perception that creative tasks are rewarding.
2. *Creativity Blocks.* The creative process isn't always smooth. Sometimes creative clients get stuck in one of the stages of idea development and implementation. When this happens, it's important to identify poor habits during clients' engagement in creative work and the psychological factors that reinforce them. This chapter looks at what happens during

the creative process, what's behind the elusive aha moment, and ways to minimize the negative impact of feeling blocked.

3. *Self-Doubts.* Even the most gifted and driven creators are unlikely to shine unless they can manage self-doubting and self-limiting thoughts. Creative confidence is necessary to help creative clients combat the rejections and uncertainty of feedback frequently found in creative domains. In addition to the intrapsychic factors that shape creators' beliefs in their creative abilities, this chapter considers the impact of the environment on an individual's sense of creative worth. The suggested interventions aim to shed light on the roots of nagging self-doubt and to increase clients' confidence in using and displaying their creative skills.

4. *Personal and Professional Relationships.* Creativity exists within a social context rich in interpersonal interactions, which have the potential to inspire, support, and guide creative people's pursuits. However, they can also introduce conflicts during creative collaborations; spark resentment stemming from social disapproval; fan feelings of rivalry, envy, and non-belongingness; and instigate other clashes. This chapter addresses the many types of social, personal, and professional relationships in creative people's lives and the potential difficulties that they imply. It focuses on ways to improve communication, resolve conflicts, and manage overwhelming feelings so that relationships have a positive effect on creativity.

5. *Trauma and Creativity.* Adversity plays an important role in motivating people to turn to creativity, especially artistic creativity, for healing and self-expression; however, clinicians must take caution so that clients avoid reliving past trauma in harmful ways. This chapter takes a look at the intersection of trauma, posttraumatic growth, and creativity. It focuses on the clinicians' role in maximizing the benefits of creative expression for trauma treatment while keeping in mind the many ways trauma itself hinders creative people's creative processes and performances.

6. *Psychiatric Disorders.* Divided into four parts (on ADHD, depression, bipolar disorder, and psychotic disorders), this chapter explores potential associations between mental illness and creative traits. Rather than looking to establish a causal relationship, it asks which psychiatric symptoms impede creative achievement, which facilitate it, and which are exacerbated by extraneous factors, such as occupational stress. With an emphasis on reinforcing creativity-sensitive treatment, each section of suggested interventions recommends ways to optimize psychological functioning without jeopardizing the cognitive and affective components (such as racing thoughts and emotional intensity) associated with high creativity.

7. *Performance and Audition Anxiety.* Performers aim for strong performances that don't just demonstrate their skills and talents to others, but become

enjoyable experiences for themselves. Unfortunately, performing and auditioning are sometimes perceived as threats, resulting in debilitating anxiety. This chapter looks at the internal and external factors that heighten performance-related anxiety, such as personality factors and pressure from audiences and critics. It addresses the role that clinicians can play in helping their clients manage their symptoms and approach performing with confidence.

8. *Artists' and Performers' Bodies.* For many artists and performers, their bodies are integral to the realization of their creative goals. The pressure placed on the body to deliver optimal results—whether those are related to the aesthetics of the "perfect dancer's body," or the tirelessness of a pianist's hands—can have detrimental consequences, such as the development of eating disorders and incidences of injuries. This chapter, divided into two sections, discusses the prevalence of eating disorders and injuries in the performing arts, the psychological and environment factors behind them, and how clinicians can strike a balance between professional growth and physical self-care.

9. *Stress in the Arts-and-Entertainment World.* Careers in the arts-and-entertainment industry tend to be unstable, arduous, and highly competitive. This world presents many occupational risks that increase the likelihood that creative professionals will experience severe stress at some point in their careers. This chapter lists the challenges and potential obstacles inherent in the creative professions, with a focus on the tools that creative clients may employ to persevere.

I hope that these nine topics augment readers' interest in their clients' creative identities and professional demands. By enhancing their knowledge of creative clients' experiences, readers can build the necessary skills to provide treatment that's sensitive to the needs of artists, performers, and other creative individuals. My hope is that this book sheds light on ways to nurture and protect a critical part of people's psychological health—their creativity.

Note

1 To protect clients' confidentiality, names, professions, and other identifying information have been changed. Most examples presented are an amalgam of various cases with similar characteristics.

Chapter 1

Low Motivation

The drive to create is powerful. Whether it's the mentally immersive experience, the challenge of combining ideas in novel ways, the relief of emotional release, the aesthetic pleasure of making art, or the gratification of solving problems, creative pursuits can be compelling. Yet, as strong as it may be, the creative drive is also fragile. Creative clients, whose relationship with their work is constantly evolving, are often troubled by fluctuations in their creative motivation. A common complaint that brings them to my office is an unwanted lack of interest in their creative work. Even when ideas are plentiful, their desire to spend time on them comes and goes: the talent, skills, and resources are there, but the passion is diminished. Somehow, their motivation for creativity becomes weak, interfering with the quality and quantity of creative output, and diminishing the psychological benefits tied to creative engagement. To understand how the creative drive can go from strong to weak, this chapter teases apart the relationship that creators have with their work, with an emphasis on motivation, enjoyment, and perception of rewards. It considers how creative motivation contributes to people's well-being, making low motivation a problem worth addressing. We'll explore the threats to motivation and investigate the role of clinicians working with clients who wish to revive their passion for their creative pursuits.

Creativity comes in many forms. It exists in the unique combination of preexisting thoughts, the authentic expression of one's individuality, and the accessing of unexplored emotional and cognitive spaces. It comes into play during the arrangement of a bouquet of flowers, the search for a solution to a software-programming problem, the composition of an original piano piece, the distinct interpretation of a well-known tune, the brush stroke of a painting, and so on. When people are being creative, meaning that they're generating new, useful, and valuable ideas (Runco, 2014; Sternberg & Kaufman, 2010), they enter into an active and dynamic relationship with their creative work that can be emotionally and mentally rewarding. Moments of creative problem solving can feel like scratching a persistent itch, and immersion in creative expression can feel like a cathartic emotional release. Completing a creative project can be elating, and the novelty of beginning a new one can become an adaptive obsession that fills creators with a sense of purpose. When things are going smoothly, motivation and creativity are intertwined as parts of a perfect partnership: people are driven by the desire to be creative simply because creativity itself is rewarding. In an ideal scenario, they're motivated because they're getting something out of being creative, and they're creative, at least in part, because they're motivated.

However, when the creative drive wavers and the perceived rewards become obscured, not only does the creative work get compromised, but a threat is posed to the creative person's overall psychological well-being. As common as changing levels of motivation are, they can be alarming as they fill creators with anxiety, guilt, and doubts about their suitability for creative pursuits.

Creative Motivation and Psychological Well-Being

How does low creative motivation affect creators' mental health? And what's special about low motivation in artistic and creative populations? To answer these questions, we need to consider the importance of creativity for creative clients' psychological well-being. We must explore the crucial role that motivation plays in enabling people to realize their potential for creative expression and innovation, and in pursuing the hard work required to achieve creative success. A novelist I once worked with, whose motivation to write had been low for 3 or 4 months, resulting in low productivity and hopelessness about her career, described her despair effectively by stating that she needed to get her creative motivation back to feel like herself again and to protect against the impulse to give up.

Another person I worked with was Sean, a visual artist who felt completely unmotivated and disconnected from his work for about 6 months. He couldn't find any joy or challenge in his art. His detachment, being so intense, flooded him with shame and regrets. He couldn't bear to talk to his parents, who had warned him that this might happen, and who would surely remind him of the career in finance he'd given up. Without a thirst for creative expression, which had fueled his motivation until that point, he had no other guaranteed gain in sight—no professional recognition, no family praise, and no money. On the contrary, all that was left was disheartenment about past sacrifices and the effort he had put into defending his choices to his family. Sean and I spent weeks on identifying motivating rewards. He reluctantly agreed to enroll in a summer residency program, which reinstilled a sense of fascination for his creative work by providing new creative challenges, enriching his knowledge base, building his confidence, and offering collaborative settings. His motivation and sense of commitment solidified, and he eventually felt the need to express himself again through his art. In his words, it was if he had "found himself."

People's self-identity and their creative identity are often closely tied together as to be indistinguishable (Weller, 2013). Rather than being a separate part, which can be turned on and off, the creative identity, once acquired, developed, and maintained, becomes a frame that filters the self and the world. The architect can't help but see structural arrangement and design, the musician can't help but hear pitch and melody combinations, and the photographer can't help but notice light and depth. Through the process of creating, creators build a mental and physical representation of their inner world (thoughts, feelings, perceptions, experiences) and its interplay with the external world (the objective, the observable, the other centered). A creative identity is centered around making, building, giving form, transforming, and experimenting, and the motivation behind it often begins during the creative person's childhood years (Botella et al., 2013). This sense of identity becomes painfully fragmented when a creative person no longer has the motivation to relate to the world in the same way. Low creative motivation breaks the link between the two identities. It weakens the desire to reach creative potential (Nickerson, 1999). Unfulfilled creative abilities result in a poor sense of creative self-identity; predict poorer creative performance (Jaussi et al., 2007); and limit access to talents, skills, and unique attributes. Creative people need to remain motivated to engage in creative work, and for good reason: creative endeavors express their uniqueness, facilitate their emotional expression, activate innovative thinking, and demonstrate their task competence.

A creative person full of ideas but lacking the energy or intention to actualize them (for example, by not applying for grants, not reaching out to connections, not spending time in the lab or studio) will watch opportunities go by, savings dwindle, and productivity plummet. In a circular pattern, being poorly motivated diminishes the quality of creative results and suspends creative energy to keep going.

Creative Motivation in Professional Artists

Aside from helping realize creative potential, motivation is important because it protects artists, performers, and other creative individuals from the adversities involved in many creative careers. Professional artists like Sean often take risks to pursue their artistic paths, despite opposition from familial or cultural norms about traditionally expected careers. A common story among the professional artists I work with is the pursuit of an artistic career despite discouragement—sometimes subtle and sometimes explicit—from their environment. Comedian Demetri Martin joked in a May 2017 interview[1] with Stephen Colbert that he dropped out of law school to become a comedian so that his family would stop being proud. Choosing a career in the arts is associated with many inherent difficulties. The stress of uncertainty about finances and success, the multitude of career-related responsibilities, the physical demands, and the frequent rejections make for a career that can be easily dismissed as impractical, precarious, and without a future. (For more about stress in the arts-and-entertainment world, see chapter 9.) A quick search on the US Department of Labor Bureau of Labor Statistics website[2] shows that in 2016 the median pay for lawyers was $56.81 per hour but only $18.70 for actors and $23.45 for professionals in the fine arts. The median pay for dancers and choreographers was $16.85 per hour, whereas it was $32.76 for accountants and auditors, and $58.77 for pharmacists. These numbers do not show us the reasons behind such discrepancies. But they do illustrate job-market trends and the financial realities associated with being a professional artist.

Even so, the inner drive for artistic immersion is strong enough to push people toward financially insecure lifestyles (Jackson, 2003). Wyszomirski and Chang (2017:10) emphasize the importance of *self-motivated creative activity* to cope with the unclear paths, multiple roles, and need for self-management associated with many creative careers. Without motivation, professional artists are vulnerable to deterrents and run the risk of prematurely giving up without achieving their creative professional goals.

The Need to Be Different

Carving out one's own creative path requires nonconformity, unconventionality, and self-guidedness. A close look at the traits of creative people (both in arts and sciences) reveals that they are less risk averse compared to the general population; they don't care much about following rules, have a need to go against the norm, and are open to new experiences (Feist, 1998; Feist, 1999; Nickerson, 1999; Runco, 2014; Simonton, 2000). When creative motivation is low, these personality characteristics become stifled and cannot emerge via creative outlets. Autonomy (the feeling of having choices and that one's voice matters), which is particularly high in creative people, is one of three drives (the others are competence and relatedness) that make people do what they do, according to Edward Deci and Richard Ryan's self-determination theory (Deci & Ryan, 2011). The need for independence characterizes creative people and, to some extent, explains why they follow creative paths; however, when motivation drops, this need remains unsatisfied. One of my clients described it as looking in the mirror and seeing a blurry image: without the motivation to demonstrate his individuality creatively, he couldn't see himself for who he truly was. The independent, self-directing, adventurous person no longer has the impetus to express and satisfy inner core characteristics. Working with artists on getting their motivation back is crucial to ensuring the fulfillment of their creative needs and goals and to securing the integrity of their sense of self.

Why Does Motivation Falter?

The paradox about understanding low motivation in creative people is that creativity is considered to be self-driving and inherently motivating. People usually like to do creative things because it feels good to do them (Amabile, 1993; Csikszentmihalyi, 1996). In light of this, what would cause someone's motivation to drop? One of the reasons for low motivation is that the creative behavior is no longer perceived to be rewarding. Creative motivation is tied to the attitude that creators hold about whether engaging in innovative thought and behavior is in some way beneficial. Motivation is affected when creative tasks are perceived to be too boring or too challenging, too silly or not fun enough, irrelevant or overdone, and so on. Beneath creators' attitudes on the value of doing creative work lies a conscious or unconscious expectation of an *intrinsic* (deriving from doing the creative behavior itself) or *extrinsic* (deriving from an outcome separate from the creative behavior) reward. A writer who feels motivated by the act of writing itself, or who sees writing as a way to express complex ideas, is intrinsically motivated, whereas a writer motivated by the goal of producing a best seller is extrinsically motivated. With remarkable consistency, conversations with my clients about what appeals to them about doing creative work are dominated by intrinsic motivators: enjoying the process itself, the satisfaction that comes from finding a solution to a problem, improving for improvement's sake, being immersed in the creative moment, and gaining a sense of competence. In contrast, emphasizing extrinsic motivators, such as high sales and social appraisal, might keep my clients preoccupied with how to achieve such goals, but it often removes the focus from the quality of creative work.

Researchers have found that intrinsic motivation tends to be most beneficial for creative activities (Amabile, 1985; Amabile, 1994; Hennessey, 2010; Ceci & Kumar, 2015). When the goal is the creative work itself, one will engage in more cognitive flexibility, try new ways of doing the same thing, demonstrate higher levels of creativity, and maintain a longer lasting and persistent drive to continue (Collins & Amabile, 1999; Ceci & Kumar, 2015; Deci & Ryan, 1999 Deci & Ryan, 2000; Kaufman & Gregoire, 2015). An interesting caveat comes from the work of Zabelina and colleagues (2013), who propose that when intrinsic motivation is associated with a sense of duty and obligation ("I ought to") rather than a sense of striving for creative expression ("I want to"), creativity is hindered.

For creative people who notice a drop in their motivation, an undetected shift from being intrinsically motivated to becoming extrinsically motivated might have occurred. Sources of motivation can start off as being intrinsic (composing music to bring new melodies to life), but then turn extrinsic (winning a music composition contest). This transition comes about when creators' needs and priorities start to change. A highly motivated writer who's affected by a bad review is at risk for a shift in her motivation: as she focuses on what reviewers and audiences think, the intrinsic motivation, a love for writing itself, gets replaced with the powerful, yet sometimes subconscious, intention of getting good feedback. Though there's nothing wrong with wanting positive feedback or to win a competition, being led by just that diminishes the strength of the intrinsic motivation, which, as discussed previously, has been linked to enhanced creativity.

Although intrinsic sources are instrumental in driving creative motivation, there are times when extrinsic factors have the same effect. Sometimes a desire for personal recognition (winning a Nobel Prize or solving a problem that improves societal conditions) is the right impetus to activate and sustain creative work. Many of today's inventions and technological advances have been the result of creative work done with the goal of finding a solution to a problem. In creative scientific domains, creativity may be fueled by the expectation that the work will lead to concrete results, rather than by the mere enjoyment of the process. Stumpf (1995) points out that the need for professional recognition is what sometimes motivates creative people to assess the quality of their ideas before sharing them. Aside from scientists, many of the performing artists I work with, such as jazz musicians who improvise onstage, emphasize how important audience responsiveness is for their motivation and creativity to be optimal. To address the powerful interaction between intrinsic and extrinsic motivation, Amabile's model of motivational synergy (1993) suggests that extrinsic rewards can sometimes enhance motivation, assuming that it's primarily intrinsically based.

Creative motivation sometimes drops in the presence of conflicting goals. For example, the desire to record a full-length solo album may conflict with the desire to join a touring band and be on the road for 2 months. The motivation to appeal to a wide range of audiences with mainstream success may contradict the motivation to experiment with a groundbreaking artistic style. Creators must often make difficult choices or try to do many things at once (increasing the likelihood of fatigue and burnout). Conflicts sometimes exist between creative and general life goals. The compulsion to work on an art project can compete with the need to spend time with a loved one. Time constraints and priority clashes make it difficult to sustain the motivation and commitment that is necessary for creative work.

Leanne, an accomplished violinist, was concerned about having lost the motivation to compose new music. She described a feeling of dread whenever she picked up the violin. In our second session, Leanne identified an internal conflict between wanting to devote time to her 16-month-old son and wanting to make sure that she wasn't neglecting her music. Time management was not the main issue; she had time to work on her music while her son was at day care. The emotional constraint was deeper than that: subconsciously, she was resisting full immersion in her creative work to maintain a sense of nonstop availability to her son. Having her son constantly on her mind made it difficult for her to concentrate and feel enthusiasm about playing and composing music. A helpful theme throughout our work together was the concept of finding a sense of balance as she worked toward integrating two identities with conflicting motivations. In Leanne's case, thinking about extrinsic as well as intrinsic motivation was helpful in kick-starting the engine that would drive her toward composing new music. Thinking about how a high level of dedication to her creative work would provide income, serve as a role model for her son, and become a way for her to release stress helped bridge the perceived gap between her role as a mother and that of a musician. Eventually, our conversation turned toward core values and about what it means to be a working mother, especially in a field easily dismissible as unstable. To preserve her motivation, we had to rebuild the foundation of what she valued and found inherently rewarding about her creative work and artistic identity. We had to go back to her childhood and reconnect with the girl who couldn't wait to pick up her instrument. Images of her 13-year-old self practicing the violin in her room, trying to match her emotions to the sound of the bow on the strings, flooded our sessions and, thankfully, helped her feel the passion she'd been talking about.

Finally, motivation is threatened by thoughts of unworthiness—"Who am I to create something?" or "There's nothing important about what I'm doing, so why bother?" Similar internal dialogues can damage the creative drive. A feeling of not being good enough preoccupies the mind with worries about appraisal and acceptance, while deflating the motivation to leave a footprint on the world via creative endeavors. It's easy enough for creative individuals to lose faith in the quality and purpose of their work. Habitually questioning the point is an impediment to maintaining motivation. (For more on the impact of self-doubting thoughts, see chapter 3.)

The Clinician's Role

Reconnecting Clients With Their Creative Drive

Not unlike relationship coaches, clinicians can help their clients reignite their relationships with their creative work. They'll help their clients find the passion for long-term creative goals and, most importantly, for the process to achieve them. At times, some perspective on the universality of clients' experiences can go a long way toward relieving the distress caused by a diminished drive. Validating and normalizing shifts in motivation protect against the temptation to denounce oneself as unfit to do the job and to abandon it altogether. Then, clinicians and clients can shed light on the rewards of creativity.

Looking Into Clients' Motivation Patterns

Sessions can begin with a general assessment and exploration of clients' past and current levels of motivation. The goal is to facilitate a discussion that creates space for clients to bring up all their concerns and observations of what has impeded or sustained their motivation so far. Areas for potential exploration include

- which parts of the creative process seem less desirable;
- when the shift began;
- clients' thoughts about the importance of their creative work;
- the personal and professional problems posed by low motivation;
- environmental circumstances and general life changes that interfere with commitment;
- whether the decrease in motivation is associated with affective and cognitive symptoms, such as persistent depressed mood, excessive worrying, obsessive ideations, and extreme distractibility; and
- the perceived enjoyment associated with intrinsic or extrinsic sources of motivation (enjoyment, challenge, competence, emotional expression, and so on).

Naming the Rewards

It's helpful when sessions articulate and reiterate the perceived rewards associated with the creative behavior. This is particularly important because conversations around motivation can be vague and abstract. They may be more focused on what clients aren't feeling ("I don't feel like doing something"), rather than on what they're feeling or, better yet, what they're gaining from being creative ("Doing this would help me feel . . ."). Eventually moving on to a conversation about how creative clients benefit from their creative pursuits—whether that's collaborating, asserting values, making money, or finding peace of mind—is necessary to visualize concrete and attainable outcomes.

An emphasis on the intrinsic, rather than extrinsic, motivation, as discussed previously, is perhaps better suited to enhance creative motivation, but there's value in including all sources of motivation. When conflicting motivational forces exist—for example, wanting to please one's editor and experiment with writing styles—clinicians can help clients balance priorities, all while keeping in mind the significance of aligning creative choices with clients' sense of self. If experimentation with a new style is what helps the writer-client reach untapped creative potential that will improve general confidence, it may take precedence over the motivation to maintain smooth professional relationships with editors.

Exploring Helpful Habits

Clinicians can investigate clients' work habits, sources of inspiration, and preferred ways of approaching creative tasks. Quite often, a reminder of what worked in the past can help clients reconnect with motivating habits and integrate them into present practices. For example, an unmotivated photographer I recently worked with was so caught up in all the ways he wasn't progressing that he hadn't noticed the harmful work habits he'd developed. Instead of starting his workday looking at other images for inspiration like he used to, he was reading the news; instead of taking walks looking for objects to photograph, he was isolated all day in his studio; instead of challenging himself with new equipment, he repeatedly used the same. One of our goals was to get back into creative habits that worked in the past by using our sessions to set clear intentions for how he wanted to spend each week.

When the past provides little inspiration for creative drive, clients and clinicians can look toward developing new habits that will increase motivation. A musician may notice that spending time alone in front of a computer makes songwriting increasingly less enjoyable. In this case, encouraging collaborations and other ways of exchanging ideas is a great way to expand on motivating work habits.

Enhancing Feelings of Autonomy

The need to feel important is especially strong when it comes to creative work. Creativity coach Eric Maisel (2005) has developed the concept of *deciding to matter* as it pertains to creative people leading meaningful lives by virtue of creating. This is tied to the permission clients can give themselves to feel important by making creative choices, taking risks, coming up with ideas, and expressing them. Even when the idea of spending another minute on a creative task seems futile, a strong sense of autonomy will secure the belief that one's feelings and thoughts are valid enough to express creatively. The role of clinicians is to explore how engaging in creative work is a conscious decision to matter and an opportunity for clients to value their individual preferences. This can be done by asking clients to think about what matters to them and to look back at times when they made their own creative decisions and exercised free will.

Emphasizing the Value of Creating

Clinicians can challenge clients to embrace the idea that they're contributing to the creative world by virtue of turning nothing into something. The act of bringing an idea to life, and of being motivated enough to carry on until completion, requires courage and confidence. Thoughts of not being important enough and of not having something meaningful to say can be explored and addressed during sessions. To do so, it may be necessary to temporarily shift the focus from the quality of creative ideas to the inherent value of conceptualizing something new.

Examining Anxiety and Other Negative Feelings

When the act of creating something causes anxiety, clinicians can investigate whether this feeling diminishes the drive to create. Anxiety about imperfect results often triggers avoidance—an effective short-term anxiety relief—as a coping response. For example, a perfectionistic actor may keep postponing character preparation and spend time on social media instead. This tactic can be confused with lack of interest, when it's essentially an effort to avoid facing the possibility of inadequate work or poor results. Clients and clinicians can discuss whether methods of tolerating anxiety will help restore motivation.

Finally, clinicians can broaden the focus of counseling sessions by looking at what else is going on in clients' lives. A death in the family may magnify the need to heal, grieve, and mourn the loss rather than to express a creative idea. Again, this might be experienced as low motivation, but it reflects the need to take care of other emotional needs.

Treatment Goals

1. Manage the "ups and downs" of motivation as they occur.
2. Understand the circumstances that cause a drop in motivation.
3. Bring motivation back to its peak.
4. Adjust to changes in creative drive.
5. Manage career goals while working through motivation struggles.

Suggested Interventions to Achieve Goals

1. *Engage in motivational interviewing.* Miller and Rollnick's seminal book on motivational interviewing (MI) (2013) looks at the processes involved in motivating clients to change. For clients who wish to increase their motivation to do creative work, clinicians can follow MI's key parts: engaging (developing a good working relationship), focusing (clarifying

direction), evoking (identifying clients' own motivations for change), and planning (developing a specific action plan). Sessions can draw a distinction between why clients want to create as opposed to why they've come to believe they should create.

> Example: When a children's book author complained of feeling unmotivated to write her third book, I inquired into what she hoped to get out of the creative activity. We discussed why writing still mattered to her, even though she already had her best seller, and what rewards she looked forward to gaining. She articulated a desire to have fun with her new ideas and to see whether they would resonate with a new age group. Our plan was for her to complete a short story a day, regardless of whether she'd end up using it later on.

2. *Suggest a motivation journal.* Journaling is commonly used during counseling to process stressful events (Ullrich & Lutgendorf, 2002), enhance self-reflection skills, and create meaning. For creative clients whose motivation has dropped, journaling can offer insight into motivation patterns. By paying attention to when, why, and how motivation changes, clients can anticipate and prepare for fluctuations in their drive to create. Journaling can help unmotivated creators clarify and articulate the factors that shape their motivations.

> Example: I once asked a theater actor to keep track of his motivation levels. He noticed that right after a big, exhilarating performance, his creative motivation would plummet. He didn't want to take classes, rehearse, or apply for new opportunities. Being aware of this pattern prepared him to face such feelings the next time they came around. He was less discouraged when his motivation dropped, and even gave himself permission to take time off without anxiety and guilt about not being productive.

3. *Improve mood.* In a meta-analytic study of 66 reports with more than 7,000 participants, Baas and colleagues (2008) found that activating positive mood (feeling happy) yields high levels of *approach motivation*, the kind of motivation necessary to take action toward something thought to be beneficial. Intuitively, this makes sense, in that the more positive we feel, the likelier we are to have more fun with creative tasks and to anticipate positive outcomes. Clinicians can ask clients to identify habits, relationships, and other factors that improve their mood.

> Example: When a mildly depressed filmmaker I worked with wasn't interested in working on new creative ideas, we began our sessions by identifying ways to feel better. Some suggestions we came up with were expressing emotions during talk therapy, taking short breaks from work, seeing friends more, and exercising. When his

mood started to improve, he began to look forward to being mentally stimulated by concepts for a new film.

4. *Find a meaningful message.* Creative people often have a message that they hope to express through their creative work. It's important to discover what that message is because clients are likelier to feel invested in subject matter that's important to them. Clients and clinicians can use the sessions to establish a sense of purpose that bridges the gap between desire and action. When this message has changed over time, or if the change itself is what led to the motivation drop, clinicians can help clients adjust to a new message that matters.

   Example: A comic illustrator I once worked with became unmotivated during a time when she was experiencing marital problems and subsequent divorce. We spent time discussing what topic would feel meaningful and relevant to her current experiences. After recognizing that she wanted to make a satirical statement about the difficulties of going through a divorce, she regained her creative motivation. Even though this was a topic she'd never considered before, the message suddenly was important to her, and she was eager to express it.

5. *Confront criticism.* Van Dijk and Kluger (2011) conducted a series of scenario experiments that demonstrated that motivation to perform tasks requiring creativity is enhanced by positive feedback. In light of the effect that positive and negative feedback can have on creative motivation, it can be helpful to explore how creative clients' motivations have been affected by criticism they've received about their work and ideas. The goal is to find new ways to interpret and internalize negative reactions so as to not threaten creators' commitment to keep creating.

   Example: A singer brought up negative online comments about her cover of a famous rock song. After processing her embarrassment, I challenged her to evaluate the comments herself. She saw merit in the view that her performance had lacked passionate persuasion, and she felt motivated by the goal of improving; however, she rejected comments about her vocal tone, maintaining the belief that the song was, indeed, a good match for her.

6. *Set goals.* Setting specific goals can be a helpful way for clients to keep their *eyes on the prize*, increasing their motivation to take action. Clinicians can ask clients to share their creative ambitions and, in specific terms, to break activities into smaller parts by listing end goals and gradual steps toward each goal.

   Example: A singer-songwriter kept setting big goals but felt unmotivated to pursue them: she wanted to release a solo album and perform at a festival, without thinking through the details of how to get there. The vagueness of her plans made it hard for her to commit to them. We broke up the goal into small steps, such as spending an hour every day learning how to use the recording software, composing parts of the lyrics, and reaching out to music show promoters. Concrete, yet small goals helped her commit to them more easily.

7. *Create memorable motivation mantras.* Clients often leave sessions feeling focused and driven; yet when the moment comes to perform creative tasks, discouraging automatic feelings and negative thoughts reemerge. To capture the insight achieved in the counseling room so that clients can connect with it when they're back in the studio, office, or rehearsal space, it's helpful to use short and easy-to-remember catchphrases.

    Example: Sean, the artist mentioned in this chapter, and I summarized concepts that resonated with him the most, such as "I care about learning," "I care about honing my skills," "This activity or moment matters to me," or "My goal is to improve, not to prove." These reminders helped him apply our conversations during moments of wavering motivation in his day-to-day life.

8. *Cultivate intrinsic motivation.* As discussed in this chapter, researchers have demonstrated the importance of doing creative work for its own sake in order to increase the drive to engage in creative tasks. Questions can circle around what clients enjoy about the process itself, what they find challenging, and what they are curious about, regardless of the outcome. The goal is to visualize a scenario in which no extrinsic gain exists, yet the person is still motivated to keep up the creative work because it's rewarding for its own sake.

    Example: A photographer I worked with was so focused on client demands and expectations that he'd forgotten about internal rewards associated with the process. To cope with his frustration, he subconsciously abandoned the work altogether. Despite proclamations such as "I want to get back to working hard," he'd subtly demonstrate the opposite by missing deadlines, repeating past ideas, and avoiding meeting new clients. By shifting the discussion onto his own interest in the work, he began to reconnect with what had originally drawn him to photography: a passion for visual self-expression and a desire to manipulate light and objects.

9. *Encourage creative collaborations.* Clinicians can consider how working on a project with new creative partners, visiting the art shows of fellow artists, and exchanging ideas with people from other creative disciplines stir up newfound motivation to work on old or new ideas. Such collaborations

sometimes run the risk of evoking harmful comparisons, especially if others are perceived as superior. However, when it comes to enhancing motivation, the advantages of collaborating can outweigh the disadvantages, making it an approach worth considering.

> Example: A filmmaker I worked with for a few months hesitated to begin new working relationships with other filmmakers because he feared he'd be betrayed or that he'd have creative clashes. After weeks of putting his projects off, he admitted to having little drive to take the lead. I urged him to reach out to old, trusted colleagues and to invite them for a brainstorming session. To his surprise, they saw eye to eye creatively, and he felt a strong desire to start bringing his ideas to life.

10. *Resolve conflicts.* Conflicting needs—such as the needs to socialize, exercise, spend time at a "day job," or fulfill other important obligations— can make it difficult to maintain a clear and solid sense of motivation for creative work. Clients and clinicians can work together to identify competing needs, weigh the advantages and disadvantages associated with each choice, and prioritize the benefits of the creative activity.

> Example: A client's desire to be in his art studio competed with his desire to spend more time with his boyfriend. He learned to compartmentalize the two desires, seeing his relationship to his art and his boyfriend as integral to his overall well-being, yet clarifying that they satisfy different sets of needs. He began to see his artistic accomplishments as an extension of the person he brings to his relationship, and worked on communicating his creative needs to his boyfriend.

11. *Encourage clients to keep busy.* Research has indicated that having a full, busy schedule is likely to increase motivation to pursue goals even when deadlines are initially missed (Wilcox et al., 2016). Clinicians can help clients identify and verbalize a sense of tentative scheduling. In light of how the potential pressure of time frames and deadlines can trigger anxiety, it's important to listen to clients regarding what schedule they consider to be busy enough to pose a challenge, yet still comfortable enough to maintain the will to keep going.

> Example: When an unmotivated guitar player complained about his lack of drive to set goals, I encouraged him to plan some events for the future (book a show weeks in advance, or announce a release date on social media) so that he'd have one thing to keep him busy per month. He noticed that even some activity during slow months brought up his creative motivation.

Additional Interventions

12.
13.
14.

Takeaways

- For the most part, ebbs and flows in creative motivation are normal; however, they sometimes cause significant distress to the person experiencing them and can be harmful to the creative process.
- Artists and creative people who feel unmotivated to pursue their creative goals are troubled by a disruption in their sense of self, purpose, and psychological and professional well-being.
- Obstacles to maintaining creative motivation are internally driven (such as changes in affect), reinforced by environmental deterrents (such as daily stress), or both.
- Clients can connect with their inner drive to engage in innovative and expressive work that's important to them.
- Mental health practitioners can help their creative clients reenergize their feelings toward their creative endeavors by helping them identify rewards, by examining their values, and by setting appropriate goals.

Notes

1 Retrieved from www.cbs.com/shows/the-late-show-with-stephen-colbert/video/dt6Rj Plk54AJnSToENmMrKUWHeZXIabQ/demetri-martin-shares-his-early-comedy-drawings/.
2 Retrieved from www.bls.gov/home.htm.

References

Amabile, T. M. (1985). Motivation and creativity: Effects of motivational orientation on creative writers. *Journal of Personality and Social Psychology, 48*(2), 393–399.

Amabile, T. M. (1993). Motivational synergy: Toward new conceptualizations of intrinsic and extrinsic motivation in the workplace. *Human Resource Management Review, 3*(3), 185–201.

Amabile, T. M., Hill, K. G., Hennessey, B. A., & Tighe, E. M. (1994). The work preference inventory: Assessing intrinsic and extrinsic motivational orientations. *Journal of Personality and Social Psychology, 66*(5), 950–967.

Baas, M., De Dreu, C. K. W., & Nijstad, B. A. (2008). A meta-analysis of 25 years of mood-creativity research: Hedonic tone, activation, or regulatory focus? *Psychological Bulletin, 134*(6), 779–806.

Botella, M., Glaveanu, V., Zenasni, F., Storme, M., Myszkowski, N., Wolff, M., & Lubart, T. (2013). How artists create: Creative process and multivariate factors. *Learning and Individual Differences, 26*, 161–170.

Ceci, M. W., & Kumar, V. K. (2015). A correlational study of creativity, happiness, motivation, and stress from creative pursuits. *Journal of Happiness Studies, 17*(2), 609–626.

Collins, M. A., & Amabile, T. M. (1999). Motivation and creativity. In R. J. Sternberg (Ed.), *Handbook of creativity*. Cambridge: Cambridge University Press.

Csikszentmihalyi, M. (1996). *Creativity: The flow and the psychology of discovery of invention.* New York, NY: HarperCollins Publishers

Deci, E. L., & Ryan, R. M. (2000). Intrinsic and extrinsic motivations: Classic definitions and new directions. *Contemporary Educational Psychology, 25*, 54–67.

Deci, E. L., & Ryan, R. M. (2011). Self-determination theory. In P. A. M. Van Lange, A. W. Kruglasnki, & E. T. Higgins (Eds.), *Handbook of theories of social psychology: Collections: Volumes 1 & 2.* Thousand Oaks, CA: SAGE Publications.

Deci, E. L., Ryan, R. M., & Koestner, R. (1999). A meta-analytic review of experiments examining the effects of extrinsic rewards on intrinsic motivation. *Psychological Bulletin, 125*(6), 627–668.

Feist, G. J. (1998). A meta-analysis of personality in scientific and artistic creativity. *Personality and Social Psychology Review, 2*(4), 290–309.

Feist, G. J. (1999). The influence of personality on artistic and scientific creativity. In R. J. Sternberg (Ed.), *Handbook of creativity*. Cambridge: Cambridge University Press.

Hennessey, B. (2010). The creativity-motivation connection. In J. C. Kaufman & R. J. Sternberg (Eds.), *Cambridge handbook of creativity* (pp. 342–365). Cambridge: Cambridge University Press.

Jackson, M. R. (2003). *Investing in creativity: A study of the support structure for U.S. artists.* Retrieved from http://webarchive.urban.org/UploadedPDF/411311_investing_in_creativity.pdf

Jaussi, K. S., Randel, A. E., & Dionne, S. D. (2007). I am, I think I can, and I do: The role of personal identity, self-efficacy, and cross-application of experiences in creativity at work. *Creativity Research Journal, 19*, 247–258.

Kaufman, S. B., & Gregoire, C. (2015). *Wired to create: Unraveling the mysteries of the creative mind.* New York, NY: TarcherPerigee.

Maisel, E. (2005). *Coaching the artist within.* Novato, CA: New World Library.

Miller, R. W., & Rollnick, S. (2013). *Motivational interviewing: Helping people change.* New York, NY: Guilford Press.

Nickerson, R. S. (1999). Enhancing creativity. In R. J. Sternberg (Ed.), *Handbook of creativity*. Cambridge: Cambridge University Press.

Runco, M. (2014). *Creativity: Theories and themes: Research, development, and practice* (2nd ed.). London, UK: Academic Press.

Simonton, D. K. (2000). Creativity: Cognitive, personal, developmental, and social aspects. *American Psychologist, 55*(1), 151–158.

Sternberg, R. J., & Kaufman, J. C. (2010). Constraints on creativity: Obvious and not so obvious. In J. C. Kaufman & R. J. Sternberg (Eds.), *Cambridge handbook of creativity* (pp. 113–130). Cambridge: Cambridge University Press.

Stumpf, H. (1995). Scientific creativity: A short overview. *Educational Psychology Review, 7*(3), 225–241.

Ullrich, P. M., & Lutgendorf, S. K. (2002). Journaling about stressful events: Effects of cognitive processing and emotional expression. *Annals of Behavior Medicine, 23*(3), 244–250.

Van Dijk, D., & Kluger, A. N. (2011). Task type as a moderator of positive/negative feedback effects on motivation and performance: A regulatory focus perspective. *Journal of Organizational Behavior, 32*, 1084–1105.

Weller, J. F. (2013). How popular music artists form an artistic and professional identity and portfolio career in emerging adulthood. *Education Doctoral Dissertations in Leadership*. Paper 43.

Wilcox, K., Laran, J., Stephen, A. T., & Zubscek, P. P. (2016). How being busy can increase motivation and reduce task completion time. *Journal of Personality and Social Psychology, 110*(3), 371–384.

Wyszomirski, M. J., & Chang, W. (2017). Professional self-structuration in the arts: Sustaining creative careers in the 21st century. *Sustainability, 9*, 1035. doi:10.3390/su9061035

Zabelina, D., Felps. D., & Blanton, H. (2013). The motivational influence of self-guides on creative pursuits: Psychology of aesthetics, creativity, and the arts. *American Psychological Association, 7*(2), 112–118.

Chapter 2

Creativity Blocks

Holly, a 33-year-old writer, reached out to me for help getting started on her career-coaching book. Every time she sat down to write, she'd have an intense feeling of being blocked, almost as if someone would erase everything in her brain. She described it as a "mental paralysis." As we thought about the factors that contributed to her block, she identified three obstacles: first, she realized that she didn't know enough about the topic. Domain-specific knowledge—in this case, the domain of career coaching—was necessary to stimulate her brain enough until an idea randomly sparked. Second, she figured that her uncertainty about how to turn thoughts into sentences stopped her from making progress. She'd have to accept that not knowing how to capture her ideas was par for the course, and it shouldn't discourage her from writing until something clicked. Third, to tackle her block caused by worries about the applicability of her ideas, she thought about the people who are professionally unfulfilled and in need of career guidance. This last point intensified her motivation, which set the creative process in motion.

To help Holly make progress with her book, she and I had to investigate how blocks halt creative behaviors by addressing the multiple factors involved (brain functions, personal traits, cultural attitudes on what's deemed creative, and environmental and chance factors). We also had to consider the psychological ramifications of being stuck. Conversely, we looked at how her psychological state—feelings, attitudes, experiences, and thoughts—kept stubborn blocks from dissolving. This chapter looks into all these factors, as it delves deeper into understanding a nuisance that vexes all types of creative people.

Creativity blocks are mental obstacles to accessing and using creative abilities. They describe the inability to be inspired by something and to be inspired to do something (Thrash & Elliot, 2004). When persistent, they frustrate the ability to channel mental energy creatively—the ability to come up with original, expressive, and useful ideas—and can even become emotionally disturbing. As discussed throughout this book, failure to reach creative potential is tied to lack of self-actualization: feeling inspired to do something predicts progress toward personal and creative goals, which are then associated with overall psychological well-being (Milyavskaya et al., 2012; Thrash et al., 2010). Being blocked leaves the creatively inclined feeling unfulfilled and those who make a living off their creative skills feeling professionally stunted.

Types of Creativity Blocks: Process and Outcome

To understand the nature of these mental obstacles, it's helpful to distinguish between process and outcome blocks. Processes and outcomes are two interconnected but distinct facets of creative behaviors (Zhang & Bartol, 2010) thwarted by different, though often overlapping, blocks. Process blocks make it difficult for creators to use their creative skills to come up with novel and useful ideas. These blocks feel like *mental itches*, a term used by Matthew Jarman (2016) to describe the uncomfortable feeling of an intense, unsatisfied need to reach a new concept or solution. This itch is relieved only when insight is finally achieved or creative sparks have finally fired. Unfulfilled, the mental itch that cannot be scratched persists like an intrusive and unsettling obsession that takes over one's thoughts and leads to feelings of frustration and unfulfillment. A young shoegaze rock guitarist I once worked with disliked all his ideas and wasn't inspired by any of them, despite sky-high motivation and good time-management skills. He was experiencing process blocks. He'd spend hours in the studio, messing around with guitar pedals and sound effects, but he'd come out feeling like he hadn't gotten anywhere. As a result, he couldn't focus on other tasks, had constant low-grade anxiety, and obsessed about coming up with the best melody and guitar sound.

The other type of block, the outcome block, torments those who have the ideas, and perhaps have even made some progress on them, but can't seem to implement them or complete the creative task. As mentioned previously, creativity blocks are about the inability to be inspired to do something as much as they are about not being inspired by something. Outcome blocks describe difficulties with seeing an idea through to its end. Very often, clients come to sessions with a plethora of ideas they are confident in and with solid motivation, but freeze up when it's time to take action. I once worked with an artist who was excited to work on a new series of portrait sketches. He spent a couple of sessions going over his plans of going to cafés and drawing people who seemed to "carry strong emotions in their faces." His face lit up when he spoke about it, and he jumped from one creative idea to another, yet every time he went to the café, he drew a few lines and then stopped. It was as if the entire creative experience was beautifully mapped out in his head, but he couldn't begin the journey that would take him to his destination: the creative product. Despite many aha moments, none of them resulted in a viable creative outcome.

Stages of Creativity

By looking into the stages of creative behaviors, we gain some insight into where and how creativity gets stuck. Though creativity stages often overlap, don't always follow a linear sequence, and might differ from one creative domain to another (for example, visual arts or computer science), many researchers and theorists have developed consistent explanatory models that give us a sense of what happens when people engage in creative work.

In the first stage of creativity, one has to be open to receiving external stimulation, making observations, using analytical skills, taking in knowledge, and identifying tasks and problems (Amabile, 1996; Carson, 2010; Heilman, 2005; Wallas, 1926). This is a stage of childlike impressionability, characterized by unfiltered receptivity. The more curious people are about a topic, the better prepared they become to use the information obtained in novel and original ways.

In the following stage, creators need to process all that has soaked in by letting the mind do its own work, both consciously (by using active imagination or manipulating mental images), and subconsciously (where brain processes are beyond their level of awareness). This subconscious process, called *incubation* (Wallas, 1926), might look like daydreaming, "sleeping on it," or just stepping away from the task. Even though someone isn't actively thinking about something, a cascade of ideas can be simmering in the background. Riter and Dijksterhuis (2014) believe that unconscious thought processes play an active role in brain behaviors that contribute to creativity (such as making associations and generating ideas). According to some authors, the period of incubation, when the creative task is set to the side, is when creativity blocks become noticeable and might obstruct the transition to the third stage (Lubart, 2010).

The third stage of creativity is marked by the elusive aha moment, when something "clicks" and develops a life of its own. It's the feeling of generating many ideas or solutions, formulating the beginnings of something innovative, and the compulsion to keep going while neurons are firing and lightbulbs are going on (Carson, 2010; Heilman, 2005; Lubart, 2010; Wallas, 1926). When creators are feeling blocked, it's this part of the creative journey that's often the most emotionally charged. The elusiveness of creativity left one composer I worked with feeling powerless. She tearfully shared her worries of not being able to find her inner creativity the same way that creativity had "found" her years ago, when she composed her most critically acclaimed piece. Being preoccupied with not accessing creativity can induce

28 Creativity Blocks

distractibility and anxiety. It's important to learn how to manage the negative feelings that come from feeling blocked to avoid worsening the block.

Finally, the stage that follows is a period of evaluation, or verification (Stumpf, 1995; Wallas, 1926), of the ideas that occurred. Decisions will be made about the relevance, appropriateness, and quality of the ideas that, hopefully, were sparked (Amabile, 1996; Carson, 2010; Heilman, 2005) during the previous stage. Unless an outcome block occurs, the right ideas will result in the implementation of an idea and the creation of the desired creative product. This last stage, as with the first, requires conscious attention (Beardsley, 1965/1976).

Creativity Blocks and Low Motivation

The idea that creative achievement is tied to psychological well-being runs throughout this book. It's likely particularly familiar to those who read chapter 1, "Low Motivation." Feeling creatively blocked shares many similarities with being unmotivated. First, whether due to creativity blocks or low motivation, the frustration resulting from not accomplishing creative goals is equally painful. The difference between not having the drive and not having the idea may seem inconsequential to someone who's trying to cope with the disappointment of unrealized creative potential. Second, creative blocks and low creative motivation both can be caused by overlapping internal and environmental factors. For example, creators who don't feel competent are less likely to maintain solid motivation and less likely to experiment with novel ideas that might lead to creative insight. Similarly, having to deal with stress in their environments, such as financial or marital problems, makes it harder to commit to devoting time and energy to creative endeavors and to have the presence of mind that's needed to spark ideas. Finally, sometimes it's difficult to distinguish between feeling blocked and being unmotivated because one state often begets the other. Struggling to come up with a good idea can suck all the motivation out of someone. Conversely, low drive to engage in creative work is likely to reduce the chances of arriving at a great idea (Lubart, 2010), given that the more time and effort people spend on a task, the likelier it is that they will generate solutions or have an aha moment (Simonton, 2004).

Despite the similarities, distinct differences occur when being blocked and being unmotivated. In my experiences with my clients, I've noticed that low motivation runs the risk of introducing feelings of guilt and self-blame—thoughts such as "What's wrong with me? Why didn't I go to the studio today?" and "I'm not a true writer; I keep putting my writing off." Creativity blocks, however, may bring up more insecurities about innate capabilities—such as thoughts about not being intelligent enough or talented enough, or just being unlucky in that inspiration hasn't spontaneously arrived. Another difference is that creativity blocks are about cognitive, mental, or perceptual breaks, whereas low motivation is more of an affective interruption of creators' senses of purpose. An architect looking for the best way to maximize space functionality could have high positive feelings toward her work and high creative engagement—spending hours on the project, coming up with many variations for the space—but still not reach a satisfying result because her brain is not going in new directions, not seeking novelty, or not making connections among different domains of knowledge. Motivation might account for the perspiration part of Edison's famous genius equation (that genius equals 1 percent inspiration and 99 percent perspiration), but inspiration is what is borne out of unblocked creative thinking.

What Causes Creativity Blocks?

For each creative person, there's a unique combination of factors that cause him or her to be blocked. A creative person with obsessive tendencies may be blocked by constant and intrusive thoughts about how to proceed with his projects. A self-doubting creative person may be blocked by quickly abandoning the beginnings of creative ideas (more about self-doubts in chapter 3). Holly's block was caused by insufficient knowledge on the topic, by resisting the inevitable twists and turns of the creative process, and by doubting the validity of her ideas.

The architect presented previously was blocked by expertise (Runco, 2014), a kind of process block that kept her stuck on tackling the architectural problem the same way she'd done in the past. Her attachment to her knowledge came at the expense of innovative thinking—of thinking outside the box. Other causes of process blocks include too little intellectual stimulation, not giving the mind enough time to wander, and putting a stop to the flow of ideas coming in. Creative people who don't run with a thought or an inspiring feeling are less likely to land on a creative idea they can then build on.

Another hindrance to generating creative ideas is a distracting environment. It's hard to become absorbed in novel and innovative thinking when there are multiple stimuli competing for the brain's attention. Taken to the extreme, however, the quest for a distraction-free moment leads to a different type of process block. Searching for the perfect moment, one that offers no external interferences to the mind's wanderings, sets up unrealistic expectations, along with the pressure of trying to meet them. Since most people's lives are filled with responsibilities, obligations, and environmental demands, waiting until nothing else is going on limits the opportunities for engaging in creative thinking. The longer the wait, the bigger the anticipatory anxiety—which further exacerbates this creative process block.

This happened to a writer I once worked with who worried that by writing just a couple of sentences after a day's worth of work, he wouldn't be able to finish his draft before the publishing deadline. As we spoke in more detail about his block, he described how he started off his writing day. Quickly, a pattern stood out. He'd start by taking care of all the things he thought might distract him. He'd first respond to e-mails (to "get that out of the way"), order supplies (to make sure he didn't "run out of ink"), gather all his previous notes (to "get organized"), repeat inspiring affirmations (to "keep doubts at bay"), and put on soft music (to "muffle the noise from nearby construction"). The emphasis on everything around the writing but the writing, in an effort to help himself, merely ended up delaying essential creative processes, such as engaging in divergent thinking and thought association and problem solving endings to his fiction stories. As a result, he got increasingly anxious about not writing.

Having too many creative thoughts to choose from (Carson, 2010) can make the task of selecting one and completing it much more arduous, resulting in an outcome block. Other explanations for outcome blocks include being too self-critical, shutting ideas down easily—often as a result of overly ambitious expectations—and finding it difficult to distinguish good ideas from bad ones. Overemphasizing end-goal success and audience reception can also block the idea-implementation stage. When a photographer thought about the many ways he could approach the same subject matter (film, narration, video, and installation) he eventually stopped strategizing because an internal voice cautioned him that using too many media would "damage his brand" and confuse his audience. Though his creative process was confident and rich in powerful ideas, his unhealthy attachment to outcome expectations escalated to a self-induced negation of ideas.

Creativity blocks don't just happen to people in the arts: scientists, entrepreneurs, and anyone who strives for originality, innovation, and aha moments run the risk of experiencing mental obstacles. Dean Simonton's book *Creativity in Science: Chance, Logic, Genius, and Zeitgeist* (2004) breaks down the elements that contribute to moments of scientific discovery, in contrast to those of artistic creation. He points out that artists work with fewer constraints (meaning that they're not usually looking for a single correct result) compared to scientists and that they rely on sensory and subjective experiences rather than the conceptual and objective. Therefore, to determine the kind of help that people need to overcome creativity blocks, it might be helpful to distinguish what kind of creative thinking they tend to rely on the most. Creativity researcher Shelly Carson (2010) points out that there are different creativity skill sets and brain states, some of which are triggered by intense emotions, whereas others are engaged in reasoning and decision making. Blocked artists might need more help with the former brain states, and blocked creative scientists with the latter. For example, though artists might feel like creativity blocks are, by and large, about the difficulties transforming affect into the most original or satisfying artistic representation (Carson, 2010), scientists might feel blocked in finding the solution to a problem. Rather than it being about emotions, scientists' blocks might be about finding the connecting thread among different forms of knowledge, which, according to Kenneth Heilman (2005), is an essential feature of creativity.

The Context of Creativity Blocks

Despite the emphasis of this chapter on the internal psychological traits that hinder or facilitate creativity, a conversation about creators' experiences with blocks would be incomplete without addressing the creative person's greater environmental context. The experience and perception of having a creative block are greatly dependent upon what's deemed to be creative in the first place. Finding out that the idea one has come up with has already been done or that it's been negatively received will make a creative effort seem futile, making the creator feel blocked.

Pointing out how people's environment shapes their experience of a creativity block hints at the culturally bound, sometimes arbitrary nature of idea assessment. It raises the question of whether one can feel successfully creative when the environment says otherwise. A creative person who judges his or her work harshly and views it as not particularly creative compared to other works around him or her is doing so in the context of external factors, such as timing, the environment's readiness to replace preexisting norms, and expert recognition. Such factors make the difference between just an image of an ordinary object and Warhol's world-famous *Campbell's Soup Cans*. Limits imposed by one's zeitgeist—the prevalent attitudes of a sociocultural environment in a particular time—will largely determine creators' own perceptions of whether what they came up with is creative or not.

The Clinician's Role

Understanding the Creative Process

To help creative clients tackle creative blocks, it's important for clinicians themselves to gain a good understanding of the creative process. They'll need to have a sense of what goes on in their creative clients' minds, and what their blocks say about where they're stuck. Clinicians can help clients by becoming knowledgeable about cognition and creativity, theories about the stages of creativity, and the basic ideas behind what facilitates creative brain arousal.

Before I began to work closely with creative populations, I approached blocked clients with a psychotherapy bias. My perspective was informed by an examination of inner conflicts, conscious and subconscious self-doubts, and the person's overall emotional state. As we'll see later in this chapter, these factors are, without a doubt, worthy of exploration. However, what was missing was a discussion of the mental processes needed to enhance creativity. For example, without an understanding of how the mind's wandering, daydreaming, and sleeping facilitate idea production (Riter & Dijksterhuis, 2014), clients might inadvertently prolong the blocked period by persisting on creative tasks without taking a break, feeling guilty whenever they step away.

Identifying the Blocked Stage

Clinicians will be better equipped to help their clients by identifying the stage in the creative process that appears to be blocked. A block in the earlier stages of the creative process could mean that the obstacle lies in accessing a state of creative flow—the full immersion in a creative activity that leads to peak performance (Csikszentmihalyi, 1997; Csikszentmihalyi, 2008). People are so conscious of their own thoughts, or so fragmented in how they approach the task at hand, that they resist the full absorption that's necessary to engage in divergent thinking. Other times, they're simply not thinking outside the box when they fixate on the same perspectives.

In contrast, if the block seems to come after the bulk of ideation has already been produced, it's likely that there's some difficulty in sifting through them to narrow them down and to make progress by building on the most appropriate one. This process, of converging and synthesizing information (Guilford, 1957; Cropley, 2006), can be hindered by the urge to keep producing ideas, perhaps due to underlying doubts about the ones already produced, or because of fears associated with bringing the creative task to completion. The clinicians' role is to help their clients identify the stage with which they struggle the most, to help them put their difficulties into words, and to provide a set of tools that'll help transition from one stage to the next.

Addressing Habits and Psychological Characteristics

Creative flow can be obstructed by psychological traits and habits that have been unintentionally reinforced over the years. Let's take the example of distractions. Too much focus on eliminating distractions creates unrealistic expectations, making it a counterproductive habit. In contrast, being constantly bombarded by phone and e-mail notifications makes it impossible to become engrossed in a task. Clinicians can help clients identify such tendencies and, when applicable, to understand the psychological underpinnings of their attachments to counterproductive habits.

Csikszentmihalyi (1997) draws a connection between the fears associated with depression and anxiety (such as the fear of being rejected and the fear of confronting one's own limitations) and the inability to enter a flow state. The counseling setting can be useful for exploring and articulating the thoughts, feelings, and behaviors that keep clients from comfortably "losing themselves" in the creative moment. Other mental health considerations are addressed in separate chapters in this book (see Chapter 5 on trauma and Chapter 6 on psychiatric disorders). Through discussions and clinical assessments, clinicians can gain insight into the psychological factors that account for clients' persistent obstacles to creative achievement.

Often, the traits that appear during moments of creativity parallel general traits in creators' lives. Overly cautious, risk-averse types will hesitate to settle on an idea with confidence, regardless of its quality: they'll doubt its worth, endlessly searching for an improvement, and resist commitment to implementation. Impulsive thrill seekers are likely to jump from one creative idea to another, but for different reasons: the need to seek novelty is so strong that they'll struggle with deep immersion in a single creative task. Clinicians can help clients recognize personality and behavioral patterns that emerge when they're engaging in creative tasks.

Unlearning Harmful Lessons About Creativity

There's often a story behind clients' experiences with creativity blocks, which can reveal useful information about how creators' pasts contribute to diminished creativity. For example, not everyone is raised in an environment that encourages and reinforces the freedom to think differently. When a creatively blocked painter discussed details about his past, he revealed countless interactions with teachers and family members that communicated a disapproval of going against the norm. Statements such as "What will people say?" and "Good kids don't rock the boat" had been drilled into him to the point that he associated originality with shame. Similarly, having learned to suppress emotions or to express only socially appropriate ones limits the exploration of different emotional states for inspiration. Clinicians can offer the supportive environment that enables clients to challenge limitations conditioned by past experiences.

Identifying Strategies to Overcome Blocks

With an understanding of where the person is blocked, the circumstances around the block, and possible explanations, clinicians can turn to what will bring about improvement in a client's creative ability: an array of tools that'll help clients put their blocks into perspective, limit their duration, and maximize the quantity and quality of creative ideas. Clinicians can begin by devoting time to picking clients' brains about what they're working on and the skills they plan to use while doing so. This demonstrates that clinicians value and validate their clients' creative identities. Then, clients and clinicians can discuss specific ideas for enhancing creativity, such as meditating, gathering knowledge, and collaborating.

Treatment Goals

1. Access creative flow.
2. Identify the type of creativity block.
3. Understand the causes of creativity blocks.
4. Develop creativity-enhancing practices.
5. Improve confidence in creative potential.

Suggested Interventions to Achieve Goals

1. *Keep at it.* This simple and intuitive intervention underscores the concept of working through a creativity block. Although it might be tempting to fantasize about giving up or moving on to a different creative project, giving something another shot, even when we think ideas have dried up, is key to unlocking creative potential. A similar concept comes from Simonton's assertion that the quality of a creative idea is the "probabilistic function of quantity" (2004:179). The more attempts, the likelier it is to yield good results.

    > Example: When a novelist I once worked with couldn't come up with an ending to her story that resonated, I suggested that she come up with a list of ideas for possible endings by the end of that week. When she came back with a long list of possibilities, but disheartened that none of them worked for her book, I challenged her to add an extra day, instead of abandoning her efforts. If nothing happened, she'd repeat the day extension, as long as she was doing her part: developing as many ideas as possible.

2. *Foster risk taking.* One of the defining personality traits among creative types is novelty seeking and openness to try new things. Clinicians can build on these traits to encourage clients to embrace challenges and

take creative risks, by trying new ideas, and by producing work that might be considered controversial. Sternberg (2006) describes these as sensible risks that help develop one's creativity. Counseling sessions can help identify fear, where it exists, and focus on tolerating the anxiety that might come from accessing and expressing unconventional ideas.

> Example: A software engineer was stuck for days on how to streamline a data-gathering process. Being a new employee in his company, he felt pressure to use the code written by other programmers and hesitated to stray from what was done before. He and I worked on improving his creative confidence so that he'd feel more comfortable approaching the problem from a new angle, despite potential resistance. When he took that risk, he opened himself up to new ways of thinking and, thus, of solving the problem.

3. *Encourage creating "in the middle of things."* Creativity coach Eric Maisel (2005) has developed the concept of creating in the middle of things, meaning resisting the urge to limit creative work to when the "time is right." He points out that there's always going to be noise, both external and internal, and that the role of the creative person is to enter a creative mode while things are going on. Clients are encouraged to see an opportunity for creative work no matter how busy, distracted, or preoccupied they are.

> Example: A photographer I worked with complained of struggling to finish his portfolio because of family visitors. I encouraged him to excuse himself from the dinner table 10 minutes earlier to go to his work area, to continue thinking about his images even when he couldn't find the time to work on them, and to spend 10 minutes per night on editing one image. The habit of committing to his creative engagements during chaotic moments helped him make enough progress so that when he did have uninterrupted time, he could mover further along.

4. *Incorporate improvisation.* Researchers have documented a positive correlation between improvisation (creating something new spontaneously) and divergent thinking (generating as many thought associations possible following a single cue) (Lewis & Lovatt, 2013; Sowden et al., 2015). Both divergent thinking and improvisation are hallmarks of creative abilities. Improvising is therefore a helpful way of training the brain to access new mental territory quickly. Rather than practicing rehearsed work or going over familiar routines, the goal is to approach the work without any preparation.

> Example: When a rock guitarist and songwriter was looking for ways to "avoid writing the same song over and over," I suggested

that he set aside 30 minutes during the day with the intention of improvising his craft. During this time, his task was to play styles he'd never ordinarily try (such as bossa nova and country) without worrying about song structure or technique. The goal was to let his brain go down new paths.

5. *Suggest sleeping on it.* Another well-documented way of spurring a creative breakthrough is to allow for the incubation period to happen. Resting, taking a break, and focusing on another task are examples of nurturing the incubation effect. This requires tamping down the urge for new ideas, so as to give the conscious mind some time off and let the subconscious mind do the work (Carson, 2010; Ellwood et al., 2009; Riter & Dijksterhui, 2014). Allowing oneself to take time off or to focus on another creative project can be difficult, in light of the mental-itch effect that comes up when feeling blocked, as described earlier in this chapter; yet doing so can improve performance and idea generation. Though this approach seems to contradict the "*Keep at it*" intervention, the key to finding a middle ground between these interventions lies in establishing a delicate balance between pushing forward and pulling back.

    Example: A highly anxious illustrator was stressed about being unable to meet her deadline. She had a vague sense of what she wanted her images to look like, but she was stuck repeating variations of the same idea. She saw merit in taking 24 hours off, but that idea fueled her anxiety, making it unfeasible. Eventually, she agreed to take 12 hours off, during which she cooked, started a puzzle, and listened to music. She returned to the task with a renewed perspective and the feeling that her previous trite ideas had gained some freshness.

6. *Chase the flow.* Inhibitions limit creativity. A state of creative flow, by its very existence, leaves little room for inhibitions. It's a state of full absorption, without worries about success or failure, with no sense of time, and with the immediately gratifying feeling of being rewarded (Csikszentmihalyi, 1997; Csikszentmihalyi, 2008). During a flow state, brain functions change in a way that favors spontaneity and a lack of restraint (Limb & Braun, 2008). These changes activate divergent thinking, thought associations, cognitive fluidity, and other tools for overcoming creativity blocks. Clinicians can work with their clients on identifying and reinforcing the conditions that bring on creative flow.

    Example: A creatively blocked actor worked with me on implementing flow-inducing practices. She tried to eliminate environmental distractions (noises, phone notifications, and so forth);

identified flow triggers, such as working early in the morning or while listening to relaxing music; and practiced staying in the moment by noticing wandering thoughts and bringing them back to the creative task.

7. *Monitor negative thoughts.* When my creative clients keep doubting their creative abilities, their creativity suffers. A time does come for judgment to play its part in evaluating the appropriateness of creative ideas, but doing so too early in the creative process causes and sustains creativity blocks. When negative thoughts pop up, it's important for clients to take notice of their frequency and intensity. Doing so helps create a healthy distance between the thought and the person, minimizing the impact of the negative thoughts' messages.

> Example: A multidisciplinary artist I worked with had been making little progress preparing for an upcoming show. After every idea that came to mind, he made a negative prediction about how it'd be received. I asked him to jot down all the negative thoughts that were popping up (that people would walk away, or that nobody would want to talk to him about his work), along with different, less negative interpretations. For example, he wrote down that some, not all, attendees might walk away, and that not being approached to discuss the work doesn't reflect audience reception.

8. *Stimulate natural curiosity.* What Shelly Carson has called the *absorb state* is our brain's ability to take in information freely, without a filter, and with a sense of wonder about what one might ordinarily take for granted (Carson, 2010; Nickerson, 1999). Sessions can focus on enhancing natural curiosity about what clients are working on. Thinking outside the box is an extension of the idea that being observant opens up new ways of processing the same information. In a similar vein, to get clients' natural curiosity going, clinicians can ask them to identify problems in need of solutions or to wonder out loud about the things that don't seem to make sense.

> Example: I once asked a client to imagine seeing the world the way children would, noticing all the things they might take for granted. Specifically, I suggested that she look at ordinary objects—a cup, a leaf, a rubber band—and try to come up with as many uses for them as possible. Another client and I talked about things that intrigued him during otherwise unremarkable moments, such as the commute to and from work.

9. *Encourage concentrative meditation.* Meditation—in particular concentrative meditation, where the goal is to stay focused on one object—has received recent attention regarding its ability to enhance cognitive flexibility

(Muller et al., 2016). Mindful concentration is also thought to increase creative performance by means of regulating attention and managing distractions (Kaufman & Gregoire, 2015). Clinicians can educate clients and provide them with resources on meditation styles and techniques.

> Example: A creatively blocked writer wanted to practice concentrative meditation by staying focused on one stimulus per meditation session. At first, she started concentrating on her breath and then moved on to a sound in the room. After 2 weeks of meditation sessions, she revisited her writing, in which she noticed more intensity and depth in her creative reflections.

10. *Consider the environment.* By reviewing of a number of studies of sociocultural context and creativity, Erez and Nouri (2010) posit that openness to experience and the pursuit of novel ideas—both of which are associated with creativity—are influenced by social and cultural factors. Of course, people are limited as to whether they can change their sociocultural context. Still, clinicians can help clients identify the environmental influences that have caused and sustained creativity blocks, and recognize when these influences get in the way of their creativity.

> Example: A client from a tight-knit religious community recalled being part of a culture that frowned upon creative expression in language, clothes, and hobbies. Despite these constraints, she applied to an art school in a different city and, for the first time, saw unlimited possibilities. It was important for her to understand how her environment had ingrained beliefs in her about taking creative risks. Understanding those beliefs helped her manage and control them.

11. *Manage time effectively.* Though, as discussed previously, it's important for creators to learn to create in the middle of things (Maisel, 2005), poor time management can worsen a creativity-conducive environment, making it difficult to overcome blocks. Zampetakis and colleagues (2010) used data from 186 participants that supported their hypothesis that individual creativity is positively related to behaviors such as organizing, managing time, and planning ahead. Creatively blocked people struggle with the content, quality, and quantity of their ideas. Still, it can be just as useful to look at the amount of time they spend on each creative task, when they do so, and how their creative goals fit into other time-sensitive responsibilities. Doing so highlights potential problems with creators' efficiency as they go through the stages of creativity.

> Example: A graphic designer I worked with tried to take care of many responsibilities at once: take the dog to the vet, clean the bathroom, and respond to apartments ads, as well as work on proposals for clients. He approached them all without a plan for the day's

Creativity Blocks   39

structure and quickly became overwhelmed with how hard it was to carve out time to build on creative ideas. I encouraged him to list the week's responsibilities and to divide them into four categories: some he'd delegate to someone else, some he'd work on for no more than 45 minutes, some he'd do first thing in the morning, and some he'd view as absolute priorities. This categorization helped him manage his time, so that that when he did work on creative ideas, he could do so for longer.

Additional Interventions

12.
13.
14.

Takeaways

- Creativity blocks—mental obstacles to thinking or acting creatively— damage creative people's psychological well-being. They threaten their confidence, the ability to enter a state of creative flow, and the realization of creative potential.
- Blocks appear throughout the stages of the creative process and can interfere with the process of coming up with a creative idea, as well as the outcome of bringing the idea to life.
- Different types of blocks have different causes: some are exacerbated by psychological traits and predispositions, whereas others are exacerbated by counterproductive working habits and conditions, and still others by limited exposure to mental stimulation.
- Counseling can help creative people identify and overcome their blocks by confronting obstacles and fears associated with the creative process.
- Clinicians and clients can work on reinforcing strategies that enhance the mind's natural curiosity, problem solving, and immersion in creative moments.

References

Amabile, T. M. (1996). *Creativity in context: Update to the social psychology of creativity*. Boulder, CO: Westview Press.

Beardsley, M. C. (1965, 1976). On the creation of art. In A. Rothenberg & C. R. Hausman (Eds.), *The creativity question* (pp. 305–311). Durham, NC: Duke University Press Books.

40 Creativity Blocks

Carson, S. (2010). *Your creative brain: Seven steps to maximize imagination, productivity, and innovation in your life*. San Francisco, CA: Jossey-Bass.

Cropley, A. (2006). In praise of convergent thinking. *Creativity Research Journal, 18*(3), 391–404.

Csikszentmihalyi, M. (1997). *Creativity: The flow and the psychology of discovery of invention.* New York, NY: HarperCollins Publishers.

Csikszentmihalyi, M. (2008). *Flow: The psychology of optimal experience.* New York, NY: Harper Perennial.

Ellwood, S., Pallier, G., Snyder, A., & Gallate, J. (2009). The incubation effect: Hatching a solution? *Creativity Research Journal, 21*(1), 6–14.

Erez, M., & Nouri, R. (2010). Creativity: The influence of cultural, social, and work contexts. *Management and Organization Review, 6*, 351–370.

Guilford, J. P. (1957). Creative abilities in the arts. *Psychological Review, 64*(2), 110–118.

Heilman, K. M. (2005). *Creativity and the brain.* New York, NY: Psychology Press.

Heilman, K. M., Nadeau, S. E., & Beversdord, D. O. (2003). Creative innovation: Possible brain mechanisms. *Neurocase: The Neural Basis of Cognition, 9*(5), 369–379.

Jarman, M. S. (2016). Scratching mental itches with extreme insights: Empirical evidence for a new theory. *Psychology of Aesthetics, Creativity, and the Arts, 10*(1), 21–31.

Kaufman, S. B., & Gregoire, C. (2015). *Wired to create: Unraveling the mysteries of the creative mind.* New York, NY: TarcherPerigee.

Lewis, C., & Lovatt, P. J. (2013). Breaking away from set patterns of thinking: Improvising and divergent thinking. *Thinking Skills and Creativity, 9*, 46–58.

Limb, C., & Braun, A. R. (2008). Neural substrates of spontaneous musical performance: An fMRI study of jazz improvisation. *PLOS One, 3*(2), e1679. Retrieved from https://doi.org/10.1371/journal.pone.0001679

Lubart, T. (2010). Models of the creative process: Past, present and future. *Creativity Research Journal, 13*(3–4), 295–308.

Maisel. E. (2005). *Coaching the artist within: Advice for writers, actors, visual artists, and musicians from America's foremost creativity coach.* Novato, CA: New World Library.

Milyavskaya, M., Ianakieva, I., Foxen-Craft, E., Colantuoni, A., & Koestner, R. (2012). Inspired to get there: The effects of trait and goal inspiration on goal progress. *Personality and Individual Differences, 52*(1), 56–60.

Muller, B. C. N., Gerasimova, A., & Ritter, S. M. (2016). Concentrative meditation influences creativity by increasing cognitive flexibility. *Psychology of Aesthetics, Creativity, and the Arts, 10*(3), 278–286.

Nickerson, R. S. (1999, 2010). Enhancing creativity. In R. J. Sternberg (Ed.), *Handbook of creativity* (14th ed.). Cambridge: Cambridge University Press.

Riter, S. M., & Dijksterhuis, A. (2014). Creativity—the unconscious foundations of the incubation period. *Frontiers in Human Neuroscience, 8*, 215.

Runco, M. A. (2014). *Creativity: Theories and themes: Research, development, and practice* (2nd ed.). London, UK: Academic Press.

Simonton, D. K. (2004). *Creativity in science: chance, logic, genius and zeitgeist.* Cambridge: Cambridge University Press.

Sowden, P. T., Clements, L., Redlich, C., & Lewis. (2015). Improvisation facilitates divergent thinking and creativity: Realizing a benefit of primary school arts education. *Psychology of Aesthetics, Creativity, and the Arts, 9*(2), 128–138.

Sternberg, R. J. (2006). The nature of creativity. *Creativity Research Journal, 18*(1), 87–98.

Stumpf, H. (1995). Scientific creativity: A short overview. *Educational Psychology Review*, 7(3), 225–241.

Thrash, T. M., & Elliot, A. J. (2004). Inspiration: Core characteristics, component processes, antecedents, and function. *Journal of Personality and Social Psychology*, 87, 957–973.

Thrash, T. M., Elliot, A. J., Maruskin, L. A., & Cassidy, S. E. (2010). Inspiration and the promotion of well-being: tests of causality and mediation. *Journal of Personality and Social Psychology*, 98(3), 488–506.

Wallas, G. (1926). *The art of thought*. New York, NY: Harcourt Brace.

Zampetakis, L. A., Bouranta, N., & Moustakis, V. S. (2010). On the relationship between individual creativity and time management. *Thinking Skills and Creativity*, 5(1), 23–32.

Zhang, X., & Bartol, K. M. (2010). Linking empowering leadership and employee creativity: The influence of psychological empowerment, intrinsic motivation, and creative process engagement. *Development and Learning in Organizations: An International Journal*, 24(5), 107–128.

Chapter 3

Self-Doubts

People who are creatively fulfilled see their creative endeavors as being worthy of pursuit. Without self-approval and belief in the work, the most touching painting will never leave the studio; the most helpful innovation won't get funding and reach the layperson; the most inspiring novel won't be submitted to publishers. I once worked with a choreographer, Mark, who had an unfaltering drive to create a dance company. Week after week, he'd bring up an idea that had just inspired him. His eyes would light up as he spoke about movements he was excited to try out with his dancers. He'd come up with a strategy to promote his company's showpiece and had researched ways to get funding. There was, however, one problem: he couldn't bring himself to start choreographing. Every time he'd try, a familiar feeling of hesitation would take over. An indistinct, but strong internal voice wondered if he really knew what he was doing. It questioned whether he could ever be "one of those great choreographers out there." A generally confident man, with logical and straightforward thinking, he couldn't bring himself to confront all the what-ifs: what if the dancers hate it? What if it fails? What if the idea for the choreography is trite? What if I'm not as good as others expect me to be? To get a better sense of what Mark and other creators with similar feelings go through, we'll take a look at self-doubts during the creative process. We'll investigate where they come from and the ingredients that build creative confidence. Last, we'll consider suggestions that mental health clinicians can use to help clients value their creative skills.

My creative clients often go back and forth on some strongly held, but inhibiting convictions: painters question whether taking time to paint is time well spent, even though they enjoy the process; photographers proclaim that the world "doesn't need another photographer," even though no other photographer has the exact perspective they do; writers doubt that starting a blog is a good idea because of their small online following, even though starting the blog is the only way to increase it; self-taught guitarists don't believe they deserve to collaborate with musicians who went to prestigious music schools, even though their talent is comparable. Unfortunately, these clients are flooded with doubts about their right to occupy space in the creative world and about the quality of the creative outcome—doubts that keep them from pursuing their creative dreams. These clients are filled with ambivalence about their worth and believe they're impostors who are fooling others into thinking that they're truly creatively gifted.

Causes of Self-Doubts During the Creative Process

Julia Cameron's internationally best-selling self-help book, *The Artist's Way*, published in 1992, quickly gained momentum as one of the most influential validations of the intrinsic value of using one's creativity. Her book, which has sparked a movement over the last decades, and whose followers set up workshops to implement its teachings, explores creative people's fears and outlines concrete steps that people can take to become creatively empowered. Cameron speaks about the deeply rooted ways artists doubt themselves through self-attacks. Regarding the recovery of people's creative selves, she says that "as we gain strength so will some of the attacks of self-doubt. This is normal, and we can deal with these stronger attacks when we see them as symptoms of recovery," and "early in our creative recovery, self-doubt can lure us into self-sabotage" (Cameron, 2002:42). Cameron is not alone in identifying this vulnerable spot for many creative people. As I perused countless self-help books, articles on creativity, and interviews with artists and creative innovators, I easily got a sense of how often people struggle to reach their creative potential because they question their abilities, worth, and legitimacy.

It's not all that surprising that self-doubting thoughts come up for creative people. The creative process, by virtue of being an exploration of uncharted territory (novel ideas that aren't tried and true), is a breeding ground for self-doubts. Doing something creatively means doing it differently—going against norms, traditions, and conventions (Kaufman & Gregoire, 2015). Naturally, these kinds of risks are likely to introduce apprehension. The subjectivity that's often involved in evaluating the quality, usefulness, and originality of creative work, particularly in artistic creativity, can instantly fill people with questions about how their work is perceived. Though there are tools and rubrics for assessing originality and value in creative ideas, such as the Consensual Assessment Technique, where independent experts rate creative products (Kaufman et al., 2008), according to (Amabile, 1996:28) the "purportedly objective scoring procedures in many of the creativity tests are, in fact, basically subjective. For some scoring procedures, results must depend on the test scorer's intuitive assessment of what is creative." As mentioned in chapter 9 on stress in the arts-and-entertainment world, a study by Lauring and colleagues (2016) confirmed the conventional wisdom that people perceive artwork to be more or less favorable according to the price of the painting and how others, particularly experts, rate the pieces.

44 Self-Doubts

When creative individuals submit a manuscript or an album for consideration, they'll have no way of accurately predicting whether it'll resonate with the recipient. They'll have no guarantee that at the end of a long and challenging creative process, their painting, song, novel, film, or theatrical performance will meet success and recognition. Mark, the choreographer mentioned previously, was troubled by these kinds of questions, as he hadn't any guarantee for how his ideas would fare. This uncertainty, perhaps due to his high need for control and stability, which was one of the issues we worked on during our sessions, was unbearable.

People in arts-and-entertainment careers are particularly susceptible to self-doubt. The high standards placed on physical appearance, the industry's competitiveness, and the repeated rejections reinforce doubts about their creative skills and talents. Evaluating creativity in sciences is different, since scientists use their creative capacities to solve problems for which the criteria tend to be clearer. A software developer might have to use divergent, associative, and imaginative thinking to write new code, but the code either works or it doesn't: the process is creative, but it has a clear-cut goal. Still, every creative process can raise doubts because every new trial brings with it chances of error. Even with a single desired destination, the road can be winding and uncertain. Again, this kind of unpredictability produces doubts about the quality of the creative process while reinforcing doubts already present.

Self-doubts in the creative process are also tied to the personal and revelatory nature of creativity. Artistic work reveals information about its creator: it tends to express its creator's emotional and mental state—feelings, thoughts, and perceptions. One of my clients, a singer who'd mostly been associated with pop-rock acts, was interested in forming a doom metal band. The content of the lyrics would be substantially different: instead of singing about love and breakups, she'd now be singing about corruption and atheism. Those were issues she'd been thinking about already, but she would be making a drastic shift in genres. For the first time, she'd be writing from her heart, and she worried that her friends, fans, and family wouldn't relate. She worried that they'd perceive her to be a troubled person. These worries resulted in her doubting the worth of her songwriting ideas.

Creative products, even when not artistic, offer a window into thinking patterns that are unique to the creative person's mind. They mirror what creators think about and how they see the world. Another client I worked with, a copywriter for an advertising agency, described a similar experience: during brainstorming sessions for advertising ideas, he felt like every spontaneous thought would be an uninvited glimpse into his creative brain. Being that he didn't feel completely safe in the group, he hesitated to speak up, fearing that he'd be negatively perceived. Revealing oneself, especially when it means carving new paths, often triggers second-guessing, overthinking, and hesitating.

The link between creativity and self-doubting thoughts can be understood by traits associated with sensitivity. Silverman (2000) and Winner (1996), in their observations of highly creatively gifted people, have noted that children and adults with extraordinary creative abilities exhibit profound sensitivity to stimuli in their environment. Creative people tend to be sensitive and overexcitable—they react intensely to sensory, emotional, intellectual, psychomotor, and imaginational stimuli (Daniels & Piechowski, 2009; Kaufman & Gregoire, 2015; Silverman, 2000). As a result, they feel things deeply, including stress (Runco, 2014), and pick up on information that generates self-doubting thoughts. Because of their sensitivity, they'll notice when something around them isn't right, such as when a drawing in their imagination differs from what they actually drew, or when a drummer stays behind the beat by a few milliseconds. Or, they'll catch a subtle change in the facial expression of a collaborator as they're presenting their creative work. Being deeply in tune with what's happening around them triggers intense thoughts, feelings, and reactions. Kaufman and Gregoire (2015:125) note that "to both the highly creative and the highly sensitive mind, there's simply more to observe, take in, feel, and process." Being able to absorb a lot from internal and external stimuli has many potential benefits: it can lead to interesting observations, point toward unusual patterns, and heighten emotional intuitiveness and the urge to externalize one's inner world through creative expression. But taking more in leaves the door open for sensitivity to criticism, rejection, and disappointment. Sensitive people are paying more attention to what's happening—including experiences that cast doubt on their creative abilities.

Luckily, even when sensitivity leads to self-doubts and insecurities, creative people can still exhibit high levels of nonconformity and autonomy. In a seeming paradox, creative people can be hyperaware of negative feedback, and still drum to their own beat. It's likely that rather than consider conventionality as a viable antidote to self-doubts (instead of saying, "I'll draw the way everyone else draws" or "I'll do whatever pleases my collaborator"), creative people find solace in their creativity as a way of dealing with the feeling of not belonging. This might be because creative pursuits are a way to channel overexcitability, or because creative expression is their way of asserting their independence when it's threatened by social norms.

The way creative people are taught to deal with their insecurities is not always helpful. Those in the arts-and-entertainment industry are particularly prone to tucking away their sensitivities, at least publicly, in order to present an overly confident persona. In competitive professions, where insecurity is often mistaken for inability, people live by the fake-it-till-you-make-it mantra. Although this resembles a desired psychological state, it can actually be a harmful one: it disguises a person's genuine feelings and keeps them from being recognized, making it difficult to address self-doubts at their root and manage them effectively.

Creative Self-Efficacy

What does high confidence look like in creative people, and why is it important? Pamela Tierney and Steven Farmer (2002) studied the construct of creative self-efficacy, an extension of Albert Bandura's self-efficacy theory (Bandura, 1977), the belief people have in their abilities to succeed. Creative self-efficacy describes the confidence people show in their abilities to think and act creatively. This type of confidence is important because it determines the persistence with which creative people tackle demanding tasks. It reinforces their commitment to trying new things (Tierney & Farmer, 2002) and going against the grain. When people have low creative self-efficacy, they wonder if the time spent on creative work is worthwhile. They underperform on creative tasks (Malik et al., 2015) and are preoccupied with nagging thoughts such as "What's the point?" and "This is a bad idea." They give up on the creative work when obstacles come up, and they avoid talking to others about it (Maisel, 2013).

A painter I worked with tried to manage her low creative self-efficacy by jumping from one idea to another. Even though she was motivated and enthusiastic, her confidence in her creative abilities was so low that she never actually made progress with any of her paintings. The first trace of hesitation would lead her to give up and, detrimentally, to redirect her attention elsewhere. The excitement of a new creative thought felt good, but as soon as things got tough—when the paintings didn't match what she'd envisioned, or she heard critical remarks—she started to doubt the entire idea.

People with high creative self-efficacy are likelier to spend time thinking about creative solutions to problems (Hsu et al., 2011) and to persevere. They see obstacles as indicators that they're tackling the task in depth. They are eager to engage in promotion-seeking behaviors such as looking for funding, representation, and sponsorship. They pursue opportunities, even at the risk of failure or rejection. A strong belief in one's creative abilities is important for creative success (Kaufman, 2002)—perhaps even more so than for creative thinking. This is because even without confidence and high creative self-efficacy, people can still engage in creative thinking (generate many ideas, make connections between seemingly unrelated pieces of information, and produce original content). However, confidence is particularly helpful when the time comes for people to promote their work, advocate for it, and ensure that it gets enough exposure. Confidence, or creative self-efficacy, protects against fear of exposure, the fear of ridicule, and the need to conform (Nickerson, 1999).

I remember feeling gratified and encouraged by the slow but steady progress made by Ben, a marketing consultant I worked with. He played guitar nonprofessionally and sought counseling to address extremely low confidence when it came to seeing himself as a guitarist. For months, he'd avoid bringing up the topics of music writing and playing during our conversations. He'd cringe and nervously fidget. He was a highly sensitive person, who idolized his musical heroes such as Bob Dylan, Hank Williams, and David Bowie, and carried their lyrics with him as he went about his day. His day-job dissatisfaction strengthened his need to go home and pour his emotions into his playing, yet he didn't dare think of himself an artist, not when he had such a deep appreciation for, as he put it, "true artistry."

As time progressed, I invited him to talk more openly about his creative ideas and his passion for playing music. I listened to him speak about the guitar melodies he'd been working on and asked questions about what he liked about them. I urged him to challenge the idea that he must be a musical hero to create, by emphasizing his innate pull toward music. During an intimate moment of equal anxiety and excitement, he shared some of his lyrics and hummed a melody during one of our sessions. It was the first time he'd done something like this during our sessions. These small moments, as difficult as they were, demonstrated to him that he could do this, even in front of another person—me. About a year after our first meeting, he'd set up his first open-mic show. The reinforcement of the self-image of a guitar player crystallized the conviction that he, in fact, was one. Without realizing it, session by session, he was building his creative self-efficacy.

Belief in creative abilities is important because it helps creative people like Ben and Mark keep going. It imbues nonartists with the feeling that they, too, can be innovative—that creativity isn't reserved for just the eminent painter or novelist (Kelley & Kelley, 2013). It helps artists, performers, and other creative professionals truly see themselves as contributors to the vast domain of creativity. It solidifies their conviction that they deserve to be seen, recognized, and celebrated. It protects against the so-called *creativity bias* (Kaufman & Gregoire, 2015), which suggests that, at least initially, audiences, evaluators, and even creators themselves favor predictability and consistency over novelty and innovation.

The Clinician's Role

Addressing Attachment to Negative Self-Perception

Clients' convictions that their creative worth is low can be persistent. Suggesting otherwise is often met with suspicion. This is one of the self-perpetuating features of poor self-confidence: it's hard to have a favorable view of oneself, even when it's backed up by convincing evidence, because such evidence tends to be disregarded. When I happened to see one my clients' paintings exhibited at a local restaurant, I told her about it during our next session. Mistakenly perhaps, I thought that my self-disclosure about the restaurants I visit, and about my being a consumer of art out in the real world, would have therapeutic value because it would serve the purpose of helping my client see herself in a positive light. I told her about the praising comments I heard from other restaurant guests. I mentioned that I found her artwork to be significantly more thought-out and technically proficient than she'd let on during our sessions.

Unfortunately, this backfired. My client, who'd been so used to being critical of her work, in part so that her harsh criticisms would temper her expectations for success, had developed an automatic suspiciousness of every positive reaction. She needed to believe that she wasn't great because, if she wasn't, failure would hurt less—it would make sense somehow. For the first time ever, she began to slip in questions about my art background. She wanted to know if I'd worked with similar cases. She questioned my positive reaction to her painting and wondered how much exposure to art I'd had. To hold onto her narrative of being an unworthy artist, she looked for ways to shift her perception of the person threatening this narrative—in this case, me.

Instead of focusing on challenging harmful perceptions, clinicians can, at least in the beginning, gently point out the presence of such defense mechanisms in order to shed light on how they interfere with creative achievement. The clinicians' role is to identify clients' attachment to negative views of their creative identities and to help clients recognize the harm that such views can cause.

Looking at Clients' Work

The previous example of the painter brings up a question that many clinicians who work with this population are curious about: when is it a good idea to look at their clients' work? Getting a sense of what clients are working on can be helpful as it can help clinicians identify discrepancies between perceived and actual features of the work. Looking at clients' work can reveal in real time clients' affective responses. Do they get anxious and fidget in their chairs? Do they seem proud and eager to share their songs, images, and so forth? Do they immediately point out the flaws? These reactions demonstrate how clients feel about the work and provide useful information regarding what sessions ought to focus on.

The advantages of inviting clients to show their work are unclear for those with low creative confidence. This is because doing so could put clinicians in a position of being asked to judge, praise, and validate the worth of works and ideas. Especially for clients with a vulnerable sense of self-worth, this runs the risk of creating a relationship of dependency, in which clients rely on clinicians for validation. When emphasis is placed on what clinicians think, the need for clients to access feelings of confidence from within gets undermined.

In contrast, clients sometimes make great progress in managing to feel proud of their creations; they look forward to sharing their joy with clinicians. In such cases, becoming part of the journey can be invaluable for clients who've come a long way. The answer to whether clinicians should look at their clients' work largely depends on whether doing so would serve the purpose of providing validation or sharing the validation already in place.

Validating Clients' Right to Create

There is, however, a different kind of validation that clinicians ought to provide. This isn't the kind that reassures clients about the quality of their creative work. Rather, it's a validation of their right to think creatively, to seek the rewards of creative expression, and to invite others to witness their creative journey. When clients excessively scrutinize their creative ideas, they hesitate to reveal them. This results in ideas becoming stuck in their minds, bouncing around aimlessly. The role of clinicians is to provide a safe platform for such ideas to come out. Clinicians can ask probing questions about what clients are working on and what they find most enjoyable about the work. They can inquire into what clients' work reveals about their personalities, and they can show interest in the creative ideas that matter most to clients. The clinicians' role is to demonstrate genuine curiosity in their clients' creative thoughts and to support their right to make a contribution, regardless of its size, to their chosen creative field.

In the same vein, it's helpful when clinicians emphasize their clients' distinctness and originality. When creative work is seen as a product of the unique combination of the creator's traits, it becomes legitimate. The emphasis is not on how it compares to other creative works, or on what people think, but on whether creations reflect their creators' inner workings. By validating clients' creative efforts as an opportunity to leave their fingerprints on the world, clinicians can move clients from comparison-based thinking ("I shouldn't produce this play because it's destined not to be of Broadway-production quality"), to thinking that recognizes the needs for self-actualization and for self-expression ("I choose to produce this play because I'm uniquely qualified to do so, and I'm the only one with these exact aesthetics, skills, and creative values and perspectives").

Encouraging Self-Acceptance

Clinicians will have more impact when they foster clients' self-accepting attitudes. Exploring—and hopefully improving—the relationship clients have with themselves sometimes requires delving into the past. Doing so offers insight into how their creative identities were perceived and shaped by influential figures in their childhoods, such as parents, extended family members, and teachers. A writer I worked with kept repeating the words "fraud" and "fake" when he'd describe his writing abilities. "I'm just pretending," he'd often say. When I asked him to think about himself as someone who was both competent and flawed in his writing skills, he asserted that he couldn't reconcile the two ideas. He tearfully revealed a series of painful interactions with his father: whenever he proudly showed his poems and essays to him,

50 Self-Doubts

his father would return them with corrections and harsh feedback. He'd tell him that "real" writers have a distinct capacity for the use of language; "real" writers evoke vivid images with just a few words; "real" writers move readers with their descriptions. This client and I spent many sessions separating his father's thoughts from his own in order to minimize his self-rejecting tendencies. Exploring clients' pasts traces the history of their fears, hesitation, and ambivalence. This helps clients draw distinctions between negative self-perceptions formed by past experiences and the feelings of self-acceptance they choose to embrace when they're pursuing creative goals.

As mental health professionals well know, restructuring the relationships people have with themselves into ones that are driven by positive self-regard can take years. Nevertheless, clinicians can begin to make an impact by modeling acceptance of their clients' flaws and mistakes. For clients who tend to judge themselves harshly after a failure, the clinician's role would be to create space for a discussion of what went wrong, to normalize the occurrence of disappointments alongside taking risks, and to engage in conversations that emphasize the potential for improvement. Without shying away from them—the goal is to accept the whole self, not just its favorable parts—clinicians can help their clients move away from knee-jerk self-attacks, and from emphasizing the negative consequences of their failures. Opportunities to model self-acceptance might come up when clients judge themselves for putting off their creative work, when they receive unfavorable feedback, when the results of their efforts don't meet their own expectations, and so forth. Clinicians can work to foster the attitude that creative accomplishments exist not in spite of failures, but because of them.

Treatment Goals

1.	Increase creative self-efficacy.
2.	Prioritize creative pursuits.
3.	Make progress in achieving creative goals.
4.	Become comfortable promoting creative work.
5.	Manage feelings from rejections and failures.

Suggested Interventions to Achieve Goals

1. *Practice cognitive defusion.* The term *defusion* is used in acceptance commitment therapy to illustrate the distinction between the person doing the thinking and the thoughts themselves. The contrasting concept is *fusion*, which describes our identification with what we are thinking. The idea is that the words we use to describe thoughts and feelings are just that—words. They can be distinguished from the accuracy of what they describe (Hayes et al., 2016). Clients aren't worthless because they had the thought that they are: rather, they're worthy people with occasional thoughts of worthlessness. When working with creative clients who doubt themselves, clinicians can use this approach to break the cycle between the thinking of words that reinforce the perception of inadequacy and the perpetuating act of fulfilling the mandate of the words.

    > Example: An illustrator and I worked on making subtle changes in the wording and thought process that accompanied persistent self-doubts. Instead of saying, "I can't do the work," I encouraged him to say, "I just had the thought that I can't do it." Instead of saying, "Everyone submitting to this competition is better than me," he practiced saying, "My thoughts are telling me that other candidates are better, but I'll apply anyway because my thoughts might be wrong."

2. *Reflect on successes.* An effective way for clients to increase their creative confidence and solidify their creative identity is to think about past successes. Even if the successes seem unimportant to the clients, reinforcing the idea that they've used some sort of creativity, at some point, and in some way can have a positive impact. It conveys the message that clients are likely to be creative or to have creative success again. Clients can draw confidence from resurfaced memories of positive experiences.

    > Example: I worked with a singer-songwriter who was recording her first album in 4 years. The gap between albums made her fear that she might have lost her songwriting and singing touch. Our sessions had turned into a list-making exercise of her insecurities: she worried that she'd no longer have an audience, that she'd mess up the chords during the recording, and so forth. One day, an old collaborator asked for her biography. Though she initially dreaded the process, I asked her to compile a list of her accomplishments, leaving the decision of whether to send it to her acquaintance for later. Thinking about all the things she'd accomplished helped her think of herself as a musician for the first time in a while, renewing her confidence for her next album.

3. *Give permission to fail.* Clients will often consciously admit that failure is part of the learning process, but subconsciously they'll hesitate, procrastinate, give up, and pass on opportunities in order to avoid it. Reframing failure as a potentially positive experience takes work. It goes against the craving for immediate positive results—to pass the audition today, to get many views on one's video, to get published right away. However, without failure, one bypasses valuable opportunities to learn, to allow time for creative ideas, and to reinforce the identity of a dedicated, persistent creator. Clinicians can work with clients on developing flexible attitudes around failing.

> Example: When a writer came up with a list of publications to which he planned to submit his work, he and I tried to normalize the possibility of failure as an outcome. We set aside time to articulate the benefits of trying despite the likelihood of being rejected. He prepared for the possibility of negative feedback and had already decided to use constructive criticism to make changes in his upcoming manuscripts. We spent time emphasizing the significance of making efforts, even though his initial goal—of getting a contract—might not be met.

4. *Foster a sense of entitlement.* Elizabeth Gilbert, best-selling author of the memoir *Eat Pray Love*, encourages people to develop their creative confidence by feeling entitled to use their innate potential for creative thought (Gilbert, 2015). This guards creative clients against painful memories of having failed before and discouraging worries about being good enough. Clinicians can work with clients to reinforce the idea that, even in the presence of inadequacies, limitations, and failures, they have the right to use their creativity. As much as possible, it's important to separate the concept of the right to create from the quality of the result. Clients' work will always have room for improvement, and success is often assessed subjectively. In contrast, entitlement to do the work in the first place can be seen a nonnegotiable, absolute right.

> Example: When a nonprofessional painter felt unworthy of spending her day painting, thinking she ought to do other things like caring for her elderly parents and housecleaning, I asked her to think about how her life might improve if she spent more time on her creative interests. She explicitly addressed benefits, such as "When I'm done with this painting, I can hang it on the wall and decorate my home" and "Painting is a healthy outlet for my negative feelings." Focusing on such positive outcomes helped her see herself as inherently deserving of using her creative potential.

5. *Introduce optimism.* It took me a while to see the value in adopting an optimistic attitude with clients. I worried that doing so negated clients' needs to express their darkest and most negative thoughts. I feared it

would cast me as the cheery friend—a figure who can't contain the sadness, defeat, and disappointment that come with having a fragile sense of self. Although it's true that clinicians should try to meet clients where they are (meaning clinicians should create a safe space for clients to express all sorts of feelings, including negativity, flaws, and anxieties), being optimistic has benefits. For creativity in particular, optimism strengthens the persistence necessary to search for innovative ideas and solutions to problems. It protects against the impulse to give up in the presence of obstacles (Hsu et al., 2011; Icekson et al., 2014). Clinicians can model expectations of positive outcomes while helping clients feel safe to voice their skepticism.

> Example: A filmmaker I worked with doubted every step of the creative process. Whether it was about finding like-minded collaborators, getting funding, or being positively reviewed by critics, he always imagined the worst outcome. Unsurprisingly, this lowered his motivation to try things and lowered his satisfaction derived from filmmaking. First, we spoke about his fears and tried to tolerate the emotional pain inherent in his hypothetical catastrophic scenarios. Then I asked him to envision the best possible outcome for each step. For example, he'd meet someone who "got him," and he'd have the creative freedom to pursue his ideas with a network to back him up. He hesitated to think this way, fearing it would make disappointment all the more upsetting; however, once I reminded him that we'd handle his negative feelings during our sessions—if things were to go badly—he reluctantly allowed himself to think optimistically. Doing so began to stimulate his desire for creativity.

6. *Build competence.* Perceiving oneself as being skilled at something sustains the conviction needed to keep doing it. When clients feel insecure about their abilities, sessions can focus on strategies to improve skills specific to the creative work. Clients will inevitably face limitations as they try to do things that are new or difficult. Acquiring knowledge and gaining expertise reinforce a sense of competence, which will hopefully lead clients to want to demonstrate what they've learned.

> Example: Ben, the guitar player presented in this chapter, managed to quiet down some of his self-doubts by enrolling in an online music composition course and taking guitar lessons. Doing so helped him develop new guitar-playing abilities and increased his confidence when jamming with other musicians. He was motivated to try new songwriting ideas under the guidance and support of his more experienced teachers.

7. *Implement habits that foster creative self-efficacy.* Some habits promote creative confidence, and some don't. Clinicians and clients can work

together to identify helpful practices and implement a routine that incorporates them. Examples of habits that protect creative clients' confidence include being surrounded by encouraging figures, getting one small thing done every day, setting the goal of working a little each day, and drawing self-comparisons instead of comparisons to others.

> Example: A disheartened novelist contacted me to regain his creative confidence. It immediately became clear that the break he'd been taking from writing—as a way of healing from a previous publication that had done poorly—exacerbated his preexisting doubts about his talents. We worked on implementing habits such as writing a short story every day, without intending to show it to anyone. Even if the story wasn't his greatest work, the habit of using his imagination daily and his experimentation with the uses of language empowered his self-perception as a writer.

8. *Build creative identity.* Clinicians can help clients develop a vocabulary that describes their identities as creative beings. To do so, sessions can focus on how they perceive themselves, with an emphasis on their innovative and outside-the-box traits. By reflecting on their individuality, artists, performers, and other creative individuals strengthen their sense of self. A secure creative identity emphasizes uniqueness instead of flawlessness. It promotes the idea that even if they don't feel omniscient or perfect, they can still offer distinct perspectives that deserve to be expressed.

> Example: I once asked a highly self-doubting painter to come up with a list of words that described her as an artist. She had an extraordinarily difficult time doing so. She reported that she didn't want to be pigeonholed, but my hunch was that, beyond that, she didn't see herself as worthy enough to be taken seriously as a painter with a trademark. When she agreed, she came up with specific, detailed words, including "minimalist," "pure," and "three-dimensional." As she continued to do so, she began to identify a place for herself in the artistic world. She wasn't "just another artist."

9. *Practice strengths-based therapy.* Strengths-based and positive-psychology interventions examine a person's positive attributes. They don't view clients as being inadequate or ill, but rather value their potential for growth. They emphasize possibilities for improvement in overall functioning (Scheel et al., 2012). This approach can be used with creative clients who doubt their abilities, as it teaches them to recognize and use their strengths during the creative process.

> Example: When I worked with a singer who always thought about her flaws, or the kind of voice she wished she had, I encouraged her to think about the unique qualities in her voice that she appreciated.

Similarly, during my work with a self-judging dancer, we spoke about the parts of her body that had helped her get to where she was, rather than focus on limitations in her movements. In both cases, the goal was to focus on what they wanted to keep, along with what they wanted to improve.

Additional Interventions

10.
11.
12.

Takeaways

- Creative clients engage in work that, by definition, is innovative, novel, and representative of their unique ways of thinking. Doing so requires them to have confidence in their creative abilities. Creative people reach their potentials by believing in their abilities to think and act creatively.
- The subjectivity of evaluating creative work, the heightened emotional sensitivity in creative people, and the competitiveness of the arts-and-entertainment industry contribute to the development of self-doubts and low creative self-efficacy.
- Creative confidence is important because it guards creators against criticism, self-attacks, and rejections.
- Clinicians can work with clients to uncover the sturdiness of their self-concepts and the strength of their self-esteem. Clients can work on gaining insight into the roots of their self-doubting tendencies.
- Counseling sessions can manage clients' negative beliefs, help them implement habits that foster a sense of competence, and empower their convictions that they have the right to create.

References

Amabile, T. M. (1996). *Creativity in context: Update to the social psychology of creativity.* Boulder, CO: Westview Press.

Bandura, A. (1977). Self-efficacy: Toward a unifying theory of behavioral change. *Psychological Review, 84*(2), 191–215.

Cameron, J. (2002). *The artist's way* (2nd ed.). New York, NY: Jeremy P. Tarcher/Putnam.

Daniels, S., & Piechowski, M. M. (Eds.). (2009). *Living with intensity: Understanding the sensitivity, excitability and emotional development of gifted children, adolescents and adults.* Scottsdale, AZ: Great Potential Press.

Gilbert, E. (2015). *Big magic: Creative living beyond fear*. New York, NY: Riverhead Books.

Hayes, S. C., Strosahl, K. D., & Wilson, K. G. (2016). *Acceptance and commitment therapy: The process and practice of mindful change* (2nd ed.). New York, NY: Guilford Press.

Hsu, M. L. A., Hou, S. T., & Fan, H. L. (2011). Creative self-efficacy and innovative behavior in a service setting: Optimism as a moderator. *Journal of Creative Behavior, 45*, 258–272. doi:10.1002/j.2162–6057.2011.tb01430.x

Icekson, T., Roskes, M., & Moran, S. (2014). Effects of optimism on creativity under approach and avoidance motivation. *Frontiers in Human Neuroscience, 8*, 105. Retrieved from https://doi.org/10.3389/fnhum.2014.00105

Kaufman, J. C. (2002). Creativity and confidence: price of achievement? Comment. *American Psychologist, 57*(5), 375–376.

Kaufman, J. C., Plucker, J. A., & Baer, J. (2008). *Essentials of creativity assessment*. Hoboken, NJ: John Wiley & Sons.

Kaufman, S. B., & Gregoire, C. (2015). *Wired to create: Unraveling the mysteries of the creative mind*. New York: TarcherPerigee.

Kelley, T., & Kelley, D. (2013). *Creative confidence: Unleashing the creative potential within us all*. New York, NY: Crown Business.

Lauring, J. O., Pelowski, M., Forster, M., Gondan, M., Ptito, M., & Kupers, R. (2016). Well, if they like it. . . . Effects of social groups' ratings and price information on the appreciation of art. *Psychology of Aesthetics, Creativity, and the Arts, 10*(3), 344–359. Retrieved from http://dx.doi.org/10.1037/aca0000063

Maisel, E. (2013). *Making your creative mark*. Novato, CA: New World Library.

Malik, M. A. R., Butt A. N., & Choi, J. N. (2015). Rewards and employee creative performance: Moderating effects of creative self-efficacy, reward importance, and locus of control. *Journal of Organizational Behavior, 36*, 59–74. doi:10.1002/job.1943.

Nickerson, R. S. (1999). Enhancing creativity. In R. J. Sternberg (Ed.), *Handbook of creativity*. Cambridge: Cambridge University Press.

Runco, M. A. (2014). *Creativity: Theories and themes: Research, development, and practice* (2nd ed.). London, UK: Elsevier.

Scheel, M. J., Klentz Davis, C., & Henderson, J. D. (2012). Therapist use of client strengths: A qualitative study of positive processes. *The Counseling Psychologist, 41*(3), 392–427.

Silverman, L. K. (2000). The gifted individual. In L. K. Silverman (Ed.), *Counseling the gifted and talented*. Denver. CO: Love Publishing Company.

Tierney, P., & Farmer, S. M. (2002). Creative self-efficacy: Its potential antecedents and relationship to creative performance. *Academy of Management Journal, 45*(6), 1137–1148.

Winner, E. (1996). *Gifted children: Myths and realities*. New York, NY: Basic Books.

Chapter 4

Personal and Professional Relationships

Artists, performers, and other creative individuals must reconcile their need for solitude—a prerequisite for insight-filled creative moments—with their need for meaningful interpersonal interactions. The literature on traits associated with creativity and artistry is filled with descriptions of autonomous, nonconformist people whose creativity flows freely when they're alone with their thoughts. Yet people's creative work doesn't exist in a social vacuum. Creators are part of a system of professional, social, and personal relationships—in which their creative work is embedded—all within the larger context of cultural and historical parameters. Though many of these relationships and systemic social practices of art and creativity appreciation have positive effects on people's creative output, as well as the course of their careers, there are challenges: creators are sometimes vulnerable to tension caused by unsettling interactions with competitors, peers, critics, and audiences, not to mention friends and loved ones with a poor understanding of their need to prioritize their work. In this chapter, we'll look at the numerous relationships in creative people's lives and the roles that they play. We'll explore when and how they become problematic for creative work, and how clinicians can help their clients navigate relationship difficulties.

To illustrate how relationships present challenges for creative clients, I thought about drawing from my recollections of my clients' accounts of distressing interactions. This task was easier than I'd anticipated: themes that kept recurring were relationships strained by envy, worries about their dedication to their creative goals getting in the way of relationships with loved ones, discomfort during networking events meant to promote their work, and anxiety about being evaluated by others. An artist I recently worked with who'd just completed a series of paintings begrudgingly talked about having to go out and promote them. She'd have to go to galleries, reach out to old connections, and post information about her work. This part of the job, which was entirely different from what she cared about (painting), was one she loathed. Another example comes from my work with an architect, who'd spent weeks coming up with a creative solution for a problem at his job, but became plagued with doubts when he was informed that his work would be evaluated by peers during a presentation. In these examples, my clients and I had to expand the focus of our sessions from intrapsychic conflicts—tension within their thoughts and feelings—to interpersonal dynamics occurring beyond their inner worlds. We had to think about how they present themselves to the world, how they relate, and how they communicate.

Aside from professional relationships, sometimes it's the personal and intimate ones that pose the biggest challenge. When people prioritize their creative work, personal relationships may suffer; when they prioritize their relationships, their creative work often gets compromised. Though every creative person's circumstances are unique, the tension and conflicting attitudes around maximizing creative potential while maintaining reciprocally satisfying relationships are familiar to many creative people.

To illustrate why such problems exist, it's helpful to turn our attention to general traits associated with the temperament of artists, performers, and other creative individuals. Creative people's dispositions and how they function in interpersonal settings vary widely: some will collaborate and get along with most people they meet, whereas others will feel so intimidated that they sabotage their success by not showing up to meetings, or even by burning bridges by withholding important industry contact from competitors. Still, certain traits that are typical of creative people help us understand how personal and professional relationships could interfere with people's creative processes and career success.

Nonconformity

Highly creative people challenge the status quo. Nonconformity, a high need for independence and autonomy, and the tendency to be doubtful of norms and authority are characteristics of creative individuals (Batey & Furnham, 2006; Feist, 1998; Runco, 2014). Their worldviews often clash with those of others, and they don't passively take things as they are. The need for nonconformity can make creative people intensely curious and likely to notice and question things that others don't, activating creative ideas that lead to innovative products and discoveries. This need, however, poses a potential conflict because creative people's work is embedded in a wider system, shaped by the influence of social norms. A creative scientist with authority-defying, nonconformist traits must still submit studies for peer review, and for good reason, as they need to be assessed by other experts before they shape decisions made in medicine, technology, and public policy. Such expert opinions, despite their merit, aren't free from bias. Someone may indeed have an innovative and useful idea but meet significant resistance from others from within and outside the field. Barry Marshall, a physicist who in a 2010 *Slate* interview (Schulz, 2010) described himself "as always making his own decisions," and Robin Warren discovered that peptic ulcer disease is a result of a bacterium, not stress. Their hypothesis was met with such skepticism by the scientific community that research-grant requests got rejected. Their idea about the causes of ulcers was so innovative, and arguably so creative, that it took years before other people accepted and recognized this contribution by honoring it with the Nobel Prize in 2005.

Similarly, many creative artists who carve their own paths are dismissed by those around them and gain recognition, if at all, only posthumously. An avant-garde composer I'd worked with spent hours each week promoting his compositions and trying to get others to listen to them. He'd gotten used to being told that his work was too "out there" and grimly joked that he was waiting to get the recognition he deserved from beyond the grave. The reality is that creative ideas are constantly being evaluated—not just by the artists themselves, but by authority figures, critics, and audiences, who often have a say in what's deemed creative and what gets recognized. Contrary to what someone would assume, creative ideas aren't always rewarded by society: they can be ignored or even punished (Runco, 2014). Highly autonomous, nonconformist creators must learn to manage the tension between their worldviews and that of others, without losing creative motivation or succumbing to self-censorship in reaction to social pressure (Maisel, 2013).

Introversion

Another creative trait that sometimes clashes with the need to be part of a wider web of social networks is introversion—the desire to remove oneself from social interactions (Oztunc, 2011). Creative people are often described as introverts because they enjoy solitude (Heilman, 2005; Caine, 2013; Feist, 1998), and they need the time away from others for reflective introspection. Some theorize that it's the very fact that creative people are introverts that drives them to seek self-expression through creative media (Rhodes, 1997). Introversion is pertinent when discussing creative achievement for two reasons. First, artists, performers, and other creative individuals must enter the outside world to present and promote their work. They must develop relationships to advertise what they do. New, useful, and original ideas can make an impact only when there's someone to receive them. For artists, performers, and creative individuals, that someone is the audience, fans, followers, art critics, booking agents, reviewers, and so forth. Introverts automatically experience conflict between their social temperament—their preference for inwardness—and the need to display an outgoing persona. At times, they must painfully fake extroversion to be perceived more positively.

A fashion designer I worked with spent years taking creative risks in pursuit of her unique style, and finally had enough material to put a representative portfolio together. A self-reported introvert, who enjoyed hearing others talk much more than she enjoyed talking, and who craved moments of solitude just minutes into conversations with others, she knew that she'd reached the dreaded stage of having to make connections. As a result, she developed high anxiety. Her anxiety was triggered by feeling trapped in a system in which she did, in fact, need others so she could succeed, and for which she had to adopt a friendlier and sunnier personality. She and I worked hard at taking small steps to confront her anxiety and ease into social interactions, such as setting up one-on-one meetings, and doing most of the networking online.

The second reason introversion is relevant for creators is that they're often required to work creatively by sharing ideas and collaborating. This might happen for members of a rock band in a studio brainstorming lyrics and melodies, a team of architects collaborating on a project, a jazz ensemble improvising onstage, a sketch comedy group bouncing ideas off each other, and so on. Introverts typically prefer to take their time reflecting on ideas and are more comfortable when they're alone (Martin, 2001). They prefer to work individually and exercise their autonomy during the creative process. No matter how extraordinary their creative talents may be, introverts placed in a social group may struggle to pursue an idea to its depth and, consequently, feel uncomfortable sharing it with others for fear that it'll be poorly received.

Groups and Collaborations

Research on team creativity shows that creativity is inhibited unless others serve as models for creative achievement (Amabile, 1996), and unless the social atmosphere fosters a sense of support, a collaborative culture, and trust among group members (Barczark et al., 2010; Binyamin & Carmeli, 2017). If the atmosphere among group members is one of cooperation and trust, social interactions can provide invaluable support, and collaborations can become a fun and stimulating exchange of creative energy leading to innovation (Sawyer, 2017). One writer-director I worked with was concerned about being creatively blocked after beginning a new job in an Internet media company. Soon after spending more time with her supervisors, engaging them in a conversation that revealed mutual aesthetic and creative values, she reported noticing an immediate flooding of ideas, which resolved her creativity blocks. Being part of a wider social network can be helpful when it enriches a person's experiences, which then become a source of creative ideas, and when it offers motivating feedback that fosters dedication and perseverance.

Without the aforementioned ingredients, a team or group can be full of talented and creative members and still produce poorer creative results than it would if each of its members were to work alone. This is because people tend to exhibit heightened sensitivity to being critically evaluated and might be less inclined to share ideas in which they're not already confident. The pressure for social approval and status recognition gets in the way of uninhibited creative curiosity (Amabile, 1996). Someone who shies away from confrontation or who has an intense need to preserve a positive social image will think twice before expressing a thought that may elicit negative reactions. Again, for highly creative people who feel compelled to challenge conventions but are inhibited by group dynamics, there is an undeniable tension.

Similarly, collaborations are rendered ineffective by poor relational skills, many of which don't come naturally to nonconforming introverts. Collaborations mean having to communicate one's creative vision clearly, listen intently, compromise when people don't see eye to eye, defend ideas when they're so innovative that they become unpalatable, and manage rejections. For example, a novelist can go into a pitch meeting with her agent feeling confident, yet when discussions about modifying her ideas begin, miscommunication and conflicts might arise. She must find a way to listen to what's suggested, and to speak up about what she believes in, without doubting the validity of her ideas or threatening the working relationship.

It's not just the lack of intergroup cooperation and social bonding that hinders creativity when working with others. The presence of other people can impede profound creative insight. On the one hand, as I mentioned earlier, many innovations and original ideas are stimulated by social interactions. Observations about what happens to others can lead to the identification of problems that result in creative solutions, such as when noticing people's need for communication sparked ideas that led to smartphones, and when seeing how students score poorly on tests leads to innovative approaches to education. Songs, paintings, poems, novels, and films are inspired by the feelings and experiences that result from the richness of human relationships, such as when romantic involvement inspires love poems and betrayals inspire revenge novels. On the other hand, solitude is considered to be a condition that fosters creative thinking. According to Kaufman and Gregoire (2015), eminent artists like Ingmar Bergman, Georgia O'Keeffe, Emily Dickinson, and Marcel Proust needed moments of solitude to produce high-quality creative ideas. A mind left alone can come up with truly innovative and creative work. As discussed in chapter 2 on creativity blocks, exposure to many stimuli, including those of a social nature, is helpful for activating creative thinking, but it's solitary reflection that allows multiple ideas to converge into a single meaningful one (Csikszentmihalyi & Sawyer, 2014).

The multiple ways that groups, collaborations, and social interactions affect creative work suggest that learning how to navigate one's presence in a larger social context is an essential tool.

Let's now turn our attention to the more personal relationships formed in creative people's lives. Artists, performers, and other creative individuals form many different types of personal relationships (Mokros & Csikszentmihalyi, 2014; Maisel, 2013; Simonton, 1984). These are tied together by emotional bonds and animated by strong feelings, and they are significantly affected by a person's creativity-driven lifestyle.

Relationships With Competitors and Gatekeepers

The reality about many creative fields, especially those in the arts-and-entertainment industry, is that the high demand and low supply in career opportunities make it difficult to stand out. This creates strong feelings of competitiveness, rivalry, envy, and resentment toward those who get lucky and those with good networking skills. Social media magnify these feelings by providing a readily available basis for comparison, even though the comparisons aren't always based on others' real attributes. I remember a musician discussing his envy of a fellow performer who'd attracted thousands of followers on Instagram and hundreds of thousands of views on YouTube. Upon trying to figure out what might've helped this person do so well, my client realized that many of these followers were fake accounts! The musician he envied had paid thousands of dollars to give the illusion of popularity. It was important for my client to recognize his own biases before comparing himself unfairly with others.

Relationships with competitors and gatekeepers can be complicated, frustrating, and rich in interpersonal dynamics. An actor might feel envy, admiration, a desire to support, and a desire to supersede, all at once, toward a classmate who's gone on to have a successful and lucrative acting career. A painter might feel contempt toward an art dealer coming for a studio visit, while feeling responsible to honor this potentially career-advancing opportunity. Artist and career coach Caroll Michels (2009:174) describes artists as "having an *attitude* about dealers and anyone else in the art world perceived to be an authority figure." One of the reasons that these relationships are troublesome is that they elicit competition and social comparisons. Social comparison theory tells us that people tend to compare themselves to those who appear to have similar characteristics (Festinger, 1954). These types of comparisons, made for the purpose of evaluating our own self-worth, make for relationships that create complex feelings (Maisel, 2013).

A jazz singer I worked with knew that she needed to form relationships with other musicians in order to set up more shows and gain publicity for her jazz group, but she found it difficult to do so. Despite her continuous efforts, she always seemed to remain on the fringe of the local popular music scene. On the one hand, she was growing angrier and angrier toward other jazz musicians who were part of the scene, and along with her anger came an obsessive tendency to follow their careers online, to exaggerate the importance of their shows, and to compare her accomplishments with theirs. On the other hand, she continued to go to show after show and try and form relationships with them. The antithesis of wanting to be part of a group of people for whom she had such strong competitive feelings culminated in severe social anxiety and overall feelings of low self-worth. Our sessions involved working through many of these antithetical feelings.

There is a positive side to being competitive. A 2011 study by Eisenberg and Thomson showed that musicians' improvised work was rated as being more creative when musicians were competing. It's up to the creative clients themselves to use their competitiveness in ways that foster creative motivation (Runco, 2014). An example of an advantageous use of competitiveness is setting up creative collaborations where members of the collaborative team are all competing to produce the most original and useful results. If the team members' needs to be better than others lead them to want to surpass their previous efforts, competitiveness can be a productive feeling.

Relationships With Teachers and Mentors

The relationship between creative people and their teachers, mentors, coaches, and other supportive experts can play a crucial role in their creative and professional development. Such influential figures can inspire mental and physical development, increase motivation and confidence, and provide invaluable guidance. Without the support of teachers, coaches, and mentors, inexperienced and self-doubting creators might hesitate to pursue opportunities, question their abilities, and second-guess their decisions. Occasionally, however, when a creative person is not adequately supported, relationships with teachers, mentors, and coaches can be a source of distress. One can be extraordinarily talented and insightful, yet produce little creative work of significance because of invalidating feedback from those assuming a position of authority in the mentor-disciple pair.

Simply feeling dismissed by teachers is enough to fill many with crippling doubts. When a painter met with me to try and regain her confidence in her art making, she recounted painful experiences during her years at art school. She'd started her academic career feeling confident and ambitious and formed a close relationship with a well-respected teacher, whom she idolized. She was acutely sensitive to her teacher's comments and feedback, and it was especially painful when her teacher didn't pay attention to her work or appeared more interested in other students. As she put it, she began to feel like she was "losing the faith of the person who made her believe in herself." My client started to doubt her abilities. She internalized the perceived rejection by her teacher in a way that convinced her to stay away from art. Years later, she connected with me to strip away the impact that this experience was still having on her so she could feel proud of her painting again.

Thomson and Jaque (2017) discuss the prevalence of abuse (emotional, verbal, physical, and sexual) toward performing artists by their teachers and coaches. Abuse, in the form of harsh criticism, often occurs during training, rehearsals, and performances, inducing intense shame that can even trigger posttraumatic stress from past incidents of abuse (Thomson & Jaque, 2017). These occurrences are an important reminder of the pivotal role that these kinds of figures play in the emotional and professional development of creative people.

Relationships With Fans, Followers, and Students

Then there are relationships in which creators themselves are the experts, impart knowledge to students, and share ideas with eager fans and followers. In these relationships, creative people's efforts are recognized, valued, and appreciated, thereby fostering their creative visions. The negative side of these relationships results from the high expectations placed by fans and audiences on creators. The stress caused by expectations of continuing creativity can reduce their motivation (Ceci & Kumar, 2015), damage their creativity, and put their psychological health at risk. In 1994, speaking to an anguished audience about Kurt Cobain's suicide, Eddie Vedder, lead vocalist of the rock band Pearl Jam, proclaimed that "sometimes, whether you like it or not, people elevate you [and] it's real easy to fall" (Hilburn, 1994). Still, creative people will seek out relationships with people who recognize their work's worth because doing so is gratifying and a validation of their talents and hard work.

Relationships With Close Loved Ones

Intimate personal relationships with close friends, family, and significant others can also be trying. These kinds of relationships are troubled by the challenging task of having to balance conflicting needs and priorities. As discussed previously, creative work requires dedication, intellectual and emotional immersion, and, to a certain degree, solitude. This is at odds with the investment required to develop and maintain close relationships. It triggers tension for creative people who must give part of themselves to the creative process and another part to their significant others, children, friends, and relatives. A freelance film producer I worked with turned down numerous opportunities because he knew that his girlfriend, who had a steady job in New York, wouldn't be comfortable with the frequent traveling. He felt suffocated by the restrictions imposed by his relationship but, more importantly, he felt unsettled by his own conflict about whether he'd even be up for taking on projects that would keep them apart. Touring performers must constantly go through the death and rebirth of relationships with friends and loved ones who've remained back home. The road offers a whirlwind of intense experiences where locations, people, venues, audiences, and schedules are constantly changing. Performers, when returning home, have to figure out how to start from where they left off and how to reconnect with people who can't identify with their experiences.

The struggle to connect with less creative people is not just due to the professional demands mentioned previously. It also stems from difficulties fitting in with those who don't share a proclivity for highly innovative thinking. Highly creatively gifted children, for example, experience a sense of nonbelongingness, of being different, and of not relating with most of their peers (Jacobsen, 2000; Winner, 1996). The fact that, from a young age, highly gifted people live with the pressure of being labeled *gifted* creates an in-group/out-group social tension, making it difficult for them to form close bonds with friends. When giftedness is associated with a sense of otherness, the tension from being different— and as a result, often misunderstood—gets exacerbated by being ridiculed, called names, and excluded, and by other hurtful behaviors. Highly gifted people in creative domains think and feel differently from most people and are at risk for recurrent feelings of being social outcasts throughout their lives, including from close loved ones.

Finally, when it comes to romantic relationships and creative lifestyles, creative professionals have contrasting views on how to balance the two. In discussions with my creative clients, especially those who are artists, many report that they only want to date other artists because they'll "get it." They want the reassurance that their partners, who've gone through similar experiences, will empathize. For example, my clients believe that their partners and spouses won't react when they need to make sacrifices, such as staying up all night working on an idea, having to travel for months at a time to promote their recent work, or needing time alone to be inspired. Other creative professionals refuse to relive the volatility and intensity of a creative lifestyle through their significant others' experiences. Perhaps they need a romantic partner with a stable and structured lifestyle, or perhaps simply to know that they won't have to compete about whose creative and professional needs will get met first. On this topic, Csikszentmihalyi and Sawyer (2014) have identified the existence of gender differences. These studies of eminent creative people have revealed that wives tend to make more professional sacrifices, such as having to move or adjust their creative career goals, to satisfy their husbands' needs. Husbands, in contrast, are supported and encouraged by their wives in the pursuit of their creative and professional goals. Another comparative study (Kirschenbaum & Reis, 1997) emphasized the difficult choices female artists faced when they needed to divide their attention between their art and their spouses and children.

The Clinician's Role

Identifying the Problematic Relationship

Whereas some relationships in creative people's lives are positive and rewarding, others prove to be challenging. Clinicians can begin by investigating the types of relationships that elicit distress. A person with deep and meaningful bonds with his spouse and friends might struggle relating on a superficial level with acquaintances; he might feel like a fraud when he's keeping up with chitchat. In contrast, someone who can easily navigate the social demands of a public event may find the emotional reciprocity of an intimate relationship intimidating. Such distinctions will put client and clinician on the same page regarding the difficulties that keep clients from forging and experiencing creativity-enhancing relationships.

Understanding the Person's Disposition

Getting to know the personality traits that shape how clients relate to others sheds light on where the problem lies. As discussed previously, artists and creative people tend to show trends in personality traits, such as an openness to experiences, the need for autonomy, low conscientiousness, impulsivity, introversion, and a high intrinsic motivation (Batey & Furnham, 2006; Eysenck, 1983; Feist, 1998; Kerr & McKay, 2013; Runco, 2014; Simonton, 1984). However, these broad descriptions don't tell us much about individual differences nor do they inform us about the way artists and creative people behave in an interpersonal setting. Does a software developer become socially anxious in a group setting, or does he thrive in it? Does a writer edit her e-mails to perfection before sending them to her publisher, resulting in communication delays? Does a fashion designer crave the social interactions at a party? Or perhaps he ruminates endlessly about a remark an acquaintance made about his portfolio, making him want to be at home working hard on it. Is a singer gregarious and charming during interactions that involve discussing her creative achievement, or does she present them in an arrogant manner that pushes people away? Does an aspiring actor take on the role of the pleaser in a romantic relationship, struggling to assert his need for solitude?

A pianist I worked with used to apologize to me excessively—when she was 5 minutes late, 5 minutes early, when she "complained too much," and when she "didn't speak enough." I couldn't help but wonder if this behavior, which in her case revealed an obsessive inclination to worry about what others thought of her, came up during her networking interactions. Indeed, she talked about hesitating to e-mail venues about playing, prefacing every social media announcement about her shows with an apology for "bombarding their feed," and avoiding approaching other musicians at public events at the risk of bothering them. Clinicians won't get a full picture of what it's like for their creative clients to be out in the world without an understanding of their core personality traits.

Determining the Root of the Conflict

Clinicians can initiate conversations that investigate the source of clients' feelings and relationship difficulties. Sometimes the problem is caused by miscommunication, tension, or conflict with someone in the client's present life: a partner who gets upset when the performer must stay out night after night performing or networking, a musical collaborator who micromanages the recording process, the team members of an architecture firm that critically challenge every decision, and so on. In such cases, sessions take on more of a problem-solving and conflict-mediation approach.

Other times, interpersonal difficulties may begin with an interaction taken from the person's present, but trigger deeper, traumatic memories from the person's past. A recording artist I worked with didn't speak up to his producer about changes made to his album. We discovered that his producer's behavior was reminding him of the powerlessness he'd felt during the years he had been bullied at school. The underlying feeling—that he wasn't worthy of success and therefore shouldn't dare go against his producer— originated from relationships formed in his early years, yet it still resurfaced during interpersonal exchanges in the present.

The clinician's role is to help the client effectively navigate the demands presented by the current social relationship without unconsciously reenacting past relationships. Similarly, clinicians can move clients toward a direction of healing: when relationships become problematic because of past trauma or abuse, sessions can focus on confronting and managing old feelings. In the case of the recording artist, we practiced applying attributes to the producer that were fundamentally distinct from those of the childhood bullies: the producer wasn't deliberately trying to cause harm (he just had a strong creative vision for the album); he didn't lack compassion for my client's desire to experiment with instrumentation (the communication between them was so poor that they didn't see eye to eye about how important experimenting was to my client).

Building Social Skills

Clinicians can help clients improve their relationships by introducing concrete solutions for smoother social interactions. For this to be most effective, clinicians must demonstrate nonjudgmental acceptance of their clients. Doing so ensures that the focus is on changing the behaviors, not changing the person. This helps clients welcome the use of tools that modify the ways they relate to others, without assuming that something is inherently wrong with them. A gentle emphasis on skill improvement sets the stage for building positive social habits. Examples of such habits include talking about one's work without monopolizing the conversation, managing conflicting feelings (such as feeling inferior and superior to peers' creative accomplishments) without damaging relationships, balancing the need for closeness and intimacy with the need for solitude, and setting boundaries with various gatekeepers without removing the element of trust from those relationships.

Treatment Goals

1. Improve the quality of relationships.
2. Ensure that creativity isn't impaired by relationship problems.
3. Develop insight into conflicts posed by social norms.
4. Build skills to improve social interactions.
5. Make the most of social and personal relationships to advance creative goals.

Suggested Interventions to Achieve Goals

1. *Include others in counseling sessions.* When possible, meeting with people who are part of the troublesome relationship is an effective way for clients to gain insight and see improvements in their interactions. Seeing the ways we behave socially, in real time, is an invaluable tool for self-awareness, one that can bring about lasting change. Rather than talk about the relationship dynamics clients have with collaborators and significant others, clients can show them in the neutrality and safety of the counseling office.

     Example: An accomplished architect had developed a contentious relationship with her employer. Their clashing personalities—the employer was an overpowering micromanager, whereas my client was a people-pleasing avoidant type—got in the way of their creative work. My client's employer agreed to come in for one session during which we uncovered some of their relationship patterns and discussed tactics for effective collaboration. The employer agreed to give my client more time to come up with ideas on her own, instead of observing the process from the beginning, and my client agreed to voice her creative ideas more regularly.

2. *Balance demands placed by close relationships.* Creative clients are often pulled in opposite directions. They try to be present for the people in their lives and at the same time dedicate themselves to their creative

work. A supportive immediate environment makes it possible for creative clients to immerse themselves in their creative endeavors without feeling ambivalent, or even guilty, about doing so. The people who are part of clients' daily lives must be on board regarding goals and schedules. This is more easily achieved when creative clients are clear about their needs and invite others to understand the importance behind a creative project.

> Example: I encouraged one of my writer clients to inform his family members that he'd be unavailable for the day, and that he'd be accessible only in case of emergency. I asked him to set a predetermined agreed-upon time frame during which he'd be working so that his partner and friends wouldn't be caught by surprise by the request. My client had to highlight that spending time on his novel wasn't meant to reject them: rather, it was his way of balancing conflicting demands.

3. *Practice talking about the work.* Many artists and creative people are more comfortable "letting the work speak for itself." They don't want to engage the audience, talk about their artistic vision, or have to convince peers about the importance of their innovative research. Yet without effective communication, the creative work gets seen by fewer people and has fewer opportunities to get the recognition it deserves. Sometimes artists and other creative professionals must participate in panel discussions at public conferences and talk about their work, perhaps at a college or university, or go on the set of a TV studio and talk one on one with a host. It's important for sessions to identify and implement ways to communicate with others about the work. The goal is to talk about the work with conviction about its significance.

> Example: A composer and I practiced 5-minute pitches on his most recent compositions. The pitches included information about what's unique about them and his personal investment in the process and outcome. He practiced communicating his experiences by saying something like "I'm trying to incorporate traditional eastern melodies as an homage to by cultural background. I believe listeners will be drawn to the fusion of various musical elements."

4. *Build confidence and assertiveness.* High confidence and a strong ego help creative achievers maintain the perseverance necessary to seek out career-advancing opportunities (Csikszentmihalyi & Sawyer, 2014; Winner, 1996). Confidence is what helps someone talk to strangers about his or her most recent book at a dinner party, send out newsletters announcing upcoming shows, listen to negative feedback without losing motivation, and tell publishers that the format of the book is wrong without the fear of being blacklisted.

Example: A musician and I role-played scenarios during which he practiced self-assured responses, such as "I appreciate being included in this performance lineup; however, I'm dissatisfied with the quality of the equipment and would suggest that you look into so and so." A photographer and I practiced dialogues such as "Good to see you again! Can I share with you some images of my latest work?" While doing so, it was helpful to address clients' anxieties arising from this kind of presentation.

5. *Encourage networking and the search for a mentor.* It's tempting, for introverts in particular, to remain isolated in a creative bubble. People know whom they know and what they know, and this may seem to be enough. Other times, creatively gifted people, especially children and adolescents, may feel excluded from the majority of their peers because of differences in interests, aptitudes, and intellectual abilities. Searching for like-minded individuals who can support, teach, and guide them offers clients many benefits, such as a confidence boost, a sense of belongingness, and the validation of their experiences.

Example: A highly creatively gifted piano player had been accustomed to being ostracized in school when his unique mathematical abilities set him apart from his peers. As a young adult, he'd come to expect that he'd always struggle with fitting in. When he complained about feeling isolated, I encouraged him to revisit his assumption that "nobody gets him" and to begin attending local seminars and workshops and auditing university music and math classes. In time, he found value in receiving external input on his creative ideas from people who seemed to understand him more.

6. *Implement beneficial competitive practices.* Competing in a healthy way can demonstrate one's worth, increase motivation for high creative performance, and offer a backdrop against which creative people challenge themselves and improve their performances. Although it's true that certain creative domains, such as the acting industry, have more supply than demand, a dog-eat-dog mentality of bringing others down to attain the few positions available can only go so far. Career longevity is achieved when clients stand out from their scene on their merit, rather than when they undermine others along the way. Similarly, frequent comparisons to others and preoccupations with their successes are unhealthy practices that promote feelings of destructive envy instead of constructive ambition.

Example: A pop-rock singer was vying for show promoters' attention. To get to them, she found herself copying the sound of another singer, who was ahead of her in terms of following and online presence. This resulted in my client trying to imitate the other singer's style, causing her to slowly lose her uniqueness. Instead of comparing her voice timbre, personality, and appearance with those of the other singer, I encouraged her to compare ambitions and goal-setting habits. This helped shift the focus of the competition to things she could control. Eventually, she felt comfortable enough even to approach the singer she'd been envying and pick her brain for career advice.

7. *Nurture relationships.* Creative clients may be too busy thinking about end goals to appreciate the value of having circles of friends and acquaintances, even if there's nothing immediate to gain. Some people may define success as getting the part or being offered a show, rather than as developing the professional relationship (Michels, 2009). However, a new perspective on what the prize is—perhaps being part of a creative community, or giving and receiving a platform for creative expression—can help reduce ambivalence about spending time connecting with others.

    Example: I once asked a photographer who was concerned about being ignored by industry professionals to call or send a message to a different person (makeup artist, photographer's assistant, art director, and so forth) each week. She made a list of people she'd collaborated with in the past and people whose work she admired and committed to maintaining some sort of contact with them in order to keep the relationship alive. As a result, she built a stronger creative and professional network so that she felt comfortable reaching out to when she wanted to execute a creative idea.

8. *See the good in others.* In *Making Your Creative Mark*, creativity coach Eric Maisel (2013) refers to people's negative sides as the shadows that come along with the light. I've often heard my clients write collaborators off because they hadn't come to their show, or cut ties with directors who'd spoken harshly to them during a rehearsal. However, clients can learn to see the positive side of such relationships. Instead of expecting collaborators to come to shows, clients can get their constructive feedback by sending them links to performance videos. Instead of counting on directors for supportive guidance, clients can think of them as opinions that reflect a portion of the audience, which they can then learn from.

    Example: When an actor I worked with dreaded rehearsing and preparing for an upcoming show because of a tense relationship with his director, he and I worked on emphasizing what their relationship could offer him rather than what it couldn't. For every disappointing interaction my client had with his director, he and I discussed a possible positive outcome: even though his director seemed to pick on him, my client saw potential for improving from the attention placed on his acting skills; even though his director

72 Personal and Professional Relationships

didn't congratulate him after the show, my client focused on the benefits of staying in touch with him after the production ended, as he might be a helpful resource in the future.

9. *Look for what feels authentic.* Having to network, schmooze, and chit-chat may feel like faking friendliness to get ahead. This is something many creative people dread, as it feels inauthentic and far removed from what they truly care about: the creative work. However, it's important to highlight that there can be authenticity somewhere in these social interactions. For example, it might be found in the desire to connect with another person, to spread the word about hard-earned achievements, or to hear someone's thoughts about a creative idea.

> Example: A painter with whom I worked off and on for many years rejected invitation after invitation to art-exhibit openings. She wrote these events off as "disingenuous and exhausting." To change her perspective, she and I tried to think about two things that felt genuine and exhilarating about being among other artists. She came up with being interested in hearing about new trends in the arts community and sharing her enthusiasm about the photorealist elements in her most recent paintings. Going out with these two authentic intentions made it easier for her to connect to others.

Additional Interventions

10.
11.
12.

Takeaways

- Relationships in the lives of creative people have the potential to be beneficial for activating and producing creative ideas; however, they often get in the way of creative immersion and optimal creative achievement.
- Personality traits, group dynamics, and competitive conditions in many creative fields can cause tensions in creative people's relationships.
- Sometimes difficulties result from the clash between a person's creative vision and the larger evaluative social context; sometimes the challenges lie in balancing the needs of the creative work with the demands of close and intimate relationships.

- Clinicians can work with clients to manage disturbing feelings, such as envy and resentment, so that they don't interfere with the creative process.
- Counseling can help clients understand and manage the interdependence between their creativity and their social environment, and work through conflicts between the two. This can be achieved by communicating effectively, fostering social bonding, and using networking to their advantage.

References

Amabile, T. M. (1996). *Creativity in context: Update to the social psychology pf creativity*. Boulder, CO: Westview Press.

Barczark, G., Lassk, F., & Mulki, J. (2010). Antecedents of team creativity: An examination of team emotional intelligence, team trust and collaborative culture. *Creativity and Innovation Management, 19*(4), 332–345.

Batey, M., & Furnham, A. (2006). Creativity, intelligence, and personality: A critical review of the scattered literature. *Genetic, Social, and General Psychology Monographs, 132*(4), 355–429.

Binyamin, G., & Carmeli, A. (2017). Fostering members' creativity in teams: The role of structuring of human resource management processes. *Psychology of Aesthetics, Creativity, and the Arts, 11*(1), 18–33.

Caine, S. (2013). *Quiet: The power of introverts in a world that can't stop talking*. New York, NY: Broadway Paperbacks.

Ceci, M. W., & Kumar, V. K. (2015). A correlational study of creativity, happiness, motivation, and stress from creative pursuits. *Journal of Happiness Studies, 17*(2), 609–626.

Csikszentmihalyi, M., & Sawyer, K. (2014). Creative insight: The social dimension of a solitary moment. In *The systems model of creativity: The collected works of Mihaly Csikszentmihalyi*. Dordrecht: Springer.

Eisenberg, J., & Thompson, W. F. (2011). The effects of competition on improvisers' motivation, stress, and creative performance. *Creativity Research Journal, 23*(11), 129–136.

Eysenck, H. J. (1983). The roots of creativity: Cognitive ability or personality trait? *Roeper Review, 5*, 10–12.

Feist, G. J. (1998). A meta-analysis of personality in scientific and artistic creativity. *Personality and Social Psychology Review, 2*(4), 290–309.

Festinger, L. (1954). A theory of social comparison processes. *Human Relations, 7*(2), 117–140. Retrieved from https://doi.org/10.1177/001872675400700202

Heilman, K. M. (2005). *Creativity and the brain*. New York, NY: Psychology Press.

Hilburn, R. (1994, May). He didn't ask for all this: Eddie Vedder always wanted his band Pearl Jam to make music that mattered: He can sometimes feel, as Kurt Cobain did, the pressure of mattering too *much* to his fans, but he's finding a way to deal with it. Retrieved from http://articles.latimes.com/

Jacobsen, M. E. (2000). *The gifted adult: A revolutionary guide for liberating everyday genius*. New York, NY: Ballantine Books.

Kaufman, S. B., & Gregoire, C. (2015). *Wired to create: Unraveling the mysteries of the creative mind*. New York, NY: TarcherPerigee.

Kerr, B., & McKay, R. (2013). Searching for tomorrow's innovators: Profiling creative adolescents. *Creativity Research Journal, 25*(1), 21–32.

Kirschenbaum, R. J., & Reis, S. M. (1997). Conflicts in creativity: Talented female artists. *Creativity Research Journal, 10*(2–3), 251–263.

Maisel, E. (2013). *Making your creative mark.* Novato, CA: New World Library.

Martin, C. R. (2001). *Looking at type: The fundamentals of using psychological type to understand and appreciate ourselves and others* (8th ed.). Gainesville, FL: Center for Applications of Psychological Type.

Michels, C. (2009). *How to survive and prosper as an artist: Selling yourself without selling your soul.* New York, NY: Holt Paperbacks.

Mokros, C. A., & Csikszentmihalyi, M. (2014). The social construction of creative lives. In *The systems model of creativity: The collected works of Mihaly Csikszentmihalyi.* Dordrecht: Springer.

Oztunc, G. (2011). Personality: Autonomy and independence. In M. A. Runco & S. R. Pritzker (Eds.), *Encyclopedia of creativity* (Vol. 2, pp. 224–227). San Diego, CA: Academic Press.

Rhodes, C. (1997). Growth from deficiency creativity to being creativity. In M. A. Runco & R. Richards (Eds.), *Eminent creativity, everyday creativity, and health.* Greenwich, CT: Ablex Publishing Corporation.

Runco, M. A. (2014). *Creativity: Theories and themes: Research, development, and practice* (2nd ed.). London, UK: Academic Press.

Sawyer, K. (2017). *Group genius: The creative power of collaboration.* New York, NY: Basic Books.

Schulz, K. (2010, September). Stress doesn't cause ulcers! Or, how to win a Nobel Prize in one easy lesson: Barry Marshall on being . . . right. *Slate Magazine.* Retrieved from www.slate.com

Simonton, D. K. (1984). Artistic creativity and interpersonal relationships across and within generations. *Journal of Personality and Social Psychology, 46*(6), 1273–1286.

Thomson, P., & Jaque, S. V. (2017). Creativity and the performing artist: Behind the mask. London, UK: Academic Press.

Winner, E. (1996). *Gifted children: Myths and realities.* New York, NY: Basic Books.

Chapter 5

Trauma and Creativity

A popular narrative on the role that psychological trauma plays in creative people's lives suggests that adversity in their pasts fuels their need for healing through creative expression. This assumption has intuitive appeal and some scientific and anecdotal merit. But does it capture the relationship between psychological trauma and creative expressions? As we shall see in this chapter, trauma can increase self-reports of perceived creativity, but it can also block the ability to enter a state of creative flow and can lower the quality of performing artists' performances. Investigating how trauma activates creativity sheds light on the factors that enhance the need for creative expression. Equally important is the reverse direction of this relationship: how creativity—in particular artistic creativity, which is rich in emotional content—shapes the ways trauma itself is processed or reexperienced. Professional artists whose subject matter is consciously or subconsciously informed by their experiences may find their creativity to be deeply restorative and healing. In other cases, overexposure to a painful memory through creative outlets can perpetuate the trauma's effects. The goal of this chapter is to clarify many of these nuances and to provide suggestions for clinicians as they treat creative clients with a history of trauma.

Emotional trauma and adversity, though far from being prerequisites for creativity, do seem to foster a proclivity toward creative expression. This has been presented through biographical data and historiometric studies that look into the pasts of highly accomplished creative artists and scientists. In *Tortured Artists*, journalist Christopher Zara (2012) writes about Pablo Picasso, Mary Shelley, Wolfgang Amadeus Mozart, and other highly influential artists and the traumatic events (deaths, illnesses, poverty, accidents, and so forth) that they experienced at some point in their lives. In *Creativity and Madness: Psychological Studies of Art and Artists*, 18 mental health professionals tie the creative achievements of artists, writers, and musicians to emotionally painful events in their subjects' pasts (Panter, 1995). Other data indicates a correlation between having lost one or both parents and creative achievement (Albert, 1971; Simonton, 1994, Simonton, 2004). This isn't to say that people can't reach high levels of creative success without trauma or adversity; however, there seems to be an association between the impact of trauma and the drive for creative expression and accomplishment.

Why Trauma Awakens the Need for Creativity

One possible reason why people with a history of trauma are drawn to creative pursuits lies in the fact that artistic media give creators the option of using symbols and metaphors to express difficult experiences. Through indirect artistic representations, trauma survivors can both access and communicate a wealth of information (emotions, memories, suppressed instincts, and so on) that they may not have wished to express more explicitly. A folk-singer-songwriter I worked with kept revisiting themes of sexual abuse through her songs, both in lyrical content and in melody. She'd been sexually assaulted multiple times during her adolescence and young adulthood and, as with many sexual abuse survivors, had kept her experiences a secret until coming to therapy. Despite her usually animated mannerisms and her warm and enthusiastic presentation, when the topic of her past traumatic experiences would come up, she'd become silent, avoid eye contact, and hesitate to speak. She'd urge me to listen to her songs instead. For her, the role of creativity was straightforward: it was a way to communicate, a way to express feelings, and a way to access an emotional state that perhaps couldn't be adequately captured during talk therapy.

Sometimes this inclination toward nonliteral communication methods isn't just a question of willingness, but a question of conscious ability. Traumatic events such as sexual and physical abuse, accidents, natural disasters, and family or community conflicts can have long-lasting psychological effects. They can lead to posttraumatic stress disorder, depression, anxiety, and adjustment disorder. But more than just psychological trauma, these kinds of events, especially when they're chronic and recurrent and start at a young age, can leave a mark on brain development and cognitive functioning, substantially affecting how such events are processed and talked about.

Chronic trauma in the form of abuse and neglect can cause memory impairment, changes in brain structure, and the inability to process emotions (Bremner, 2005; Stien & Kendall, 2003; Swart, 2010). Similarly, severe and acute stress caused by trauma affects the amygdala, hippocampus and prefrontal cortex, and other brain areas in ways that seem to compromise the brain's ability to remember events and regulate emotions surrounding them (Van der Kolk & Fisler, 1995). In light of the powerful emotional effects of trauma, and its imposed limitations on the brain's ability to recall and describe accurately, it isn't surprising that trauma survivors would turn to activities that require more fluid uses of the brain: instead of remembering accurately, one can abstractly represent; instead of describing verbally, one can show using the body, the voice, or a melody.

The Benefits of Expressive Therapies

Dance therapy, drama therapy, music therapy, art therapy, and other expressive therapies are approaches to treatment that are supported by two fundamental principles: first, they're a useful form of self-expression, especially when verbal communication falls short; second, they can tap into one's emotional state by uniquely bridging mind and body (Malchiodi, 2003). This means that they help transform a disturbing emotional sensation into something concrete and physical. The act of turning affect and memories into tactile and sensory experiences is a beneficial intervention, often used with children and adults with cognitive impairments, such as Alzheimer's disease and schizophrenia, as well as in treating the general population. Drawing, for example, is often used as a way to visually represent vulnerable experiences and make sense of them by creating some type of narrative (Steele & Kuban, 2003).

James Pennebaker (2004) has spent decades conducting research on the mental and physical health benefits of expressive writing, in particular writing that specifically addresses past trauma. Again and again, he has documented improvements in people's feelings with regard to the painful events they wrote about. Creative people who regularly engage in making art for work or as a hobby have the opportunity to use this kind of nonverbal expression to their advantage. By doing something that comes naturally—namely, creative expression—they're exploring, confronting, and perhaps even repairing old trauma. If there's a silver lining to being troubled by the past, for creative people it's that they can deal with the past better through their emotionally restorative creative skills.

How Trauma Affects the Creative Process

Given the well-documented benefits of expressive therapies, when I first started working with creative clients with histories of trauma, I made some naïve assumptions. I figured that a day in a rehearsal studio or an hour of creative brainstorming would provide the kind of distraction and emotional catharsis that would relieve, or even heal, many trauma-related symptoms. Allow the mind to wander freely, I thought, get to an emotionally rich place, and let the process speak for itself. However, I hadn't accounted for the way that having been through something traumatic changes how creative thoughts, processes, and outcomes are experienced. For example, trauma affects performers' skills and their emotional reactions during and after their performances (Kenny, 2011; Swart, 2014). Thomson and Jacque (2017) give the example of a performer who's trying to focus on the performance but is triggered by his or her increased heart rate, bringing up memories of a rape or an attack. Trauma doesn't just affect artists who go onstage: nonperforming artists' subject matter, and their motivations to pursue it, can be heavily informed by their traumatic pasts, as they often seem to approach themes of trauma-based conflict through their work (Forgeard, 2013; Malchiodi, 2003; Knafo, 2004).

Discovering this was an important lesson I learned while working with Jake, an accomplished multidisciplinary artist. Jake used photography, sculptures, installations, and films to capture the multiple layers of his creative ideas. His initial presentation was one of a well-put-together man, whose positive, goal-oriented, and confident style matched the critical acclaim he'd gained from this artwork and installations. Yet, beneath the surface, he was emotionally heavy, consumed by self-defeating and negative thoughts. He sought counseling to address feelings of depression and, as he put it, of "living in the past." In his 20s, he'd experienced the sudden death of his brother, a victim in a drunk-driving accident. An insightful and eloquent man, Jake knew how to talk about the stages of grief, about the lasting impact the loss had on family dynamics, and about the many ways this experience had been informing his subject matter. In fact, he admitted that most of the work he was known for involved themes of anger (toward the drunk driver) and sadness (about missing his brother). His work was full of symbols and representations of feelings of emptiness and revenge, and his video installations full of narratives of deadly accidents.

Trauma had made Jake eager to find resolution through art—which had paid off in his achievement of professional success. The cost was that he kept reliving a deeply painful and traumatic experience—one he'd never effectively dealt with. Despite his ability to intellectualize and talk about the traumatic event with ease, he'd developed the habit of feeling subliminally. What we explored was how his overexposure to his past, and how relying on it in order to get work and make money, came at the expense of treating his hopeless thinking, suicidal ideation, and posttraumatic stress. Willing to show his pain to everyone but himself, he saw life only through art. Eventually, Jake found it helpful to think about new themes in his creative projects. He reignited his interest in existential art and worked on representing feelings of "otherness" and the angst of searching for meaning. Shifting creative directions gave him the chance to work through the trauma caused by his brother's death, without associating expectations of career success.

Emotional damage from reliving experiences isn't the only way trauma affects creativity. Trauma can limit a person's range of emotions and block access to the emotional space that typically gives rise to artistic expression. Unlike the person who can transform an intense and emotionally traumatic experience into a creative one (Carson, 2010), a common experience for some severely traumatized individuals is to become particularly good at *repressing* their emotions, *dissociating* from them, and *fragmenting* the traumatic memories (Van der Kolk & Fisler, 1995). These defense mechanisms, set in place to protect conscious awareness from too much exposure to painful emotions, make it difficult for artists and other creative individuals to access the past and effectively confront it during the creative process.

Another multidisciplinary artist I worked with was troubled by how detached she'd become toward her pieces. She was uninspired and felt confused about the underlying significance of her work, calling it all "nonsense and meaningless." She liked to show me pictures of her work and to send me links to write-ups about her pieces. What seemed immediately apparent to me was the contrast between the images in her work (childlike, conjuring themes of innocence) and the emotional tone of our conversations, which were filled with descriptions of past physical abuse by her father. My thought was that pointing out this discrepancy would help her develop a sense of creative purpose: she'd either embrace the healing quality of reenvisioning life through the eyes of her childhood self, or abandon her current style and develop one that better reflected her emotional world. Unfortunately, any conversation on the topic was met with short, one-word answers. Articulating these feelings was so emotionally disturbing that the approach lost all its effectiveness. The emotions associated with her past were simply too strong for her to try and connect them to what she did for a living. She needed to keep the abused child and the active artist separate, and to work on the trauma independently. In this case, we had to spend more time accepting the dissociation of her two selves rather than working against it.

At this point, let's reiterate a distinction brought up throughout this book between creative individuals in the arts and those in nonartistic creative domains. Even though there are similarities in cognitive functions, such as flexibility, divergent thinking, and insight resulting from idea generation, the two groups (artists and scientists) have been shown to differ in personality traits and in their use of emotions during the creative process (Feist, 1998; Simonton, 2004). Unlike scientific creative pursuits, which tend to be driven by a desire to solve problems and innovate, artistic pursuits tend to access and express powerful emotions. The role that emotions play in unlocking or compromising creativity after trauma is arguably more instrumental for artistic than nonartistic creative work. Even so, there are indications that regardless of creative domain, people who've been through trauma report high levels of self-perceived creativity. This effect may have something to do with the way adverse experiences shape key psychological traits, such as resilience, as well as the ability to search for purpose through spirituality and creativity.

Posttraumatic Growth and Posttraumatic Stress

Marie Forgeard (2013) conducted a study that included creative people in a wide range of domains (entrepreneurial, verbal artistic, math and science, performance, visual artistic, interpersonal, and problem solving). To understand the role that adversity plays in fostering creativity in highly creative people, and whether this creativity is an indication of *posttraumatic growth* (positive psychological change following a traumatic event), she looked at how physical assaults, illnesses, natural disasters, accidents, and other traumatic events increase people's perceptions of their creativity. Though the design of the study doesn't allow for conclusions of causation, it did indicate that higher levels of distress caused by adversity predicted higher levels of self-reported creativity. Some explanations for these findings include that adversity is what inspires people to want to express themselves or to solve a problem, and that trauma makes people likelier to turn to creative engagement as a way of coping and of making sense of traumatizing experiences. Research on post-traumatic growth can help those working with traumatized clients to focus on the positive changes brought about by negative past experiences, such as creative inclinations, and not just the harmful ones.

The other side of posttraumatic growth is posttraumatic stress. The effects of posttraumatic stress disorder (PTSD) become quite apparent in per-forming artists. To understand this, it's helpful to circle back to the way trauma—and to a greater extent PTSD—compromises brain-related func-tions. Chronic trauma and PTSD have been associated with memory and cognition impairments (Bremner, 2006). During a highly stressful experi-ence, such as performing for an audience, traumatized performers will enter a state of high cognitive arousal, during which they need to concentrate and be focused. At the same time, they need to be calm and "in the zone," with excellent memory skills, when performing memorized material (Swart, 2014). They need to have focused awareness of what's going on around them when they're performing with others. Performers with a history of trauma, especially chronic and severe trauma, often struggle to manage the anxiety that naturally occurs during this state due to the brain's knee-jerk activa-tion of a heightened fear response (Swart, 2014). With their attention and memory skills compromised, and with a sharper perception of danger, per-formers may find themselves in a scenario that simulates the traumatic expe-rience before and during performances. Stien and Kendall (2003) explain that a hyperaroused state triggers a trauma-like reaction, typically the fight-or-flight response. Unfortunately, the hyperarousing state of being onstage, showcasing meaningful and, at times, personal work while being evaluated by others, is fertile ground for trauma reactivation. This process results in severe stage fright and feelings of being blocked, paralyzed, or "choking under pressure" (Engelhard et al., 2012). Lastly, negative onstage experiences, such as falling or forgetting lines, can themselves become a source of trauma. Unless adequately processed, the embarrassment and disappointment from public failure can interfere with the quality of future performances because of fear that history will repeat itself.

The Clinician's Role

Assessing Openness to Incorporating Creativity

Clinicians may encounter two types of creative clients with a history of trauma. First, there are those who'd rather focus on their psychological symptoms and experiences, without connecting them to their creative work. In these cases, it's important for clinicians to work within clients' boundaries, and to keep discussions on the creative process separate from their trauma-induced concerns. Then there are those who'll go as far as to bring samples of their work to sessions to share how treatment has affected what they do. Clinicians can ask willing clients to talk about how their traumatic pasts inform their creative ideas, processes, and results. For example, if painters suggest themes of abuse and neglect in their paintings, clinicians can ask about what the images represent and what feelings they stir. Another example comes from my work with an entrepreneur who was chronically deprived of food and other basic necessities because most of the family's money had been spent to support her mother's drug addiction. Our sessions explored how being neglected throughout her childhood fostered the desire to compensate by developing—and making money from—innovative technological gadgets.

Clinicians can inquire into what clients' work reveals about their pasts and how their pasts have shaped their creative behaviors. These are questions that can be difficult to answer for even the most self-aware and psychologically oriented person. Clinicians can try to notice patterns, symbolisms, and subtle connections. Again, the goal is to develop insights about a territory that's explored more comfortably in indirect and nonexplicit ways. Sessions can consider whether traumatic memories and events act as a resource for clients' artistic content, or if creative endeavors serve as a distraction from uncomfortable feelings. Clinicians can delve into whether creativity provides cathartic healing or triggers unwanted trauma reenactments. These questions matter because they emphasize clients' ownership of how the creative process affects them, and they suggest that clients can exert control over the conditions under which trauma-induced feelings reemerge.

Approaching Trauma With Caution

Regarding whether to encourage artistic endeavors as an outlet for the psychological effects of trauma, clinicians are to proceed carefully. Too much exposure to the trauma that gets triggered by creative self-expression can become psychologically disturbing, especially when it breaks down the defenses held in place to protect the person from it (Swart, 2014). To work on developing a psychologically healthy narrative of the traumatic event, one that doesn't cause posttraumatic stress, it might be necessary to hold off from artistic representations, at least until the effects of reliving the trauma become clear. Approaching the traumatic events with caution will create breathing room for clinicians and clients to understand the internal dialogue around painful events. It'll allow them to reframe such dialogues so they don't produce intense emotional and physical reactions, and so clients can derive meaning from their traumatic past.

Whenever such concerns are absent, clinicians can encourage clients to participate freely in the art forms of their choice, perhaps by referring to art therapists, so as to take advantage of the well-documented positive effects of expressive therapies. In the counseling room, they can urge their clients to use their creativity to communicate or evoke images and memories of trauma, and they can point out parallels between events in clients' personal lives and symbolic representations in their creative work. Clinicians ought to take the necessary time to build a trusting and comfortable relationship; doing so will help clients feel safe to talk about painful events, to reveal vulnerabilities associated with their creative work, and to explore its meaning.

Understanding How Trauma Affects Performers

Clinicians who work with performers, especially those with performance anxiety, can think about whether their clients are affected by disturbing memories before and during auditions and performances (see chapter 7 for more on performance and audition anxiety). Since memory repression, fragmentation, and dissociation are common trauma-defense mechanisms, clinicians can explore whether the activation of memories compromises the quality of performances. Sometimes memories are explicit and straightforward ("Being looked at by hundreds of people makes me feel vulnerable in the same way I was vulnerable when I was in an accident" and "Playing the partner in a marriage with domestic violence reminds me of my own abusive relationship"), or they can be more subconscious or somatically represented, in the form of physical discomfort or vague feelings of distress during a performance. The clinicians' role is to support clients in managing anxiety from old memories and, when invited to by clients, to inquire into how performing opens them up to deeply rooted vulnerability.

Understanding How Trauma Blocks Creativity

Sometimes clinicians will work with clients who block their feelings altogether as a response to the emotional overload associated with past trauma. This poses the risk of clients developing creative blocks: clients will find it difficult to enter a mental and emotional space that's conducive to creative expression. Clinicians can investigate which emotions triggered by the traumatic event are likeliest to get blocked (for example, rage, shame, and fear) and explore how avoiding them interferes with the creative process. Sometimes, a natural progression for clients will be to choose to express these feelings gradually through their creative work. Clinicians and clients can keep track of disturbing symptoms that result from this process.

Integrating Trauma Responses

Clinicians can consider the applicability of bringing together clients' fragmented responses to traumatic events by using their creative expression. The goal is to integrate disjointed memories, emotional reactions, and conflicting thoughts and feelings associated with the traumatic event. A sudden panic attack one day, a terrifying nightmare the other, and an unexpected outburst of anger followed by emotional dissociation are examples of how one's reactions around a difficult life experience can get processed in chopped-up and incoherent ways. Clinicians can think about how clients' creative endeavors manage to bring all these fragmented pieces together. For example, a creative brainstorming process, a solo performance, and the word choices in a metaphor-filled poem can help clients access, and bring together, feelings of strength and vulnerability, of shame and pride, of hopefulness and despair.

Treatment Goals

1. Improve confidence in creative abilities when they are compromised by traumatic history.
2. Manage the impact of PTSD symptoms on performances.
3. Promote creative growth and healing from past trauma.
4. Create content that's informed by traumatic feelings and memories.
5. Use art and creativity to regulate emotions.

Suggested Interventions to Achieve Goals

1. *Inquire into the trauma-creativity relationship.* The nuanced relationship between trauma and creativity is discussed in this chapter. Trauma can block access to emotions, impair cognitive functions, and paralyze creative performers. In other cases, it can motivate resilient people to use their creativity to grow and heal from disturbing events. An open-ended and explorative discussion can help clients understand more about how

trauma has affected them. No two cases are alike, so keeping an open mind and creating a safe space for the revelation of details will help clients gain more insight.

> Example: When I worked with an actor who was struggling with a role, I asked him open-ended questions, such as "What it is like to play the role of an accident survivor?" and "What kind of similar experiences have you had in the past?" These simple questions were enough to get him to talk about embodying a character that reminded him of the helpless person he identified with when he was bullied throughout his school years. In hindsight, the connection between his past experiences and his current creative struggles seemed obvious. However, without exploring it in our sessions, he was unable to recognize its emotional impact.

2. *Desensitize through creativity.* The idea behind desensitization is that trauma survivors can gradually build the necessary tolerance to confront painful memories without avoiding or reacting intensely to them. As traumatic memories are explored from least to most anxiety provoking, clients are asked to use relaxation techniques to counter the anxiety being triggered (Glass, 2006). Creative activities are a great tool for desensitizing because they accomplish two tasks at once: they help explore painful memories (through art making, storytelling, and so on) and help combat any anxiety due to the calming effects of being in an immersive state of creative flow (Csikszentmihalyi, 1996).

> Example: I once asked a guitarist to work on composing a piece that would evoke memories from a time when he was in a car accident. He chose to do so by writing his own "soundtrack" to the experience: midway through the song, he inserted a loud, distorted crash to simulate the moment of the accident. Toward the end there was silence, intercepted by horn instruments, to represent his inability to move (silence) in the middle of a busy city street (horns). During our sessions, we prioritized gradually confronting and getting relief from the anxiety triggered by this creative journey.

3. *Look for clues in the creative work.* Clients and clinicians can uncover themes of trauma in the client's body of work. Sometimes, themes are explicit and clearly identified (for example, a spoken-word performer whose poetry is about sexual assault); other times, they're full of symbolism, sometimes through omission (as in the case of a visual artist who avoids the depiction of any colors, symbols, or objects that could remind her of the perpetrator). The need to do this kind of digging speaks to the tendency of trauma survivors to internalize traumatic memories in fragments rather than to develop detailed story lines (van

der Kolk & Fisler, 1995; Stien & Kendall, 2003). For disturbing events to be included in a healing conversation, and become part of a client's consciousness, a good place to start is to look into the subconscious expressed creatively.

> Example: A contemporary dancer agreed to show me a video of her most recent choreography, which she described as emotionally draining and exhilarating. Together, we looked for clues in what her movements showed us instead of relying only on what her words told us. A mixture of vulnerable and aggressive dancing—slow and delicate, manic and syncopated—represented her conflicting self-identities: a victim and a trauma survivor.

4. *Utilize expressive therapy methods.* Expressive therapies use creativity because it eases the process of discussing traumatic events, it helps distract people from them, and it can be emotionally restorative by reenacting memories in a safer environment. Expressive writing about traumatic events, for example, can be a useful therapeutic tool for ameliorating the psychological effects caused by trauma (Baikie & Wilhelm, 2005). Clinicians, if not trained so themselves, can refer clients to art therapists. They can encourage clients to continue to use a creative medium of their choice, and even to experiment with a new one. Professional artists in particular may find that by using a different tool or medium of creative expression, they're less concerned with the quality of the results.

> Example: I once worked with a highly creative adolescent girl who'd been sexually assaulted at a concert a few months before she was referred for treatment. To make use of her craft-making skills, she agreed to create a collage that represented her reactions to the painful event. I encouraged her to look for images that conveyed themes of trauma and resilience. She picked and used images in silence for most of the first three sessions. Eventually, she started to describe the images she chose, her process in finding them, the memories they represented, and the feelings they elicited.

5. *Build cognitive skills.* Creative work often requires strong memory and concentration skills, as with performing artists who have to memorize parts, or scientists who have to stay focused on a line of inquiry for extended periods. When chronic trauma compromises the brain's ability to use certain cognitive skills effortlessly, even the most motivated and creative people will struggle to produce their best work. To help with this, sessions can incorporate cognition-enhancing practices, including physical exercise, neurotherapy (brainwave training), and meditation, many of which have been shown to improve cognitive functions (Rabipour & Raz, 2012). These interventions don't address traumatic events

directly but deal with their effects on the cognitive skills necessary for creative functions.

> Example: A PhD candidate in philosophy sought out help because she kept forgetting important deadlines and struggled to stay focused on writing her dissertation. While providing context for these concerns, she revealed a history of chronic problems with regulating her attention. She described early memories of trying to do homework while having to listen to her parents' aggressive arguments. To counter the compromising effects of the trauma on her memory skills, she engaged in cognitive-building activities by learning a new language and practicing 30 minutes of daily meditation.

6. *Refer to an eye-movement desensitization reprocessing (EMDR) specialist.* This method works by targeting memories that are not easily accessible through conscious cognitions or that are too painful to be discussed directly (Shapiro & Forrest, 2016). Therefore, they require the help of some type of external bilateral stimulation (such as eye movement or hand tapping) to be identified and, most importantly, reprocessed until they are no longer disturbing. EMDR has been used to treat trauma that has caused performers to have severe anxiety, as well as other types of artists to feel creatively blocked. Clinicians will need to have additional training to implement this approach.[1]

> Example: I referred an actor I once worked with to an EMDR specialist to address the trauma that contributed to his severe performance anxiety. The specialist asked him to talk about the disturbing event and the negative thoughts they elicited ("Having been attacked during an armed robbery makes me think I'm powerless") and the impact he noticed that it had on his performances ("Thinking I am powerless makes me doubt my creative worth"). While doing so, my client alternated hand taps so that both body and mind were engaged in the memory reprocessing, and so that he could focus on developing psychologically healthier thoughts ("Having been attacked makes me think that I still have the power to create").

7. *Address self-blame.* Trauma survivors often go through phases of blaming themselves for events because they believe they could somehow have prevented them (Davis et al., 1996). These feelings are common and important to discuss, as they can open up a dialogue about resilience (how the person has recovered), coping strategies (how the person has chosen to deal with the negative feelings), and growth (how the person has psychologically matured). In contrast, sometimes these feelings can keep a person stuck in a cycle of self-directed anger. Creative clients can redirect anger and self-blame onto an external object, through creative and symbolic representations.

Example: A writer I worked with journaled about the traumatic event from the perspective of a compassionate caretaker rather than the perspective of a trauma survivor. With an emphasis on gentle affirmations ("The story's character did the best he could under the circumstances"), she used her words and creativity to reinforce empowering narratives and to reduce feelings of self-blame.

8. *Trust the anxiety.* Performers with a history of trauma run the risk of developing "distrust of the arousal cycle" (Levine & Frederick, 1997:127), which means that any anxiety caused by the performance will be interpreted as a sign that something threatening is happening—similar to the threatening nature of the traumatic event. This kind of misreading of physical cues has a negative effect on the quality of the performance (Swart, 2014), as it may cause performers to associate emotional arousal with danger and to experience symptoms of performance anxiety. Sessions can focus on helping clients learn to trust this cycle by recognizing symptoms of anxiety, tolerating them, and normalizing them within the context of the high-pressure moment of a public performance.

    Example: During sessions with a solo pianist, we established that he'd been associating preperformance jitters with the nervousness he'd had as child when his father would make him memorize school-book chapters and demand that he repeat them correctly. When he got things wrong, he'd get ridiculed and sometimes physically reprimanded. During sessions, we worked on accepting the state of anxiety for what it was—a natural state of arousal caused by the present circumstances—and on trusting that it's supposed to be there, unlike the posttraumatic anxiety from his past.

Additional Interventions

9.
10.
11.

Takeaways

- Many artists, performers, and other creative individuals have a history of adversity and trauma.
- There's merit to the belief that traumatic events fuel the need for creative expression. This is because those with a history of trauma are

88 Trauma and Creativity

drawn to creative media as alternatives to the verbal expression of their experiences.

- Creative pursuits can help trauma survivors heal from negative posttraumatic effects and can convey useful information about how trauma has been internalized and processed.
- Sometimes the psychological effects of emotional trauma can blunt creative abilities and increase performance anxiety, especially for performing artists with PTSD.
- Clinicians and traumatized creative clients can pay attention to what clients' work reveals about their experiences, while ensuring that boundaries and defenses set in place to protect from severe stress reactions are maintained.
- Counseling can help clients understand the role that trauma has played in their paths as creators. It can maximize the benefits of representing traumatic experiences through creative expression, help clients integrate fragmented memories, and manage trauma-related anxiety during performances.

Note

1 For information on how to practice EMDR, visit www.emdr.com.

References

Albert, R. S. (1971). Cognitive development and parental loss among the gifted, the exceptionally gifted and the creative. *Psychological Reports, 29*(1), 19–26.

Baikie, K. A., & Wilhelm, K. (2005). Emotional and physical health benefits of expressive writing. *Advances in Psychiatric Treatment, 11*, 338–346.

Bremner, J. D. (2005). *Does stress damage the brain? Understanding trauma-related disorders from a mind—body perspective.* New York, NY: W. W. Norton & Company.

Bremner, J. D. (2006). Traumatic stress: Effects on the brain. *Dialogues in Clinical Neuroscience, 8*(4), 445–461.

Carson, S. (2010). *Your creative brain: Seven steps to maximize imagination, productivity, and innovation in your life.* San Francisco, CA: Jossey-Bass.

Csikszentmihalyi, M. (1996). *Creativity. The flow and the psychology of discovery of invention.* New York, NY: HarperCollins Publishers.

Davis, C. G., Lehman, D. R., Cohen Silver, R., Wortman, C. B., & Ellard, J. H. (1996). Self-blame following a traumatic event: The role of perceived avoidability. *Personality and Social Psychology Bulletin, 22*, 557–567.

Engelhard, I. M., Sijbrandij, M., van den Hout, M. A., Rutherford, N. M., Rahim, F. R., & Kocak, F. (2012). Choking under pressure: Degrading flashforwards related to performance anxiety. *Journal of Experimental Psychopathology, 3*(2), 158–167. doi:10.5127/jep.024111

Feist, G. J. (1998). A meta-analysis of personality in scientific and artistic creativity. *Personality and Social Psychology Review, 2*(4), 290–309.

Forgeard, M. J. C. (2013). Perceiving benefits after adversity: The relationship between self-reported posttraumatic growth and creativity. *Psychology of Aesthetics, Creativity, and the Arts, 7*(3), 245–264.

Glass, J. (2006). Working toward aesthetic distance: Drama therapy for adult victims of trauma. In L. Carey (Ed.), *Expressive and creative arts methods for trauma survivors*. London, UK: Jessica Kingsley Publishers.

Kenny, D. (2011). *The psychology of music performance anxiety*. Oxford: Oxford University Press.

Knafo, D. (Ed.). (2004). *Living with terror, working with trauma: A clinician's handbook*. Lanham, MD: Jason Aronson.

Levine, P. A., & Frederick, A. (1997). *Waking the tiger: Healing trauma*. Berkeley, CA: North Atlantic Books.

Malchiodi, C. (Ed.). (2003). *Handbook of art therapy*. New York, NY: The Guilford Press.

Panter, B. M. (Ed.). (1995). *Creativity & madness: Psychological studies of art and artists*. Creativity and Madness, 1. Burbank, CA: Aimed Press.

Pennebaker, J. W. (2004). *Writing to heal: A guided journal for recovering from trauma & emotional upheaval*. Oakland, CA: New Harbinger Publications.

Rabipour, S., & Raz, A. (2012). Training the brain: Fact and fad in cognitive and behavioral remediation. *Brain and Cognition, 79*(2), 159–179.

Shapiro, F., & Forrest, M. S. (2016). *EMDR: The breakthrough therapy for overcoming anxiety, stress, and trauma*. Philadelphia, PA: Basic Books.

Simonton, D. K. (1994). *Greatness: Who makes history and why*. New York, NY: Guilford Press.

Simonton, D. K. (2004). *Creativity in science: Chance, logic, genius, and zeitgeist*. Cambridge: Cambridge University Press.

Steele, W., & Kuban, C. (2003). Using drawing in short-term trauma resolution. In C. Malchiodi (ed.), *Handbook of art therapy* (pp. 162–175). New York, NY: The Guilford Press.

Stien, P. T., & Kendall, J. (2003). *Psychological trauma and the developing brain: Neurologically based interventions for troubled children*. New York, NY: Routledge.

Swart, I. (2010). *The influence of trauma on musicians* (Unpublished doctoral dissertation). University of Pretoria, Pretoria, South Africa.

Swart, I. (2014). Overcoming adversity: Trauma in the lives of music performers and composers. *Psychology of Music, 42*(3), 386–402.

Van der Kolk, B. A., & Fisler, R. (1995). Dissociation and the fragmentary nature of traumatic memories: Overview and exploratory study. *Journal of Traumatic Stress, 8*(4), 505–525.

Zara, C. (2012). *Tortured artists: From Picasso and Monroe to Warhol and Winehouse: The twisted secrets of the world's most creative minds*. Avon, MA: Adams Media.

Chapter 6

Psychiatric Disorders

When I tell people that I'm a mental health counselor who works with creative clients, the first thing they usually want to know is whether artists, performers, and other creative individuals are more prone to mental illness. This hypothesis is a common one. The incidence of psychiatric symptoms in people from various creative fields, combined with the veil of mystery surrounding the sources of creativity, makes for a tempting assumption—that creativity is tied to mental illness. Some researchers and theorists consider the links between the two strong enough to make a case for a dynamic, nuanced relationship, whereas others see no reason to assume that creativity and mental illness are, in some way, predictive of one another. Though there isn't enough evidence to make conclusive remarks, we do know that mental illnesses are prevalent across creative populations, and that creativity and mental illnesses have overlapping traits. Establishing a causation is beyond the scope of this book. However, in this chapter, light will be shed on the role of clinicians who work with creative clients with mental health concerns. It's important to explore the psychological experiences of creative clients with symptoms of psychiatric disorders, so that creative clients diagnosed with psychiatric disorders receive counseling from mental health professionals well versed in the creativity-psychopathology relationship.

Attention deficit hyperactivity disorder (ADHD), depression, bipolar disorder, and psychotic disorders are four diagnoses whose relationships to creativity have received a lot of attention. This chapter looks at some of the interactions between each of these diagnoses and creative traits. It considers the overlap between traits associated with psychiatric disorders and those associated with creative achievement. It discusses reciprocal reinforcement, which occurs when the intensity of the creative process reinforces psychiatric symptoms, and when psychiatric symptoms enhance qualities needed for creative expression. Last, it addresses career-induced risk factors. An example of this is when the stress of working as a performing artist—erratic schedules, frequent rejections, unstable income, and so on—triggers a preexisting predisposition to feelings of isolation, hopelessness, and other symptoms of depression.

Appreciating the role that psychiatric symptoms can play in clients' creativity is pivotal. Artists who seek psychiatric counseling often report to me that prior treatment experiences didn't take their so-called creative temperament into consideration. Sometimes they'd have a different view regarding what they considered to be optimal mental health functioning from that of their clinicians. A narrow focus on reducing symptoms, for example, runs the risk of undermining the role that such symptoms play in shaping people's creative identity—an integral part of their overall self-identity. A 26-year-old recording producer I worked with came to counseling 3 years after having been diagnosed with bipolar disorder. The psychiatrist who'd initially diagnosed him had prescribed mood stabilizers and antianxiety medication for symptoms of irritability, difficulty sleeping, and racing thoughts—treatment that he'd been following for about a year. When he came to my office, he said he'd barely slept in 5 days because he'd been trying to perfect the sound on the album he was producing. He recognized this behavior as a possible precursor to a manic episode—which was why he scheduled a session. However, he was having mixed reactions to how he felt. On the one hand, he felt alarmed, as he worried that it might lead to other symptoms of bipolar disorder, which might take him back to the hospital; on the other hand, he felt reassured by the familiarity of his feelings. He knew that some of his best work had been done in this exact state: feeling highly focused, with rapid thought associations. He wanted to understand how to live with—rather than eliminate—symptoms, such as severe changes in mood and levels of energy, while monitoring them so they wouldn't lead to destructiveness.

The archetype of the *mad artist* often inspires sweeping generalizations regarding creative individuals and their proneness to mental illness. To understand how psychiatric diagnoses affect creative populations, and therefore to develop a helpful set of treatment interventions, it's important to carve out distinctions that allow for a richer exploration and understanding of the interplay between mental illness and creativity. Clinicians who want to develop effective treatment approaches for their creative clients with psychiatric diagnoses mustn't overlook differences across the following:

- *Types of creativity.* Are we discussing the ability to generate large quantities of novel ideas, reach the elusive aha moment, solve problems, express oneself uniquely, invent useful objects, or make connections between seemingly unrelated ideas? Certain forms of creativity, such as divergent and flexible thinking, are possibly enhanced by overinclusive thinking, typical a feature of ADHD and mania, whereas making connections among creative ideas and implementing them are likelier to be stunted by such features.

92 Psychiatric Disorders

- *Types of creative professions.* A music composer who spends most of his time in solitude will face different psychological triggers from those of an actor who deals with the pressure of frequent auditions and performances. Similarly, depression in a software engineer, whose creative skills are useful for solving problems, may have a different impact than it does on a depressed writer, who reflects on her experiences with low mood through writing. It's important to recognize how the professional environment and demands interact with psychiatric symptoms.
- *Types of mental illness.* When people wonder if creative people are likelier to have a mental illness diagnosis, my response is often "Which diagnosis of them all?" A social phobia diagnosis may have little to do with a writer's ability to generate many ideas for the ending to a novel, whereas a diagnosis of bipolar disorder is likelier to affect the creative content and motivation, resulting from extreme fluctuations in mood and thought patterns.

Despite the aforementioned differences, research data suggests the frequent presence of certain clusters of psychiatric symptoms in some creative groups. By virtue of these findings, which will be discussed in the following four parts (on ADHD, depression, bipolar disorder, and psychotic disorders) it's important to pay attention to how such symptoms affect clients.

Many clients come to find that the nature of the relationship between their diagnoses and creativity is complex. For example, my work with a writer diagnosed with major depression revealed an inverted-U relationship between symptoms of depression (such as low energy and hopelessness) and creativity: when she was experiencing no symptoms of depression, she felt virtually no need to find a creative outlet, but when she was too depressed even to get out of bed, she couldn't access the will to take action. Her creativity flourished only when her depression was at the "right" level—strong enough to signal the need for comfort through creative expression, but weak enough to allow for the drive that would enable her to work.

Each one of the four parts of this chapter looks at research findings and clinical observations from the perspective of how each diagnosis affects the lives and work of creative individuals. A causal connection between these disorders and creative achievement is far from clear, but evidence for the incidence of particular psychiatric disorders in creative populations suggests that symptoms and treatment require creativity-sensitive approaches. Each part takes a close look at the role clinicians must play in helping their creative clients manage psychiatric symptoms while maximizing potential for creative achievement.

Part I: Attention Deficit Hyperactivity Disorder

One of the most popular TED talks of all time is Sir Ken Robinson's talk[1] on how the school system undermines creativity. He addresses schools' overreliance on ADHD diagnoses, which come at the expense of identifying creative tendencies. He presents a powerful example of a fidgety and hyper student in the 1930s who was told by her school that she had a learning disability—what according to Robinson would be described as ADHD today. Fortunately, however, she was guided by a specialist to pursue dancing and went on to become a successful dancer at the Royal Ballet School. Perhaps one of the reasons this talk became so popular is that it presented an example that echoes the sentiment of many who see a connection between ADHD and a disposition for creative traits: even though ADHD symptoms sometimes signal the presence of heightened creativity (Saltz, 2017; Kaufman, 2014), there needs to be a system in place that recognizes this kind of potential. Distractibility is not always an impediment; it can be a chance to observe and absorb new sources of stimulation. Hyperactivity is not always an impulse-control problem; it can be energy that's used creatively. Mental health clinicians can become part of such a system that fosters creative potential, while addressing and treating disruptive symptoms.

The effects of ADHD on creative achievement come in many forms. Larry, a photographer I worked with, had been diagnosed with ADHD in college. When he heard the term, he thought it made sense and that it explained his struggles with organizing his thoughts. However, despite the struggles, he considered his diagnosis to be a tool for creative thinking. During one of our sessions, he proudly shared a concept for a cosmetics photo shoot he was looking forward to starting. He described his diagnosis as a "blessing in disguise" because his disorganized thought process helped him come up with unexpectedly interesting photography ideas. In contrast, other ADHD-diagnosed people, who also have no shortage of creative content, find it so difficult to focus their thoughts or manage their time that they're unable to complete ideas. One Broadway singer I worked with kept missing out on important auditions because of his difficulty with managing his time. He was motivated and comfortable onstage and generally optimistic about passing the audition. This helped us rule out the possibility of other obstacles to getting to his audition, such as anxiety-induced avoidance, low motivation, or negative expectations about the outcome. The only thing that got in the way of his creative success was his ADHD. To address his concerns, our sessions focused on time management, setting feasible goals, and reinforcing helpful habits, such as writing down reminders for audition dates in multiple places.

Let's look at where science stands regarding the relationship between ADHD and creativity. Research in the field has paid attention to the ability of ADHD-diagnosed individuals to demonstrate cognitive flexibility by engaging in *divergent thinking*, the ability to generate a large number of new responses to a given stimulus. A 2006 study by Anna Abraham and her colleagues gave examples of toy ideas to a group of a ADHD-diagnosed adolescents and to a control group. They found that the ADHD group came up with more ideas for toys that differed from the examples, compared to the control group (this was called the *recently activated knowledge task*). However, when the task was to invent practical and useful toys, the ADHD group didn't do as well. Similarly, Holly White and Prit Shah (2006) compared ADHD and non-ADHD groups and found that the ADHD group was stronger in the ability to generate new ideas, whereas developing and expanding on such ideas was stronger in the non-ADHD group. In 2011, White and Shah found that adults with ADHD had more real-life creative achievement than adults without ADHD. These findings are consistent with the idea that creative clients with ADHD will have a plethora of thoughts for what creative ideas to work on but are likely to need help in turning these thoughts into reality.

Cognitive thinking patterns associated with attention deficits share many similarities with the thought processes that result in creative ideas, mostly having to do with how the brain filters a stream of information. Zabelina and colleagues (2016) studied artists with a record of real-life creative achievements and demonstrated that *leaky attention*, the kind of attention where unrelated stimuli enter freely into one's cognitive attention span—in ADHD terminology, distractibility—played a part in artists' creative associations. Leaky attention, however, is not always good news: it's likely to impede performance during laboratory divergent-thinking tasks and to make it harder for those with ADHD to focus on problem clarification and idea implementation (Zabelina et al., 2015; White & Shah, 2011). Creativity in people with ADHD can benefit from their intensely vivid imaginations (Kaufman & Gregoire, 2015). In the right context, such as when brainstorming plot developments for a script, their overactive imaginations can turn from a trait that interferes with focusing to one that helps come up with unique ideas.

A clear understanding of how creative traits and symptoms of ADHD overlap is important for the prevention of a misdiagnosis. ADHD diagnoses often take place during childhood, following quick observations made by teachers or cursory screenings made by evaluators. Sometimes creatively gifted and talented children spend a lot of time daydreaming, act out due to boredom, and do not follow rules or social norms. The book *Misdiagnosis and Dual Diagnoses of Gifted Children and Adults: ADHD, Bipolar, OCD, Asperger's, Depression, and Other Disorders* by Webb (2005) presents many examples of how gifted and talented children are misclassified as having ADHD when in fact they are showing behaviors consistent with distinct abilities. As discussed earlier, an impediment in the eyes of one person may be a gift in the eyes of another. Clinicians must consider the role that symptoms play for creative functioning to avoid rushing into a potentially inaccurate diagnosis.

The Clinician's Role

Maximizing Benefits, Minimizing Impairment

ADHD can have multiple effects on creative clients. The clinicians' role is to help identify the treatment that keeps the good and tackles the bad. ADHD bombards clients with creative ideas, yet makes it hard for clients to implement them. Larry, the photographer mentioned previously, described his brain as a bottle without a cap that kept filling up with ideas. When he compared himself to his peers, he noticed that his mind was working at a much faster rate. On the one hand, this felt good to him: his brain took him to new and exciting places. On the other hand, staying focused on goals and prioritizing were constant struggles. Because of his conflicted feelings, he didn't know how to proceed with treatment. Was there even a problem that he needed to address? If so, would the treatment have an all-or-nothing effect on his creativity? Our sessions focused on getting him to know his condition and cultivating feelings of self-acceptance as a way of approaching the treatment-planning process with openness. Though he eagerly embraced characteristics of his condition that made him a better photographer, such as richness in creative ideas, he didn't know how to manage the ones that got in his way, such as disorganization. He decided to consult with a psychiatrist for medication so that, as he put it, he could finally "put a cap on the bottle." Though this course of treatment may not apply to every creative client, in Larry's case, his creativity didn't suffer. Instead, he was able to work on one isolated concept at a time, while still generating many exciting ideas. It's important for clinicians to approach treatment with an awareness of which symptoms impair creative achievement and which don't, so they can maximize benefits and minimize impairment.

Establishing an Accurate Diagnosis

Due to the frequent misdiagnosis of ADHD (Ford-Jones, 2015), it's important for clinicians to think about the conditions under which the diagnosis came about and whether it accurately reflects clients' experiences. A misdiagnosis can be harmful because it steers clients away from fully understanding the implications of their symptoms and experiences. This applies to clients who self-diagnose. I've often worked with clients who interpret traits associated with high creativity to indicate the presence of ADHD (based on online searches) only to expect reduced abilities as a result. In a self-fulfilling manner, the anticipation of a struggle begets the feeling of struggling during creative processes. In contrast, a thorough assessment that results in a reliable diagnosis of ADHD comes as a relief to some who are wondering why, despite a plethora of creative ideas, they find it difficult to understand, organize, and execute creative tasks. Once an accurate diagnosis has been established, clients and clinicians can work on setting specific goals and strategies for treatment.

Understanding Brain-Activation Patterns

To get a sense of how ADHD affects clients' creative processes, clinicians can look into brain-activation patterns during moments of increased creativity.

Typically, individuals with ADHD show higher levels of cortical activation than people without ADHD—meaning they're more vigilant—when they need to sustain focus for a goal-oriented task (Loo et al., 2009). Depending on whether the creative task at hand requires sustained or more fluid attention, creative clients will likely face different sets of challenges. For example, the process of composing e-mails with the intention of sending them out to agents is a sustained-focus task that might benefit from eliminating all distractions, whether environmental (such as noise), or psychological (such as negative thinking), so as not to burden the brain's efforts to remain activated. In contrast, a task that doesn't rely as heavily on sustained attention, such as brainstorming concepts for a film or a photo shoot, might benefit from looking at many images, listening to music and sounds that inspire new ideas, and other ways to stimulate the brain.

All creative people will get distracted at some point during a creative task; however, unlike creative clients who don't have ADHD, those who do might need more help to sustain high levels of cortical activation during tasks that require focused attention. At the same time, low cortical activation allows for an unfocused, "leaky" attentional style, which can be helpful for creativity that relies more on inspiration. One of the roles of clinicians is to help creative clients with ADHD gain a better understanding of their thinking styles and needs during different creative processes.

Strengthening Self-Esteem

People diagnosed with ADHD are thought to have a negative self-concept (Shaw-Zirt et al., 2005), perhaps resulting from years of academic and professional disappointments (Tuckerman, 2007). Clinicians can identify clients' internalized thoughts about their diagnoses and highlight the positive connections between their unique thinking traits and their creativity. They can validate clients' creative potential (for example, by clearly articulating how an active and uninhibited imagination correlates with high creativity) in order to strengthen their self-esteem. A comprehensive understanding of how ADHD helps or hinders the creative process will make clients more self-aware, more open to seeking help when necessary, and more confident in using their symptoms to their advantage.

Improving Social Functioning

Clinicians and clients can explore how having ADHD affects their social interactions. Professional artists' careers can go forward by establishing relationships, networking, and saying the right thing at the right time. Yet clients with ADHD commonly feel disheartened when they "blow it" by impulsively making an inappropriate remark, by not speaking at all because of competing thoughts, by forgetting to return a call, or by making a bad impression by being late to a meeting. These behaviors can negatively affect the quality of their social relationships, which in the creative world can be instrumental to finding supportive scenes and advancing one's career. (For more on the role of relationships in the lives of creative people, see chapter 4.) Clinicians can investigate clients' social skills and suggest ways to improve them. Role-playing dialogues and discussing time-management options can help address many of these concerns.

Treatment Goals

1. Develop insight into the relationship between ADHD and creativity.
2. Implement time-management habits that help move creative goals along.
3. Improve self-esteem caused by cognitive and social impairment.
4. Distinguish helpful from unhelpful distractibility.
5. Remain focused enough to complete creative projects.

Suggested Interventions to Achieve Goals

1. *Improve time-management skills.* Some creative clients with ADHD consciously reject the idea of adhering to schedules. They'd rather take life moment by moment and remove time constraints from the creative process. For others, managing time is a necessary tool to make the most out of the hours spent on creative tasks. For example, self-employed and freelance artists who make their own schedules can get more done, over time, when they follow some type of daily structure. Clients and clinicians can work together to identify feasible schedules that encourage unconstrained creative thinking, yet allow clients to commit to time-specific goals. Time management can be facilitated with the help of smartphone applications, alarms, calendars, to-do lists, tentative time lines, and deadlines.

    Example: The Broadway singer described previously and I worked on identifying what he wanted to spend time on and for how long,

98 Psychiatric Disorders

as well as the importance attached to each task. I asked him to try to stay as close as possible to the desired time frame, even when initial attempts were unsuccessful. Working around an approximate schedule helped him feel free to delve deeper into creative brainstorming without feeling lost as to when he needed to transition to the next step.

2. *Encourage mindfulness and sustained attention.* A telltale sign of ADHD is difficulty regulating and sustaining attention. Mitchell and colleagues (2015) reviewed the research surrounding mindfulness, such as shifting conscious attention onto one's breathing and the present moment, and found promising results: experimenting with the idea of "being present" and nonjudgmentally observing what's happening with one's cognitive and emotional experiences help increase attention on given tasks. This approach can help creative people stay with an idea longer and, hopefully, see it through, from early conception to the production stage.

    Example: When a fashion designer complained to me about her mind wandering during the process of compiling work for a portfolio to show to potential clients, I asked her to STOP (stop, take a breath, observe, and proceed) (Goldstein, 2012). I challenged her to stay focused on every step—from selecting pieces that show her best work, to adding labels—and to notice the impulse to check her e-mail or do other unrelated things. With practice, she was able to spend more time on each task and take proactive steps, such as putting her phone on airplane mode.

3. *Prioritize.* According to ADHD specialist Thomas Brown (2013), ADHD can cause cognitive executive functioning impairment in those with otherwise high IQ and high levels of creative interests. Struggling to prioritize tasks according to importance and time sensitivity is an example of this kind of impairment. Sessions can focus on which tasks seem to be more important and on ways to maximize concentration on each one. Doing so helps organize clients' thoughts and intentions.

    Example: When a ballet dancer with ADHD had to think about signing up for auditions, choreographing a new dance piece, practicing, and finding dance teacher gigs for extra income, she quickly became overwhelmed by each task's demands—which resulted in her avoiding everything altogether. Though these tasks seemed equally important to her, by discussing the advantages and disadvantages associated with each one, we worked on focusing her attention on what had greater short-term consequences. Auditioning for a well-known show seemed more crucial than coming up with an idea for a new dance piece. In our sessions, we gradually made our way to tasks with fewer long-term consequences.

Psychiatric Disorders 99

4. *Consider medication management.* Clinicians can consider referral for psychiatric evaluation and possible administration of stimulant drugs to minimize distractibility and inattentiveness. It's important to think about possible side effects and about how medication might affect creativity, as some evidence suggests that stimulants can limit the breadth of creative thinking (Smartwood et al., 2003). Medication, however, can help creative people gain more control over the creative process and persist until goals have been completed.

> Example: A musician and band leader I worked with found it difficult to keep up with the administrative tasks of his creative career. Specifically, he always felt that he was behind when he had to set up band members' schedules, book rehearsal spaces, and remember to bring music and lyric sheets. When he met with a psychiatrist, they discussed taking an appropriate dose right before planning such tasks, but to avoid taking it when he needed to write songs, play guitar, and brainstorm ideas.

5. *Practice social skills.* Artists and creative individuals who want to make professional connections often need to talk about their creative projects in a coherent and self-assured way. A good first impression with potential collaborators, clients, and buyers can be extremely important, yet symptoms of ADHD can get in the way. Impulsivity and inattentiveness can cause people to say things they regret, to forget important points in conversations, and to make poor decisions. Clients can describe how they handled social interactions and role-play during sessions in order to practice and rehearse desired reactions to social situations.

> Example: A filmmaker with ADHD hesitated to go to social events because she thought she'd sabotage them by saying too much or not saying the right things. In our sessions, we focused on how to pick up on body-language social cues (such as diverted eye contact and constricted body posture), how to sustain attention during conversations, how to stay on topic, and how to decide what information she wished to disclose during small talk with other artists.

6. *Introduce dialectical behavioral therapy.* DBT was originally developed as an approach to treat personality disorders and self-harming behaviors. Its interactive and didactic emphasis on emotion and cognition regulation makes it a helpful tool in understanding and changing thoughts and behaviors. Some of its principles have been adapted for the treatment of adults with ADHD (Hesslinger et al., 2002). When working with creative populations, the concepts of emotion regulation and impulse control—two of the fundamental tenets of DBT—ought to be explored within the context of creative expression. Though the goal of DBT

100 Psychiatric Disorders

would typically be to learn how to manage emotions and impulsivity, it's important for creative clients to balance this goal with that of having wide-ranging emotions and spontaneity—two features that allow for openness to creative expression.

> Example: During my work with a writer who struggled to finish many of her story ideas (but could easily keep coming up with new ones), we incorporated some DBT concepts to sustain focus and concentration. She practiced identifying immediate emotions, such as the impulse to give up on a story when she had distracting thoughts or when the task seemed too frustrating. Then she practiced DBT's opposite-to-emotion action technique: she continued to work, even if it was only for 5 minutes longer, despite the frustration.

7. *Work with symptoms.* Clients whose creative identities and livelihoods depend on their mind-wandering tendencies should work with the symptoms, not against them. Instead of eliminating all or many of their symptoms, clients and clinicians can focus on how to make the most of them. This might look something like identifying what's positive about what Zabelina (2015) describes as their *leaky attention* filter, and using that to expand the range of their creative ideas.

> Example: To highlight the idea that symptoms can be incorporated during treatment, I encouraged a graphic designer to suspend all cognition filtering when he brainstormed new logos. He allowed his easily distractible mind to jump freely from thought to thought, giving himself permission not to think about results. Initially, the focus was on quantity, rather than quality, to highlight the contribution of his diagnosis to having a highly prolific brain.

Additional Interventions

8.	
9.	
10.	

Part II: Depression

Depression can be dangerous for creativity as it diminishes qualities that are much needed for the pursuit of creative goals. It weakens motivation, which needs to be high so as to sustain the effort to try things over and over. It numbs pleasure, when passion and enjoyment enable full immersion in creative experiences. It lowers confidence, which needs to be high to manage rejections and criticism. It brings down energy, which is necessary for putting creative ideas into action. It sometimes impairs cognitive functions that are often required for creative problem-solving tasks (Rock et al., 2014). When creative people are depressed, their appetite for mental stimulation and idea production is likely to go down. A meta-analytic study of 25 years of mood-creativity research found that fluency and originality—two features of creativity—were stronger for those with positive mood (Baas et al., 2008).

Yet, perhaps paradoxically, creativity can emerge out of both positive and negative emotional states. Though it's more common for depression to take away the desire to engage in many facets of life, including the creative one, some characteristics associated with depression are helpful for the kinds of thought processes and emotional states that are conducive for creativity. This idea is consistent with the *inverted-U* hypothesis (Abraham, 2014), which suggests that mild or subclinical degrees of depression enhance parts of the creative process. In addition, as much as creativity draws from feelings of depression, it also ameliorates them. All the layers of this paradoxical relationship are teased apart in this section, which describes the ways depression affects creative thought and behavior.

Jane, a novelist I worked with, had spent 2 years caring for her sick sister, who eventually died from cancer. During those years, she was brainstorming ideas for a new novel but did little more than focus on her sister's psychological and physical well-being. After her sister's death, Jane, who was in her 50s at the time, began to have debilitating symptoms of depression. She wasn't new to them, as she'd been having depressive episodes since adolescence, but this time around they felt worse. She'd sleep 15 hours a day, eat one meal in 24 hours, isolate herself from friends, and break into four to five crying spells a day. The loss of her sister had left her feeling numb, making her the one who now needed care. Basic survival, not writing, had become her first priority. When, despite overwhelming reluctance, she did manage to put some effort into writing, she'd write a few paragraphs and then stop because of how tired—physically and emotionally—she felt. Unfortunately, her inability to finish a chapter made her feel even worse. Depression sucked every last bit of creative motivation out of Jane, who felt pain and despair about every aspect of her life.

Such feelings are familiar to many depressed creators. Yet, despite everything that depression takes away (motivation, positivity, cognitive skills, and so on), it also makes important additions that turn it into an asset for creativity. The first addition is the overflow of negative feelings, which will eventually be in desperate need for expression. Creativity, especially artistic creativity that's rooted in the expression of emotions, comes in to fulfill that role. Psychologists Maja Djikic and Keith Oatley (2014) propose that artists are prone to an "emotion-driven preoccupation" to express their sensitivity and emotional volatility through artistic representations, such as writing a novel. The need for creative expression will therefore likely be stronger for those who experience extreme emotions, including despair, disappointment, and hopelessness, as is the case for depressed people. For creativity coach and author Eric Maisel (2007), depression is almost unavoidable for creative people in the arts because it's what fuels the daunting task of finding meaning through their creative endeavors. Psychiatrist Gail Saltz (2017:124) writes that many of the feelings that people with depression experience might be "deeply unpleasant, but they can also yield spectacular work."

The second way in which depression contributes to creativity is through its association to ruminative thinking, one of depression's most common cognitive symptoms. Rumination deepens depressed people's absorption in ideas that need to be expressed and problems that need to be solved. In a 2014 study, Jones, Roy, and Vekuilen assessed how musicians approached their preparation and performance of a piece. They found that musicians scored higher on rumination—repetitively thinking about the causes and nature of the distress—than nonmusicians. They also found that rumination, rather than brooding, which is focusing on negative emotions and inaction, was related to improved musical skills (musicianship, expressiveness, and tone). Verhaeghen and colleagues (2005) reached a similar conclusion in their exploration of the relationship among creativity, mood, and self-reflective rumination. They found that self-reflective rumination benefited the seriousness of creative endeavors and the search for creative outlets.

Ruminating is often a part of creators' journeys. An unexpected observation about Jane, my novelist client, was that this time around depression affected her creativity differently from when she'd been a teenager. Up until now, her depressive episodes felt like an explorative emotional journey, one that encouraged self-reflection, introspection, and deep emotional sensitivity. She'd usually ruminate on betrayals and dwell on disappointments, yet despite—or perhaps because of—her intense sadness, she'd find creative release through her writing. In fact, she attributed the deep level of emotional complexity found in her writing to these feelings. When she began counseling following her sister's death, she painted a vivid picture of the contrast between how her depression affected her writing then and how it was affecting it now. Instead of actively engaging in understanding her feelings, she was now passive. Instead of feeling curious about her depression, she became apathetic. Instead of transforming her experiences through literary representations, she was withdrawing in agony. The difference seemed to be in the way her brain was working around her new depression: instead of reflecting, she was detaching.

We worked hard on differentiating these types of depressed thinking, and we tried to hear her inner voice regarding her sister's death. Was there something about this experience that she needed to express? In trying to move past the emotional numbness, we investigated how grieving her sister's death made her reflect on her own mortality. It wasn't long, upon striking a chord, before Jane began to reflect on themes of meaning and purpose. Her depression persisted as she remained isolated and hopeless, but her interest in exploring these themes in her writing began to resurface and pick up momentum.

A helpful summary of the way positive and negative mood influence creativity comes from Kaufmann and Kaufmann (2014:226) who write that "positive mood promotes broad and shallow processing whereas negative mood leads to a narrower but deeper processing." Depression can be thought of as a hindrance for the energy needed to produce quantity, but it increases the emotional intensity needed to produce quality. Similarly, behavioral neurologist Kenneth Heilman (2005) draws a distinction between depressed people's ability to have innovative ideas and their struggle with testing and implementing them—often a result of their low energy, low motivation, and feelings of hopelessness.

Regarding the way creativity affects feelings of depression, evidence suggests that engaging in creative tasks is itself a way to reduce negative feelings (Carson, 2010; Stuckey & Nobel, 2010). Perhaps this is because creative work distracts from negative thoughts or allows for the expression of otherwise unaddressed inner conflicts. It could also be because of relaxation induced during moments of heightened immersion in creative work, or because it increases depressed people's self-esteem by reminding them of their skills and talents. Young and colleagues (2013) contemplate this question as they interpret research results that document a higher incidence of depressive symptoms in teens who pursue artistic activities. Clinicians and clients can use sessions to address whether their creative work helps decrease feelings of depression.

The Clinician's Role

Exploring the Interaction Between Depression and Creativity

Sessions can begin by trying to understand the extent to which depression fuels or halts creativity. Initial assessment can include questions about moments of heightened creativity and their connection to sadness, negative thinking, hopelessness, social isolation, and other feelings typical of depression. Sometimes strong feelings of sadness will culminate in the composition of a heartfelt song, one that "writes itself," but sometimes preoccupation with negative thoughts make the songwriting process feel like pulling teeth. On a case-by-case exploration, the clinicians' role is to shed light on whether clients' feelings of depression—before, during, and after creative work—tend to find release and expression in their creative pursuits or they merely get in the way of creative achievement.

Interpreting Depressed Feelings

Clinicians can investigate what the depression is about: what thoughts accompany negative feelings, what are the triggers, and what makes them worse? The goal is to uncover common themes associated with feeling depressed. For example, depression is sometimes a reaction to having experienced a loss (the separation from a loved one, the abandonment of a dream, the rejection of oneself as being worthy, the inability to attach emotionally, and so on). Clinicians can help clients identify any underlying and internalized feelings, and see if clients can confront them, or even heal, through their creativity. For artists and performers, confronting the loss could be accomplished by giving depressive themes a voice via art making and performing. Depression that relates to a loss of self-worth, for example, could be addressed by asserting one's worthiness through the act of making a creative contribution to one's chosen field. If depression is about the loss of autonomy, the depressed person may want to turn to creative work that involves taking risks.

One client understood his depression to be about feeling unpopular and disliked in his competitive music school. As much as he tried, he never managed to feel accepted and never became part of an in-group. His depression grew as he confronted the reality of how others perceived him: talented and quirky, but not particularly socially engaging and charismatic. Initially, we worked on improving his social skills. Maybe he wasn't engaging enough in conversation or communicating effectively. However, as his depression persisted, we began to see that what lay at the core of his feelings was a sense of self-rejection, the unmourned loss of all the things he naturally was not. Our work prioritized self-acceptance, with a gentle abandonment of the mask he'd been forcing himself to wear. Remarkably, the process of finding comfort in his own skin began to reflect changes in his creative work. He made riskier choices in his music compositions, hesitated less to challenge professors' and peers' expectations, and displayed more confidence in trusting his aesthetic opinions about his work. All the years of self-rejection, which had been sustaining his depression, had been symbiotically coexisting with his creative habits. The more creative freedom he allowed himself, the more confident he felt. Conversely, as his confidence increased, so did his creative flexibility.

Encouraging Creative Habits

Sometimes clinicians must encourage clients to pursue their creative interests simply for the psychological benefits of engaging in creative work. Keeping the brain occupied with creative tasks effectively distracts clients from negative thoughts and feelings of sadness, making them a great coping tool. In addition to being a distraction, the act of finding oneself deeply absorbed in a rewarding creative task—such as problem solving, generating new ideas, combining thoughts in a unique way, and so on—encourages a positive emotional state (Csikszentmihalyi, 1996). The counseling room is an excellent setting for encouraging and fostering creative habits that help reduce feelings of depression.

Coping With Depression Triggered by Occupational Stress

According to a UK survey study with 2,211 musician participants, 68.5 percent of the respondents self-identified as having suffered from depression (Gross & Musgrave, 2016). The study concluded that the depression was not a direct result of the creative pursuit—in this case, music; rather, it was associated with having a career in music (see chapter 9 for more on stress in the arts-and-entertainment world). When depression is tied to the occupational demands of a creative profession, clinicians should work with clients on strengthening their coping abilities. Rejections, criticism, erratic schedules, income instability, and other stressors associated with creative professions often trigger depressive symptoms, especially in those already prone to mood disorders. Clinicians can help clients tolerate feedback, manage self-doubt, and reframe thoughts of hopelessness. Those who are sensitive to criticism are likely to consider giving up on their careers after getting poor reviews. The clinicians' role might be to work with such clients on anticipating and preparing for a wide range of audience reactions and distinguishing the actual negative consequences from cognitive catastrophizing—a common thought habit in people with depression. An example of catastrophizing might be thinking that a poorly attended show signals career failure.

Distinguishing Between Ruminating and Brooding

Clinicians and clients can identify the subtle differences between brooding in a negative emotional state and reflecting in a way that promotes emotion regulation through creative expression. As discussed previously, ruminating can be a way to work through negative feelings that activates the need for creativity. Clinicians can work with clients to identify and encourage this kind of purposeful thinking. The role of clinicians is to point out ruminative

Treatment Goals

1. Develop insight into the way depressive episodes affect creativity.
2. Keep depressive episodes from interfering with creative goals.
3. Reenergize motivation and pleasure that comes from creative work.
4. Improve mood so that creative abilities can flourish.
5. Increase the depth and breadth of creative content.

Suggested Interventions to Achieve Goals

1. *Encourage art activities.* In a study by Young and colleagues (2013), depressed teens tended to choose art-related activities more than non-depressed teens. Though the reasons behind this finding are unclear, some explanations suggest that artistic activities improve mood—which in turn leads to more creativity (Baas et al., 2008)—and decrease symptoms of depression. This could be because art-related activities offer a sense of in-group identification (both to adolescents and to adults) with others who share the same interests, or because art becomes a vehicle for communicating complex and overwhelming feelings. Clinicians can encourage their creative clients to regularly engage in artistic activities.

   Example: A depressed hospital administrative assistant was unhappy in his job, which he found to be completely devoid of creativity. When he opened up about his interest in reading and writing fiction, we made sure to incorporate weekly writing sessions that he would do between our meetings. This led him to look for local writing workshops. After a month, his identity as a writer began to take shape, and he'd found an outlet to release negative feelings. He reported rediscovering the ability to enjoy small moments, such as exchanging writing ideas with his workshop classmates.

2. *Listen to clients' inner voices.* Creative people have a voice that's looking to be heard. This voice might come in the form of a creative solution to a problem, an expression of a feeling that resonates with audiences, or a telling of a story that moves. However, depression can make it difficult for creators to listen to their own voices, as they get overpowered by negative thoughts and low motivation. As a result, the quality and quantity of the creative work suffers. Through nondirective open-exploration and free-association techniques, clinicians can guide clients toward revealing their inner voices that have been obscured by the emotional depletion caused by depression.

> Example: A depressed columnist was so consumed by thoughts of worthlessness that he couldn't relate to any subject enough to write about it. His depression had convinced him that his ideas about the public school education system weren't worth sharing. "What value does my view have?" he'd wonder out loud. My goal was to create a space for him to access and use his voice. By gently inquiring into his writing ideas, and seeing whether there was something in his personal experiences that made this topic worthy of being talked about, he connected with his own struggles of overcoming social injustices in educational opportunities. I encouraged him to pay attention to this voice and to put it to use through his writing.

3. *Identify challenges.* This idea borrows the basic principles behind problem-solving treatment for depression, which emphasizes the importance of identifying the problems that contribute to current feelings. Clinicians can work with clients to articulate what they're having a difficult time with. Is the depression lingering from a past experience? Does it relate to current rejections from industry professionals? Is it unrelated to the artistic or creative work but exacerbated by it, such as when financial difficulties arise? Perhaps it's a combination of many factors. Identifying challenges sets the stage for moving toward a solution-oriented approach.

> Example: When a severely depressed installation artist couldn't leave the house to go to his studio to continue his work, we initially looked at what was getting in his way. This revealed a debilitating cycle: his financial troubles led to guilt and frustration about not having enough success as an artist. These feelings made him too depressed to work, and the depression in turn resulted in low

productivity. As a result, his poor sales started the cycle all over again. We identified the challenge of the financial issue, and temporarily shifted the focus to finding a part-time job. Though it didn't feel good to take on a job that was unrelated to his career, it offered him some immediate relief and a mild, yet noticeable, improvement in his mood.

4. *Establish the right work pace.* Severe depression weakens the motivation and energy of creators, who then go on to mislabel their feelings as mere laziness: they think they're flawed and undeserving of success because they don't work hard for it. This kind of thinking is unproductive, as it induces guilt and self-blame. Instead, clinicians can work with clients on correcting harmful mislabeling and establishing a work pace that's suitable for clients' needs. Instead of setting many big goals, clients can begin to tackle one small goal, even if it's at a much slower pace; they can alternate working on different projects to avoid obsessing over the success of a single one; or, they can manage their time so it promotes small doses of daily engagement in the creative work.

    Example: A depressed Broadway performer who spent the little energy she had teaching dance classes in the mornings had no energy left to prepare for, and attend, auditions for herself. Since her low mood made her lose steam early in the day, making it nearly impossible to remain upbeat enough to complete other tasks, we experimented with scheduling changes, such as teaching classes later in the day and setting a limit on the number of students she was willing to take on. Doing so helped her cope with the fatigue and stress of auditioning.

5. *Encourage persistence through rumination.* Mood disorder and creativity researchers consider negative mood to activate a persistent "targeted search for a solution" (Kaufmann & Kaufmann, 2014:22). This means that someone with ruminative depressive traits will stick longer with an activity, feeling compelled to solve a problem. Though this kind of persistence leaves little room for breaks, making it exhausting, it can lead to deeper, well-honed creative skills. Clients and clinicians can work to use such traits to the creative person's advantage. Instead of redirecting clients' ruminative thoughts, as clinicians are often trained to do, clients can be invited to dig even deeper into their persistent thoughts. This allows clients to fully understand the creative possibilities attached to their persistent thoughts.

    Example: When a guitarist ruminated for days about which songs to play at his show, I thought about how ruminating on a single task could be an effective way for him to avoid dwelling on negative expectations from his performance—something he had tended to do. Instead

Psychiatric Disorders   109

of taking his rumination as an indication of pathological thinking, this musician and I thought about how the selection of songs symbolized his search for a desired creative outcome. His persistent thoughts helped him feel that by answering the question of which songs to play, he had more control of the quality of the creative results.

6. *Recognize accomplishments.* The self-perpetuating nature of depression is that it reinforces the thoughts that seem to cause it. Successful artists with depression often notice only the failures and rejections: they have a so-what attitude toward successes and emphasize ones that haven't yet been accomplished. At times, they will focus on others' achievements while downplaying their own. Clinicians can direct attention toward clients' accomplishments and help them pause to notice what has gone right. Though deeply ingrained self-defeating attitudes might contribute to initial resistance, the goal is to build habits of seeing the positive along with the negative.

   Example: A depressed poet would always rush to share with me that his poems had been turned down for publications, almost as if the letters provided evidence for his claims of being a failure. When at last he got a letter of acceptance, weeks passed before he brought the news up in session—I seemed to be more excited about it than he was. I asked him to keep track of things that might be considered successes, even if in his eyes they weren't, and to revisit this list daily.

7. *Manage occupational triggers for depression.* Being a creative professional introduces emotional stressors that heighten negative feelings. Many professional creative domains (performing arts, music, visual arts, and so on) are highly competitive, unpredictable, and emotionally draining. As a result, despite being talented and driven, creative clients might experience depressive episodes that could further sabotage their prospects for success and creative fulfillment. Sessions can focus on identifying occupational difficulties and on helping clients manage the feelings of depression that they trigger.

   Example: A musical theater performer struggled to feel motivated to go to auditions. He'd become depressed and take weeks to recover from rejections, thought that applying for opportunities was a waste of time, and dwelled on how his voice sounded worse than other candidates' voices. During one session, he tied his depression to his frustration with his career. "This is not a meritocracy! It's all about who you know, and how lucky you get," he proclaimed. Our work involved tolerating his sadness and frustration, as he accepted some the terms of the career he had chosen, and empowering him so he

110 Psychiatric Disorders

could rely on what he could control: his efforts to improve, to make connections, and to persevere.

Additional Interventions

8.	
9.	
10.	

Part III: Bipolar Disorder

One of the most thoroughly investigated psychiatric diagnoses among creative people is bipolar disorder. An apparent connection between bipolar disorder and creativity has captured the interest of psychologists for years. The mood volatility of Emily Dickinson, Vincent Van Gogh, Sylvia Plath, Robert Schumann, and other famous artists has been extensively investigated by psychobiographers, who've identified indicators of bipolar disorder. The idea that creativity is tied to this disorder was popularized in *Touched With Fire*, a 2015 film, which borrows its title from the seminal book written by Kay Redfield Jamison. That book, published in 1993, draws connections between the artistic temperament and the severe mood elation found in bipolar disorder. Many creativity researchers have tried to distinguish fact from myth regarding the presence of bipolar traits in creative people. Critics of the connection between bipolar disorder and creativity see no direct link between the two—if anything, they consider creativity to be associated with high mental health rather than psychopathology. They've accused some research studies of biases, such as having too small a sample, having too loose definitions of creativity, and having inconsistent measurements of creativity and bipolar disorder traits (Dietrich, 2014; Schlesinger, 2012; Rothenberg, 2001).

Other theorists and researchers have stood behind decades of empirical evidence supporting a connection between some features of bipolar disorder and some forms of creativity (Andreasen, 1987; Bilder & Knudsen, 2014; Carson, 2011; Furnham et al., 2008; Johnson, 2016; Ludwig, 1994; Silvia & Kaufman, 2010). Kyaga and colleagues (2013) studied large samples—more than one million people listed in Swedish national registries—of individuals across professions, and with various clinical diagnoses, and found that bipolar disorder was overrepresented in those with creative professions. In particular, more than other creative professions, being a writer increased the likelihood of a psychiatric diagnosis, including bipolar disorder. Kyaga and his colleagues (2011) had also previously found that people with bipolar disorder and their healthy siblings were overrepresented in creative professions (both in the arts and sciences). Shared creativity characteristics—specifically, a preference for novel and asymmetrical figures—were observed between people with bipolar disorder and people in creative fields (Santosa et al., 2007). Similarly, people with bipolar disorder reported more temperamental commonalities with creative control groups than with those in healthy groups (Nowakowska et al., 2005). Furnham and colleagues (2008) found hypomania to be a strong predictor of creativity in adolescents. These are just a handful of a large number of studies that demonstrate that bipolar disorder symptoms are associated with expressions of creativity.

Three concepts help explain the connection between clients' creative natures and their bipolar disorder experiences. The first pertains to the overlapping cognitive mechanisms between a manic state and a highly creative one. *Divergent thinking*, an indicator of creativity that refers to the ability to come up with a broad range of responses to a given stimulus, is likely present during creative thinking and during mania (Johnson et al., 2012). The rapid thoughts and flight of ideas that happen during manic states mirror divergent-thinking processes and allow for the cognitive disinhibition that gives rise to novel and flexible thoughts. Similar to what happens with ADHD-diagnosed creative clients, the same brain functions that produce psychopathology symptoms under some conditions produce creative thoughts under others.

The idea of overlapping traits takes us to the second concept: the *shared vulnerability* model put forward by Shelly Carson (2011, 2013). This model highlights the shared genetic components between creativity and psychopathologies such as schizophrenia and bipolar disorder (Power et al., 2015). Carson suggests that whether the genetic predispositions manifest in psychiatric disorders or in creative achievement depends on other factors, such as IQ, cognitive flexibility, and sources of motivation. A combination of factors determines whether traits linked to creativity—traits that, in varying degrees, are found in most people—make some people vulnerable to psychopathology and others prone to creative achievement. For example, according to Carson's model, novelty seeking is a shared trait that forms the foundation for a creative person's motivation to pursue novel forms of self-expression, and at the same time leads to potentially destructive impulsivity found in manic or hypomanic behaviors.

Last, the creativity-bipolar connection is additionally understood by the effects of *mood elevation*. Hypomania, a less intense expression of mania, increases feelings of motivation, decreases the need for sleep, and triggers feelings of ambition and excitability. These mood shifts are likely to bring about changes in behaviors that foster creativity (Richards & Kinney, 1990). With elated affect and expanded energy, creators are ready to believe in their ideas, commit to them, and implement them. Psychiatrist Gail Saltz (2017) argues that history is filled with creative contributions by people with bipolar disorder; mood elevation fosters the psychological state that helps bring such contributions to life.

Working with creative clients who have bipolar disorder warrants a thorough understanding of the bipolar-creativity relationship. Doing so means looking at symptoms through the lens of the potential for creative achievement. One all-around creative person I worked with—he painted, sang in a band, wrote lyrics, and designed clothes—had a long history of hypomanic, and sometimes manic, episodes. Occasionally, during our sessions, his gestures would become exaggerated and his speech pressured, and he would make bizarre references to his conversations with the "art spirits" that brought him divine inspiration. For the cautious therapist, all this might have led to a referral for a psychiatric evaluation; however, working closely with this person revealed the parallel between these facets of his disorder (high energy, racing thoughts, and unusual thought content) and the desperate need to express his highly creative nature. The more we understood and recognized this connection, the less scared he became of his own bizarre thoughts, which he began to see as an extension of his distinct cognitive and affective capabilities.

Despite the ways in which mania is associated with creative thinking and achievement, there are clear limits to its benefits. Richards and Kinney (1990) have examined the rise in creativity that comes with the mood elevation that typically occurs during the manic state of bipolar disorder, and point out that in severe cases, mania hinders creativity. Severe mania can impair cognitive functioning and lead to delusions that may trigger psychotic episodes. Clearly, this compromises the ability to carry out creative tasks or to produce results of creative value. On the other side of the bipolar disorder scale, severe depression can cause emotional numbness, anhedonia, and apathy, which also diminish the ability to think and act creatively. On top of that, the extreme energy that comes with inflated mood can have a crash-and-burn effect, which can damage a creative career (Saltz, 2017). In such cases, treatment that addresses bipolar disorder symptoms is crucial. Creative clients often hesitate to seek out treatment, especially medication, for fear that it will blunt their creativity and strip them of their creative identity. To address such concerns, it's important to consider the intensity and severity of symptoms, as well as the duration and modality of the recommended treatment.

The Clinician's Role

Addressing How Symptoms Help the Creative Process

Clinicians can help clients recognize the potential for creativity associated with their diagnosis. One way to do this is to anticipate the onset of symptoms and their effect on creators' mood, impulsivity, thought content, and so on. I once worked with a college student with bipolar disorder, predominantly the hypomanic type, who'd learned to anticipate the next hypomanic episode and would plan to work on his essays accordingly. He'd noticed that his creative energy tended to increase drastically every 3 to 4 weeks. He needed less sleep, he could focus better, and his thoughts were rich in creative content. He knew he could use these energy shifts to his advantage, and had learned to "own" the process.

Similarly, freelance artists and other creative professionals who have some control over their work schedules can take mood fluctuations into consideration as they make choices about when to work on what. Though, as we'll see later, symptoms are unpredictable, and hypomania is likely to escalate to a manic episode, clinicians can help arm their clients with knowledge about how their symptoms come and go and how they affect creative output.

Preparing for Mood Volatility

As much as creators strive to anticipate mood fluctuations, the reality is that bouts of depression and mania are hard to predict. The erratic symptoms of bipolar disorder, compounded by the transience of creative inspiration, can catch creators by surprise and cause significant anxiety. It's important to understand how mood volatility affects the pace at which creators work, especially when they're expected to meet deadlines. Clinicians can work with clients to create an environment that minimizes this type of anxiety by carefully watching for triggers of abrupt mood changes, and by expanding supportive resources for when they can't tackle creative and professional demands.

Preparing for mood volatility was helpful for a theatrical director I worked with, who paid close attention to when she felt "off." When manic, she usually had an uncontrollable urge to redefine the artistic vision for her plays, or to work all day without taking a break. When depressed, she'd go days without leaving the house, and her plays were the furthest thing from her mind. She couldn't predict which reactions she'd have, or when. We worked on accepting this facet of her condition and took steps to ease the disruption: we'd double up on counseling sessions, delegate tasks to trusted colleagues, and try to stay close to her average creative input baseline.

Assessing the Interaction of Bipolar Traits

Johnson and colleagues (2016: 33) underscore that "multiple qualities related to bipolar disorder have been hypothesized to drive creativity including divergent thinking, impulsivity, ambitiousness and positive affectivity." The interaction of bipolar disorder traits that each person displays is unique and ought to be assessed on a case-by-case basis. This makes it imperative that clients and clinicians work together to understand which traits are more salient, and whether they help or damage creativity. For example, some clients may notice a pattern of negative mood with high impulsivity, which could raise a red flag for self-harming behavior, as well as lower creative output. Conversely, someone with high energy and positive affect will be more inclined to seek creative outlets and feel hopeful about the creative results. Assessing the presence and unique combination of bipolar traits helps clients and clinicians assess risks and benefits.

Protecting Creativity During Treatment

Creative clients may seek reassurance that treatment, whether talk therapy or medication, won't interfere with their creativity. It's important to pay attention for signs of diminished creativity brought on by treatment, and to understand clients' individual concerns. Clinicians can offer the reassurance that, contrary to the fear that treatment reduces creativity, the right kind of interventions protect a creative career. Medication, for example, might reduce the intensity of sporadic creative peaks but compensate by ensuring a steady flow of creativity over time (Saltz, 2017). Psychiatrist Albert Rothenberg (2001) recommends that mental health professionals help their creative clients with bipolar disorder establish an artistic identity that's independent of their diagnosis. Coming from the perspective that creativity flourishes despite a bipolar disorder diagnosis—rather than because of it—and that treatment improves creativity, he cautions that the inaccurate emphasis on a connection keeps clients from seeking help.

Distinguishing Between Confident and Delusional Thinking

Creative clients with bipolar disorder sometimes want to know if there's ground for believing in their ideas, or if they merely reflect a euphoric, overly ambitious mental state. Clinicians aren't there to evaluate the work itself, but they can guide the process of putting the person's own goals and perceptions in perspective. For example, thoughts of grandiosity, commonly experienced during mania, help protect clients from sensitivity to criticism about their creative work, which can be detrimental to their motivation. On the other hand, they also cause creators to set too many high goals without checking the quality of the process along the way. I once worked with a writer who felt extremely secure in the quality of her writing. During hypomanic periods, she'd proclaim herself to be the best writer in the world, whose book would change others' lives. When her book received some unfavorable comments from colleagues and editors, she didn't flinch: she continued revising and working on her book with the same amount of enthusiasm. When her hypomania subsided, she interpreted the same comments differently and lost faith in her ideas. Clinicians and clients can work together to establish the foundation for the kind of outcomes clients expect to see, and to identify the ways in which their disorder changes their perceptions of how they're doing.

Psychiatric Disorders 115

Treatment Goals

1.	Develop insight into how bipolar disorder episodes influence creativity.
2.	Prepare for the onset of manic and depressive symptoms by recognizing triggers.
3.	Boost creativity during hypomanic episodes.
4.	Improve the perception of the diagnosis and reduce stigma.
5.	Regulate mood to stabilize the flow of creative output.

Suggested Interventions to Achieve Goals

1. *Use hypomania as a creative tool.* The hypothesized connection between hypomania and increased creativity suggests that clients can use hypomanic experiences—such as moments of inflated energy and racing thoughts—to reinforce creative thinking and behavior. This can be achieved by identifying how hypomania presents for each client, by taking advantage of changes in mood and thought content, and by managing stress so that hypomanic phases are less likely to lead to severe mania.

    Example: A writer and I carefully looked for mood, behavior, and creativity patterns. We quickly identified that a decreased need for sleep correlated with more creative energy. When she noticed that she couldn't sleep, and when her thoughts began to feel a little expansive, she'd immediately prioritize doing creative work, especially at night. To help manage her hypomania, she minimized added stressors, such as agreeing to help colleagues or making plans with friends.

2. *Introduce a mood journal.* Keeping track of moods helps clients understand more about the ebbs and flows involved in mood disorders. It's always reassuringly surprising when clients come to sessions armed with a sense of self-awareness. They share how equipped they felt to respond to depression or mania when it struck seemingly without warning. By virtue of how common cycles are in mood disorders and in creativity

(Goodwin & Jamison, 2007), clients will benefit from journaling about how they feel, the events that precipitated their feelings, and the reactions that followed.

> Example: A client with various creative outlets (singing, acting, blogging) was frequently baffled by the changes in her mood and her inability to stay on task. I asked her to jot down her feelings as soon as she woke up and right before she went to sleep, and to keep track of any events that might be linked to these feelings. She soon made illuminating connections between accepting too many job opportunities and developing manic tendencies.

3. *Address stigma.* Social stigma associated with a diagnosis of mood disorders can be damaging to clients' mental health (Kinney & Richards, 2014). It can cause creative clients to feel shame and to avoid looking for professional opportunities, fearing that they'll be seen as mentally unstable. A strengths-based approach, based on positive-psychology principles, aims to increase well-being by focusing on virtues rather than weaknesses (Seligman, 2002). Clinicians can explore the extent to which clients have been negatively perceived by others on the basis of their diagnoses, as well as the extent to which they've internalized and believed such perceptions. During sessions, a clear emphasis on aptitudes and talents highlights creative clients' strengths and conveys an empowering message about their potential.

> Example: A writer I worked with was immensely ashamed of her bipolar disorder diagnosis and had spent most of her life hiding it from others. She decided in therapy to focus on how some of her best writing, which helped her cope with adversity and contributed to her psychological well-being, occurred as a result of her mood fluctuations. To reinforce this perspective, instead of emphasizing labels such as "bipolar disorder sufferer," we used terms such as "mood fluidity" and descriptions like "prolific writer whose diagnosis informed her writing voice."

4. *Stabilize mood.* Extreme emotional highs and lows can be exhausting and can weaken the focus necessary to persevere with an idea from start to finish. Because of the way severe manic episodes can overwhelm one with nervousness about losing control (Johnson et al., 2016), stabilizing one's mood can help establish a balanced work pace. To do so, clients can minimize stress triggers and experiment with different approaches to treatment: they can consider changing diet and sleep patterns, increasing the number of sessions, or switching from individual to family sessions or from talk therapy to medication. The goal is to become vigilant about potential mood-swing triggers and to respond to ups and downs proactively.

> Example: A fashion designer I worked with suffered from frequent mood swings that interfered with her workflow. Some weeks she

was highly productive, making the company she worked for happy. Other times, she could barely get out of bed, let alone engage in creative work. She found it helpful to identify and stay away from emotional triggers in order to have even-keeled reactions. She discussed her feelings in therapy, something she hadn't been doing with her friends and family, and met with me twice a week to make sure she was monitoring how daily events were affecting her. The goal was to help her gain emotional balance.

5. *Consider medication management.* Pharmacological approaches for bipolar disorder have come a long way. Though research is continuously conducted to bring people better results, medical treatment today is more successful in treating acute manic, depressive, and mixed episodes and in preventing the recurrence of severe, rapid mood cycling (Keck & McElroy, 2015). Many creative people hesitate to take medication, fearing that it'll reduce their creative skills. However, certain forms of creative thought and behavior (for example, identifying appropriate solutions to problems and maintaining stable levels of motivation) can be enhanced by the use of medication. Appropriate dosages and types of medication that don't blunt emotions or cognitive abilities can restore clients' creativity.

> Example: When a writer I worked with was having such severe manic symptoms that they began to introduce intense paranoid delusions, she agreed to consult with a psychiatrist who was sensitive to her need to engage in creative thinking for her writing. She began pharmacological treatment to address severe cognitive disorganization, harmful delusions, and potentially dangerous impulsive behaviors—all of which impaired her ability to think creatively—along with overall functioning. Her writing did take a back seat for a few months, but when her symptoms began to decrease, she adjusted her medication to help her regain the necessary cognitive and emotional tools to start writing again.

6. *Reflect during depression.* For clients whose bipolar disorder episodes follow a succession of depression and mania, sessions can become opportunities to reflect deeply on the thoughts and experiences that come up during moments of depression. The end goal is to express these thoughts and feelings creatively during the higher energy phases of hypomania. The euphoria, impulsivity, and rapid thinking that tend to accompany hypomanic episodes are highly conducive to taking action, whereas the hyperfocused ruminating during depressed episodes adds depth and meaning to the creative ideas that'll, hopefully, get expressed once the depression has subsided.

> Example: I once asked an illustrator to "catch himself" during moments of depression, and to reflect on the nature of his feelings

so that he could eventually base his creative work off them. He reported having noticed that his feelings of hopelessness were connected to a recent family loss that brought up thoughts about his own mortality and the fact that he's not "living life to the fullest." He agreed to attempt to turn to these thoughts for inspiration for his drawings once feelings of hypomania—more energy and impulsivity—would start to resurface.

7. *Dispel myths where they exist.* A potential, albeit unintentional, mistake on the part of clinicians who work with creative clients with bipolar disorder is to overestimate the contribution of their disorder to their creative potential (Rothenberg, 2001). At the fear of quashing creativity, clinicians overemphasize the idea that symptoms enable creativity and ignore clear signs that they ought to be addressed. Creative clients may then be less inclined to seek treatment for symptoms whose management wouldn't impair creative abilities.

   Example: A photographer whose severe manic episode resulted in a hospitalization was reluctant to continue take medication after being released. His concern was it would numb his desire to continue to take pictures. He believed that being an artist meant losing touch with reality every so often. We examined his assumptions by looking at how his condition affected the quality of his work. He revealed that his mania was associated with extremely disorganized thinking and low motivation, and that his preoccupations with his delusions resulted in pictures that he described as "nonusable." Confronting the reality of how his symptoms worsened his creative abilities increased his willingness to continue with treatment.

8. *Introduce overall lifestyle changes.* General lifestyle habits such as sleep, exercise, diet, work-life balance, and stress management affect the recurrence and intensity of bipolar disorder symptoms (Russell & Brown, 2005; Sylvia et al., 2013). An emphasis on overall wellness will not only help reduce relapses but also limit the spiraling of hypomanic episodes, keeping them at a place that remains beneficial to creative goals. Clinicians can help clients pay attention to which habits bring about desired results.

   Example: After a romantic breakup, the mood and personality of an actress with bipolar disorder changed rapidly. A previously introverted and hesitant person who had been stable for the first 6 months of our sessions, she now constantly sought out company and participated in four or five creative projects at once. Though her creativity was flourishing, the stress of the breakup had triggered a mild resurfacing of bizarre ideation. We immediately targeted lifestyle factors to ensure that she'd stay in the safe zone. She reduced her creative responsibilities from five to three at a time, made sleeping 6 hours a priority, kept track of foods that helped her feel better, abstained from alcoholic substances, and practiced daily meditation. As a result, she felt that she was prioritizing lifestyle balance and self-care, while still spending time on her creative endeavors.

Additional Interventions

9.
10.
11.

Part IV: Psychotic Disorders

When I worked with Luke, a 21-year-old college student with an academic major in math and a minor in art, I often struggled to discern what he was feeling and kept losing the thread of the conversation. Right when I thought one of his stories was about to reach a conclusion, he'd go into a different one, making me scratch my head about a connection between the two. The unexpected addition of information in a conversation (such as a new name or a new event), brought up as if it had been mentioned all along, would leave me wondering if I hadn't caught or had misheard part of the conversation. An event such as a rejection or a loss, which would ordinarily elicit feelings of sadness in my other clients, would be discussed with complete apathy. Luke, who presented with symptoms of schizotypal personality disorder—a personality disorder that affects thought content and social functioning— was remarkably different from many of my other creative clients. There was, however, one important similarity: like my other clients, he made rapid associations, could come up with many new ideas, and was interested in drawing connections between seemingly unrelated concepts. All these cognitive faculties helped him excel in his classes. As we'll see later in this section, many researchers and theorists believe that the connection between creative abilities and psychotic disorders, such as schizotypal personality disorder, schizophrenia (which affects cognitive, affective, and behavioral functioning), and schizoaffective disorder (a condition that presents with symptoms of schizophrenia and mood disorders), is not random. Thoughts and behaviors like the ones Luke displayed are often seen as an expression of the same brain functions that enable creativity.

Psychosis is characterized by a loss of touch with reality. It involves bizarre or inappropriate behaviors, unusual thoughts, odd beliefs, and a distorted sense of perception, all ultimately defined by a disconnect with the real world. Unlike their nonpsychotic counterparts, psychotic people tend to have nonlinear thinking, don't filter their thoughts, and have disorganized thought patterns. What has caught the attention of many researchers, mental health professionals, and artists themselves is the fact that some defining features of creativity are similar to features of psychosis. For example, loose, *overinclusive thoughts* not constrained within rigid boundaries (Eysenck, 1993) and *magical* and *unusual experiences* stemming from vivid and unconventional imagination appear in both highly creative and disordered thinking (Lindel, 2014).

Decreased latent inhibition, the inability to filter out irrelevant stimuli, is present in people who are prone to psychoses and to those who are highly creative (Carson et al., 2003; Barrantes-Vidal, 2014). Meta-analyses from 32 studies (Acar & Runco, 2012) showed a strong relationship between creativity and psychoticism, with uniqueness used as an index of creativity (uniqueness is one measure of creativity; others include appropriateness, usefulness, idea production, and cognitive fluency), and psychosis measured by the Eysenck Personality Questionnaire. Thoughts and behaviors in people with psychotic symptoms have been repeatedly linked to creative traits (Burch et al., 2006; Preti & Vellante, 2007; Schuldberg, 2005). Some studies show that similar brain activity patterns are activated in those who are highly creative and those with schizotypal characteristics while they engage in some type of creative thinking activity (Fink et al., 2014). Kyaga's population study (2011), mentioned in part III of this chapter, revealed that patients with schizophrenia were represented in artistic occupations in greater numbers compared to control groups, while their healthy siblings were overrepresented in creative occupations (both artistic and nonartistic).

The aforementioned findings were echoed in the experiences of Lisa, a painter with symptoms of schizotypy, such as peculiar thoughts, rambling speech, and bizarre social behavior. Sometime toward the end of our second year working together, I noticed that she made less sense each time I saw her. Discussions of day-to-day stress and relationship worries were replaced with tangents about her "unique relationship with nature," her desire to withdraw from friends and family, and her persistent superstitions about the bad things that might happen were she to stop wearing mismatched socks. She spoke in metaphors and analogies and recited philosophical quotes every two to three sentences. Though she had some insight into how these thoughts might sound—"I hope I'm not freaking you out," she'd say—it was clear that she was decreasingly interested in the external, real, and objective world. In the meantime, I looked for clues that would explain the change in her behaviors and thoughts by inquiring into how she was spending her time. She'd stopped socializing and had quit her part-time job, which made me worry that she might regret these actions later. One day I wondered what she'd been doing during her newfound free time. She took out her cell phone and started to show me pictures of what seemed like hundreds of paintings and drawings. There were canvases in many sizes, large and intricately colored marker designs, and pencil sketches, all of which depicted mythical creatures, godlike entities, archetypal figures, and imaginary worlds. Though she physically existed in the real world, her artwork was an undeniable product of the world constructed by her magical, delusional thinking. Her creative work mirrored the bizarre reality that existed in her head.

Creative people in the arts—such as painters, sculptors, poets, and writers—who have psychoses are frequently found to have so-called positive schizotypy (odd or magical thinking, unusual physical perceptions, impulsivity), whereas creative scientists are hypothesized to exhibit some of the negative symptoms (lack of empathy, unusual social behavior) (Nettle, 2006). There's support for the idea that positive symptoms tend to help people engage in unconventional thinking (Mohr & Claridge, 2015). A study of 100 artists found that heightened positive schizotypy symptoms were predictive of the ability to enter a creative flow-like state (Nelson & Rawlings, 2010).

It's important to remember that the type of creativity (artistic and non-artistic) and the type of psychotic traits being measured (negative and positive) reveal nuances in the relationship between the two. These differences are crucial for appreciating the effect that psychosis has on creativity, and consequently on creative clients' needs. For example, when social anhedonia makes it difficult for creative scientists to bounce ideas off of others, sessions can focus on improving social skills. In contrast, when overinclusive thinking makes it difficult for a writer to narrow down her ideas, sessions can emphasize convergent-thinking tactics.

It's difficult to determine one causal factor that accounts for the connection between psychosis and creativity. The many genes involved in psychotic symptoms and the wide variation in the ways creativity plays out make for a complex picture. Multiple genes, in particular dopamine receptor genes, have received attention, specifically as they pertain to novelty seeking and shared cognitive processes between psychosis and creativity (Kozbelt et al., 2014). Carson's (2011) shared vulnerability model (discussed previously in the section on bipolar disorder) comes up again, as it describes how cognitive disinhibition is present both in creativity and psychosis; however, it's factors such as IQ and cognitive flexibility that will determine whether this shared vulnerability will turn into creative achievement or not. It's a complicated relationship, yet still one that's been recurrently found in scientific research and in anecdotal observations of artists and other creative people who are disconnected from reality, but uniquely capable of generating a large number of new thoughts and ideas.

Artists who think and act in psychotic ways and who seek out counseling are something of a paradox. If the impairment is, in some way, the source of the creative capacity, then what should be targeted during treatment? It can be creatively detrimental, albeit tempting, to want to introduce more "objective reality" into a process that relies heavily on being removed from it. In the next section we will look at how clinicians can walk this thin line.

The Clinician's Role

Understanding Psychotic Clients' Needs

Clinicians can start by looking at the reasons that drove creative clients with psychoses to seek out counseling in the first place. Creative clients with severe psychotic disorders who, for example, have extreme delusions that pose a threat to themselves or others will most likely be under psychiatric care for medication administration. In such cases, counseling often supplements treatment from a psychiatrist, especially in settings with higher levels of care, such as inpatient facilities and day-treatment programs, making symptom management the main objective. Creativity may come up, but clinicians needn't assume that discussion of creative work ought to be prioritized. Doing so might interfere with clients' need to reach a baseline stability in basic functioning—something that's often compromised in people with disorders in the schizophrenia spectrum.

In contrast, creative clients whose psychotic state poses minimal risk are likely to benefit from a focus on their creative work. They might be interested in treatment that incorporates art therapy, or that helps them manage their creative potential and channel it appropriately. For example, a graphic designer with schizotypal personality disorder who works for a large company that's keen on following rules, dress codes, and traditional work schedules may seek treatment that fosters his unconventional inclinations, while keeping bizarre behaviors from jeopardizing his work. A science PhD student who's trying to keep odd ideation and flat affect under control in order to remain focused and goal driven in her creative work might be looking for treatment that emphasizes the creative problem solver, not the social outcast. Clinicians can start off by assessing the degree of severity posed by the symptoms and the need to prioritize clients' creative nature.

Evaluating the Psychotic Symptoms' Impacts on Creativity

As discussed previously, symptoms in the psychotic spectrum can be categorized into positive (an overflow of bizarre thoughts and experiences) and negative (the absence of feelings, disinterest, apathy, and so forth). Positive symptoms tend to correlate with enhanced creativity. Clinicians can work with their clients to clarify the differences between the two, and take advantage of the positive symptoms, where they exist. An example of this might be to encourage clients to brainstorm and free associate so that idea fluency is enhanced by positive symptoms. To help clients manage anhedonia, a negative symptom, clinicians can encourage them to spend time with people who share similar creative fascinations.

Regarding the overall impact of psychotic symptoms, as with other psychiatric conditions, the inverted-U model can be used to guide treatment. When the flood of bizarre, odd, and irrelevant thoughts becomes overwhelming, a client will not have the clarity needed to see a creative idea through, both in terms of coherence and execution (Abraham, 2014). In a 2015 overview of relevant research, Mohr and Claridge suggested that the further one goes in the direction of psychoticism, the more difficult it is to integrate the thoughts generated in the earlier stages into a meaningful and useful product. Alternatively, dulling the cognitive processes responsible for vivid and unusual thoughts could limit the range of creative ideas. The role of clinicians is to keep this delicate balance in mind as they help clients manage their symptoms' impact.

Assessing the Need for Medication

A person with a psychotic disorder has a high risk of decompensating and of complications that lead to severe impairment of functioning (paranoid delusions, aggressive impulses, and self-harming ideation). The work between clients and clinicians will be easier after conducting a psychiatric evaluation to determine the usefulness of antipsychotic medication. Someone with schizotypy may decide that symptoms are manageable enough to be in treatment without taking medication, whereas someone with chronic schizophrenia will likely benefit from reducing debilitating symptoms before becoming fully rededicated to reaching creative goals.

Treatment Goals

1. Understand how positive and negative psychotic symptoms affect creativity.
2. Regulate cognitive dysfunction when it impairs creative ability.
3. Establish consistency of treatment, whether psychiatric or psychotherapeutic.
4. Maintain interest in creative activities when compromised by symptoms.
5. Take advantage of creative abilities enhanced by psychotic symptoms.

124 Psychiatric Disorders

Suggested Interventions to Achieve Goals

1. *Connect psychotic symptoms to the correct diagnosis.* A correct diagnosis is a starting point for the development of a treatment plan. Psychotic symptoms and episodes are present in more than one disorder; therefore, creativity-sensitive treatment approaches will vary. Diagnoses of schizophrenia and schizoaffective disorder, both of which are characterized by psychotic symptoms such as auditory and visual hallucinations, might call for pharmacological treatment, which could have an effect on creative abilities. A diagnosis of schizotypy is likely to point to short-term, goal-oriented therapy that includes a focus on thought and emotion identification. In contrast, psychotic symptoms that are part of a depressive or manic episode will call for treatment for the underlying mood disorders.

   > Example: An audio engineer sought treatment following acute psychotic symptoms: he believed that his studio partners were bugging his apartment and were planning to change his locks. Some background history revealed chronic and severe episodes of depression. This most recent occurrence was triggered by intense feelings of rivalry, followed by an argument with colleagues. Rather than treat the paranoid thoughts as an indication of a cognitive disturbance as the primary cause, we focused on addressing the mood disorder that triggered them.

2. *Identify the role played by schizotypal traits.* For Batey and Furnham (2008), the optimal combination of schizotypal traits that's most conducive to creative thinking looks something like this: a highly unusual imagination, a touch of impulsivity, and low levels of cognitive impairment. Of course, this combination will look different for each client. Clients and clinicians can work together to identify which of these three ingredients (imagination, impulsivity, and cognitive abilities) plays an active role in clients' creative work, and to what extent, and which need to be addressed during counseling. Through clinical observation, a brief mental status screening (such as the Mini Mental Status Exam), and by asking clients directly, clinicians can look for clues about clients' overall functioning, the salience of schizotypy traits, and their creative context.

   > Example: To get a better idea of how the condition of a writer who'd been referred to me affected his creativity, I asked him to give examples of times when he acted impulsively or had unusually imaginative thoughts, and to describe the creative state that followed. He reported that he sometimes found it difficult to censor what he'd say in social settings, that his thoughts were often chaotic, and that he sometimes thought others could hear his thoughts. Unlike the

Psychiatric Disorders   125

first two, the last state would usually happen right before writing a piece he'd later be proud of. We worked on gaining insight into the association between each of his traits and his creative output.

3. *Build social skills.* People with psychotic disorders tend to have social skill deficits, especially in severe cases such as schizoaffective disorder and schizophrenia. Because of inappropriate social behavior, individuals with these disorders have limited, or even completely impaired, interpersonal relationships. Depending on the severity of the condition and the level of care (inpatient or outpatient), the means of developing and maintaining social relationships will vary. For clients actively seeking connections with peers and professional networks, whether it be in the creative world or not, working on the quality of their social interactions will help improve overall functioning (Bellack et al., 2013).

> Example: A painter with psychotic-disordered thinking found it difficult to show his paintings to others. Most of the time he had no interest in socializing with people; when he did, he didn't know how to talk about his paintings, didn't feel understood, and struggled to connect. In our work together, we worked on how to read others' body language, to maintain eye contact when talking, to keep an appropriate physical distance, and to show interest in others by asking questions.

4. *Evaluate for comorbidity with substance abuse.* Some findings suggest that about half of schizophrenic patients will abuse substances at some point in their lives (Dixon, 1999; Thoma & Daum, 2013). Since both conditions cause cognitive impairments, it's difficult to ascertain what preceded the disordered thinking—the substance abuse or the mental illness—making it difficult to determine the nature and extent of the impairment in relation to creative work. Whether delusions and hallucinations are caused by the active substance or the psychiatric disorder has implications for the focus of treatment and the applicability of the psychosis-creativity parallel.

> Example: I once asked a poet and rapper to share more about his substance use after he casually mentioned being "high while writing that." I inquired into the kind of substances he was using and how often he used them. He openly discussed using marijuana on a daily basis. He agreed to monitor any early signs of psychotic thinking after smoking. He noticed that smoking seemed to exacerbate bizarre thinking, which he welcomed because it fueled his creative writing, in addition to paranoia, which he regretted because it made him feel unsafe. Our sessions continued to expand on substance-consumption habits while considering the idea of reducing the extent of their use.

5. *Include the family*. Family intervention has been shown to reduce relapse and hospitalization rates (Bird et al., 2010). For creative people, especially those whose professional demands (schedule irregularity, social isolation, and income instability) pose a high risk for relapse, it's important to garner the participation of supportive family members. Once a consistent and reliable support system is in place, creative people with psychotic disorders can more safely turn their attention to their creative work without the stress that comes from a unsupportive or uninvolved familial environment.

> Example: When a 20-year-old economics student began therapy for feelings of depersonalization and derealization, he was preoccupied with worries about developing schizophrenia (which ran in his family) and couldn't focus on his studies. He found solace in his guitar, which he played for many hours every day. We decided to include his parents, who initially objected to any disruption of normalcy in their son's life. They thought that acknowledging that something was wrong would make things worse, and urged him to keep studying, to spend less time on the guitar, and to get negative thoughts out of his head. Through family sessions, we focused on giving my client the space to express his concerns, and spoke to his parents about the benefits of creative expression, even at the temporary expense of a formal education.

6. *Use art to communicate*. Louis Sass (1994) has made a strong case for the way creative work, in particular modern art, can offer insight into the minds of schizophrenic patients. Concepts such as *hyperreflexivity*—an exaggerated sense of self-consciousness—and social isolation, both of which apply to schizophrenic individuals (Moe & Docherty, 2014), are complex forms of self-awareness that can be expressed through schizophrenic people's outside-the-box artistic perspectives. When verbal communication falls short, art is a way to replace or supplement it. Clinicians can engage in the individual's seemingly bizarre and incomprehensible thinking by paying attention to their creative work.

> Example: Luke, the 21-year-old presented in the beginning of this chapter, enjoyed painting and taking pictures. His symptoms of schizotypy made it difficult for him to engage in abstract thoughts about his self-concept. For example, it took two 45-minute sessions for him to come up with an answer to the question "How do you think others see you?" To facilitate this process, I wondered if his paintings revealed something. In fact, when he showed me self-portraits, there was a consistent theme of drawing himself to be significantly larger than he was in real life, with dark colors, and with Xs instead of eyes. This helped us open up a conversation about what his artistic

choices might have meant, such as seeing himself as an outcast who gets noticed everywhere he goes.

7. *Refer to a psychiatrist for medication.* Creative people who are administered antipsychotic medication are deeply troubled about the potential diminishment of their use of imagination, memory, divergent thinking, and other creative faculties. To figure this one out, it's important to understand which symptoms are, in fact, interfering with the person's creative abilities and the extent to which they do. Since psychotic episodes are preceded and accompanied by cognitive impairments (Hill et al., 2010), it's likely that medication, especially second-generation antipsychotics, which show promising results regarding improving cognitions, prevents such episodes. However, a possible side effect might be the loss of interest and emotional apathy, in which case creativity is also negatively influenced. Clients and clinicians need to weigh the pros and cons of starting antipsychotics and to consider how improvement in some areas, such as cognitive abilities, might bring about improvement in creative achievement.

> Example: I once worked with a photographer on antipsychotic medication who noticed that daydreaming, visualizing, and using abstract cognitive skills had become difficult, despite achieving stability in overall functioning. I encouraged him to bring up this concern to his prescribing doctor and discuss alternative options regarding doses and types of medication. Though he hesitated to experiment with different medications, he agreed to work with his psychiatrist until they found a combination that minimized cognitive disorganization, yet allowed for overinclusive, divergent thinking.

Additional Interventions

8.
9.
10.

Takeaways

- Creative clients share many cognitive, affective, and behavioral characteristics with people who have diagnoses of ADHD, depression, bipolar disorder, and psychotic disorders.

128 Psychiatric Disorders

- This correlational relationship does not imply causation, but it does point toward the direction of shared mental processes.
- Sometimes these processes work toward the creative clients' advantage, such as when cognitive disorganization generates a vast number of creative ideas. Sometimes, however, they interfere with optimal creative functioning, such as when delusional thinking makes it difficult to assess the quality of those ideas.
- Counseling can help clients understand the effects of their diagnoses on their creativity. It can address treatment needs for psychiatric symptoms that harm creative thinking and behavior, as well as work with the symptoms that facilitate them.
- Clinicians can help their clients feel empowered by emphasizing how their psychiatric diagnoses facilitate processes associated with creative achievement.

Note

1 TED (Technology, Entertainment, Design) is a nonprofit organization that publishes videos exploring ideas in science and culture; see www.ted.com/talks/ken_robinson_says_schools_kill_creativity.

References

Abraham, A. (2014). Is there an inverted-U relationship between creativity and psychopathology? General commentary article In A. Abraham (Ed.), Madness and Creativity: Yes, No or Maybe? *Frontiers in Psychology, 5*, 1–3. doi:10.3389/fpsyg.2015.01055

Acar, S., & Runco, M. A. (2012). Psychoticism and creativity: A meta-analytic review. *Psychology of Aesthetics, Creativity, and the Arts, 6*(4), 341–350.

Andreasen, N. C. (1987). Creativity and mental illness: Prevalence rates in writers and their first-degree relatives. *American Journal of Psychiatry, 144*, 1288–1292.

Baas, M., De Dreu, C. K. W., & Nijstad, B. A. (2008). A meta-analysis of 25 years of mood-creativity research: Hedonic tone, activation, or regulatory focus? *Psychological Bulletin, 134*(6), 779–806.

Barrantes-Vidal, N. (2014). Creativity and the spectrum of affective and schizophrenic psychoses. In J. C. Kaufman (Ed.), *Creativity and mental illness* (pp. 169–204). Cambridge: Cambridge University Press. doi: 10.1017/CBO9781139128902.013

Batey, M., & Furnham, A. (2008). The relationship between measures of creativity and schizotypy. *Personality and Individual Differences, 45*, 816–821.

Bellack, A. S., Mueser, K. T., Gingerich, S., & Agresta, J. (2013). *Social skills training for schizophrenia: A step-by-step guide* (2nd ed.). New York, NY: Guilford Publications.

Bilder, R. M., & Knudsen, K. S. (2014). Creative cognition and systems biology on the edge of chaos. *Frontiers in Psychology, 5*, 1104.

Bird, V., Premkumar, P., Kendall, T., Whittington, C., Mitchell, J., & Kuipers, E. (2010). The *British Journal of Psychiatry, 197*(5), 350–356. doi:10.1192/bjp.bp.109.074526

Brown, T. E. (2013). *A new understanding of ADHD in children and adults: Executive function impairments*. New York, NY: Routledge.

Burch, G. S. J., Pavelis, C., Hemsley, D. R., & Corr, P. J. (2006). Schizotypy and creativity in visual artists. *British Journal of Psychology, 97*, 177–190. doi:10.1348/000712605X60030

Carson, S. (2010). *Your creative brain: Seven steps to maximize imagination, productivity, and innovation in your life.* San Francisco, CA: Jossey-Bass.

Carson, S. (2011). Creativity and psychopathology: A shared vulnerability model. *Canadian Journal of Psychiatry, 56*(3), 144–153.

Carson, S. H. (2013). Creativity and psychopathology: Shared neurocognitive vulnerabilities. In O. Vartanian, A. S. Bristol, & J. C. Kaufman (Eds.), *Neuroscience of creativity* (pp. 175–203). Cambridge, MA: MIT Press.

Carson, S., Peterson, J. B., & Higgins, D. (2003). Decreased latent inhibition is associated with increased creative achievement in high-functioning individuals. *Journal of Personality and Social Psychology, 85*, 499–506. doi:10.1037/0022–3514.85.3.499

Csikszentmihalyi, M. (1996). *Creativity. The flow and the psychology of discovery of invention.* New York, NY: HarperCollins Publishers.

Dietrich, A. (2015). The mythconception of the mad genius. *Frontiers in Psychology, 5*, 79. http://doi.org/10.3389/fpsyg.2014.00079

Dixon, L. (1999). Dual diagnosis of substance abuse in schizophrenia: Prevalence and impact on outcomes. *Schizophrenia Research, 35*(1), 93–S100.

Djikic, M., & Oatley, K. (2014). On the fragility of the artist: Art's precarious triad. In J. Kaufman (Ed.), *Creativity and mental illness.* Cambridge: Cambridge University Press.

Eysenck, H. J. (1993). Creativity and personality: Suggestions for a theory. *Psychological Inquiry, 4*, 147–178.

Fink, A., Weber, B., Koschutnig, K., Benedek, M., Reishofer, G., Ebner, F., . . . Weiss, E. (2014). Creativity and schizotypy from the neuroscience perspective. *Cognitive, Affective, and Behavioral Neuroscience, 14*(1), 378–387.

Ford-Jones, P. C. (2015). Misdiagnosis of attention deficit hyperactivity disorder: "Normal behaviour" and relative maturity. *Paediatrics & Child Health, 20*(4), 200–202.

Furnham, A., Batey, M., Anand, K., & Manfield, J. (2008). Personality, hypomania, intelligence, and creativity. *Personality and Individual Difference, 44*, 1060–1069. doi: 10.1016/j.paid.2007.10.035

Goldstein, E. (2012). *The now effect: How a mindful moment can change the rest of your life.* New York, NY: Atria Books.

Goodwin, F. G., & Jamison, K. R. (2007). *Manic depressive illness* (2nd ed.). Oxford: Oxford University Press.

Gross, S. A., & Musgrave, G. (2016). *Can music make you sick? Music and depression: A study into the incidence of musicians' mental health, Part 1: Pilots Survey report.* University of Westminster: MusicTank Publishing.

Grosul, M., & Feist, G. J. (2014). The creative person in science. *Psychology of Aesthetics, Creativity, and the Arts, 8*, 30–43.

Heilman, K. M. (2005). *Creativity and the brain.* New York, NY: Psychology Press.

Hesslinger, B., Tebartz van Elst, L., Nyberg, E., Dykierek, P., Richter, H., Berner, M., & Ebert, D. (2002). Psychotherapy of attention deficit hyperactivity disorder in adults. *European Archives of Psychiatry and Clinical Neurosciences, 252*(4), 177–184. doi:10.1007/s00406-002-0379-0

Hill, S. K., Bishop, J. R., Palumbo, D., & Sweeney, J. A. (2010). Effect of second-generation antipsychotics on cognition: Current issues and future challenges. *Expert Review of Neurotherapeutics, 10*(1), 43–57. doi:10.1586/ern.09.143

Jamison, K. R. (1996). *Touched with fire: Manic-depressive illness & the artistic temperament* (2nd ed.). New York, NY: Free Press Paperbacks.

Johnson, S. L., Moezpoor, M., Murray, G., Hole, R., Barnes, S. J., & Michalak, E. (2016). Creativity and bipolar disorder: Igniting a dialogue. *Qualitative Health Research, 26*(1), 32–40.

Johnson, S. L., Murray, G., Fredrickson, B., Youngstrom, E. A., Hinshaw, S., Bass, J. M., . . . Salloum, I. (2012). Creativity and bipolar disorder: Touched by fire or burning with questions? *Clinical Psychology Review, 32*(1), 1–12. doi:10.1016/j.cpr.2011.10.001

Jones, M., Roy, M., & Verkuillen, J. (2014). The relationship between reflective rumination and musical abilities. *Psychology of Aesthetics, Creativity, and the Arts, 2*, 219–226.

Kaufmann, G., & Kaufmann, A. (2014). When good is bad and bad is good: Mood, bipolarity, and creativity. In J. Kaufman (Ed.), *Creativity and mental illness* (pp. 205–235). Cambridge: Cambridge University Press. doi:10.1017/CBO9781139128902.014

Kaufman, J. C. (Ed.). (2014). *Creativity and mental illness*. Cambridge: Cambridge University Press.

Kaufman, S. B., & Gregoire, C. (2015). *Wired to create: Unraveling the mysteries of the creative mind*. New York, NY: TarcherPerigee.

Keck, P. E. Jr., & McElroy, S. L. (2015). Pharmacological treatments for bipolar disorder. In P. E. Nathan & J. Gorman (Eds.), *A guide to treatments that work*. Oxford: Oxford University Press.

Kinney, D. K., & Richards, R. (2014). Creativity as "compensatory advantage": Bipolar and schizophrenic liability, the inverted-U hypothesis and practical limitations. In J. Kaufman (Ed.), *Creativity and mental illness* (pp. 295–321). Cambridge: Cambridge University Press.

Kozbelt, A., Kaufman, S., Walder, D., Ospina, L., & Kim, J. (2014). The evolutionary genetics of the creativity—psychosis connection. In J. Kaufman (Ed.), *Creativity and mental illness* (pp. 102–132). Cambridge: Cambridge University Press. doi:10.1017/CBO9781139128902.009

Kyaga, S., Lichtenstein, P., Boman, M., Hultman, C., Langstorm, N., & Landen, M. (2011). Creativity and mental disorder: Family study of 300,000 people with severe mental disorder. *British Journal of Psychiatry, 199*(5), 373–379.

Kyaga, S., Lichtenstein, P., Boman, M., Hultman, C., Langstorm, N., & Landen, M. (2013). Mental illness, suicide and creativity: 40-year prospective total population study. *Journal of Psychiatric Research, 47*(1), 83–90.

Lindel, A. K. (2014). On the interrelation between reduced lateralization, schizotypy, and creativity. *Frontiers in Psychology, 5*, 813.

Loo, S. K., Hale, T. S., Macion, J., Hanada, G., McGough, J. J., McCracken, J. T., & Smalley, S. L. (2009). Cortical activity patterns in ADHD during arousal, activation and sustained attention. *Neuropsychologia, 10*, 2114–2119.

Ludwig, A. M. (1992). Creative achievement and psychopathology: Comparison among professions. *American Journal of Psychotherapy, 46*(3), 330–356.

Ludwig, A. M. (1994). Mental illness and creative activity in female writers. *The American Journal of Psychiatry, 151*(11), 1650–1656.

Maisel, E. (2007). *The Van Gogh blues: The creative person's path through depression*. Novato, CA: New World Library.

Mitchell, J. T., Zylowska, L., & Kollins, S. H. (2015). Mindfulness meditation training for attention-deficit/hyperactivity disorder in adulthood: Current empirical support, treatment overview, and future directions. *Cognitive and Behavioral Practice, 22*(2), 172–191. doi:10.1016/j.cbpra.2014.10.002

Moe, A. M., & Docherty, N. M. (2014). Schizophrenia and the sense of self. *Schizophrenia Bulletin, 40*(1), 161–168.

Mohr, C., & Claridge, G. (2015). Schizotypy—do not worry, it is not all worrisome. *Schizophrenia Bulletin, 41*(Suppl. 2), 436–443.

Nelson, B., & Rawlings, D. (2010). Relating schizotypy and personality to the phenomenology of creativity. *Schizophrenia Bulletin, 36*(2), 388–399. doi:10.1093/schbul/sbn098

Nettle, D. (2006). Schizotypy and mental health amongst poets, visual artists, and mathematicians. *Journal of Research in Personality, 40*(6), 876–890.

Nowakowska, C., Strong, C. M., Santosa, C. M., Wang, P. W., & Ketter, T. A. (2005). Temperamental commonalities and differences in euthymic mood disorder patients, creative controls, and healthy controls. *Journal of Affective Disorders, 85*(1), 207–215.

Power, R. A., Steinberg, S., Bjornsdottir, G., Rietveld, C. A., Abdellaoui, A., Nivard, M. M., . . . Stefansson, K. (2015). Polygenic risk scores for schizophrenia and bipolar disorder predict creativity. *Nature Neuroscience, 18*(7), 953–955.

Preti, A., & Vellante, M. (2007). Creativity and psychopathology: Higher rates of psychosis proneness and nonright-handedness among creative artists compared to same age and gender peers. *The Journal of Nervous and Mental Disease, 195*, 837–845.

Richards, R., & Kinney, D. (1990). Mood swings and creativity. *Creativity Research Journal. 3*(3), 202–217.

Robinson, K. (2006, June). *Do schools kill creativity?* [Video file]. Retrieved from www.ted.com/talks/ken_robinson_says_schools_kill_creativity?language=en

Rock, P. L., Roiser, J. P., Riedel, W. J., & Blackwell, A. D. (2014). Cognitive impairment in depression: a systematic review and meta-analysis. *Psychological Medicine, 44*, 2029–2040.

Rothenberg, A. (2001). Bipolar illness, creativity, and treatment. *Psychiatric Quarterly, 72*(2), 131–147.

Russell, S., & Browne, J. L. (2005). Staying well with bipolar disorder. *Australian and New Zealand Journal of Psychiatry, 39*(3), 187–193.

Saltz, G. (2017). *The power of different: The link between disorder and genius.* New York, NY: Flatiron Books.

Santosa, C. M., Strong, C. M., Nowakowska, C., Wang, P. W., Rennicke, C. M., & Ketter, T. A. (2007). Enhanced creativity in bipolar disorder patients: A controlled study. *Journal of Affective Disorders, 100*(1–3), 31–39.

Sass, L. (1994). *Madness and modernism: Insanity in the light of modern art, literature, and thought.* Cambridge, MA: Harvard University Press.

Schlesinger, J. (2012). *The insanity hoax: Exposing the myth of the mad genius.* New York, NY: Shrinktunes Media.

Schuldberg, D. (2005). Eysenck personality questionnaire scales and paper-and-pencil tests related to creativity. *Psychological Reports, 97*(1), 180–182.

Seligman, M. E. P. (2002). Positive psychology, positive prevention, and positive therapy. In C. R. Snyder & S. J. Lopez (Eds.), *Handbook of positive psychology.* Oxford: Oxford University Press.

Shaw-Zirt, B., Popali-Lehane, L., Chaplin, W., & Bergman, A. (2005). Adjustment, social skills, and self-esteem in college students with symptoms of ADHD. *Journal of Attention Disorders, 8*(3), 109–120.

Silvia, P. J., & Kaufman, J. C. (2010). Creativity and mental illness. In J. C. Kaufman & R. J. Sternberg (Eds.), *The Cambridge handbook of creativity.* Cambridge: Cambridge University Press.

Silvia, P. J., & Kimbrel, N. A. (2010). A dimensional analysis of creativity and mental illness: Do anxiety and depression symptoms predict creative cognition, creative accomplishments, and creative self-concepts? *Psychology of Aesthetics, Creativity, and the Arts, 4*(1), 2–10.

Smartwood, M., Swartwood, J. N., & Farrell, J. (2003). Stimulant treatment of ADHD: Effects on creativity and flexibility in problem solving. *Creativity Research Journal, 15*(4), 417–419.

Stuckey, H. L., & Nobel, J. (2010). The connection between art, healing, and public health: A review of current literature. *American Journal of Public Health, 100*(2), 254–263.

Sylvia, L. G., Salcedo, S., Bernstein, E. E., Baek, J. H., Nierenberg, A. A., & Deckersbach, T. (2013). Nutrition, exercise, and wellness treatment in bipolar disorder: Proof of concept for a consolidated intervention. *International Journal of Bipolar Disorders, 1*(1), 24. https://doi.org/10.1186/2194-7511-1-24

Thoma, P., & Daum, I. (2013), Comorbid substance use disorder in schizophrenia: A selective overview of neurobiological and cognitive underpinnings. *Psychiatry and Clinical Neurosciences, 67*, 367–383. doi:10.1111/pcn.12072

Tuckerman, A. (2007). *Integrative treatment for adult ADHD: A practical, easy-to-use guide for clinicians.* Oakland, CA: New Harbinger Publications.

Verhaeghen, P., Joorman, J., & Khan, R. (2005). Why we sing the blues: The relation between self-reflective rumination, mood, and creativity. *Emotion, 5*(2), 226–232.

Webb, J. T. (2005). *Misdiagnosis and dual diagnoses of gifted children and adults: ADHD, bipolar, OCD, Asperger's, depression, and other disorders.* Tucson, AZ: Great Potential Press.

White, H., & Shah, P. (2006). Uninhibited imaginations: Creativity in adults with attention-deficit/hyperactivity disorder. *Personality and Individual Differences, 40*, 1121–1131.

White, H., & Shah, P. (2011). Creative style and achievement in adults with attention-deficit/hyperactivity disorder. *Personality and Individual Differences, 50*(5), 673–677.

Young, L. N., Winner, E., & Cordes, S. (2013). Heightened incidence of depressive symptoms in adolescents involved in the arts. *Psychology of Aesthetics, Creativity, and the Arts, 7*(2), 197–202.

Zabelina, D. L., O'Leary, D., Pornpattananangkul, N., Nusslock, R., & Beeman, M. (2015). Creativity and sensory gating indexed by the P50: Selective versus leaky sensory gating in divergent thinkers and creative achievers. *Neuropsychologia, 69*, 77–84.

Zabelina, D. L., Saporta, A., & Beeman, M. (2016). Flexible or leaky attention in creative people? Distinct patterns of attention for different types of creative thinking. *Memory and Cognition, 44*(3), 488–498. doi:10.3758/s13421-015-0569-4

Chapter 7

Performance and Audition Anxiety

Right before he went onstage, Steve, a saxophone player with decades of experience playing the saxophone, would convince himself that his audience consisted of highly accomplished musicians. These musicians, he thought, would most likely be critical of his playing. More specifically, they'd find his technique to be poor, his performance to be flat, and his movements to be too jerky. When I asked him what evidence led him to that conclusion, he shrugged his shoulders and admitted to not having any. Even so, the anticipation of important critics was some kind of preperformance cognitive ritual he'd developed and reinforced throughout his career—one that filled him with anxiety about performing. Despite years on the saxophone and a profound passion for his art, his outlook on the entire performing experience was marred by persistent self-perceptions of inferiority, which were only worsened by his strong need to be praised. This kind of pressure triggered a series of overwhelming physical symptoms of anxiety. With shaky hands, shortness of breath, and feelings of depersonalization, he was having a series of reactions that were compromising the quality of his performances and confirming his fears of failure. He desperately wished to change these reactions but was at a loss as to how to start.

Steve's ordeal is a variation of an experience shared by many performers. Anxiety associated with performing and auditioning is perhaps the most common mental health concern among performing artists. Demonstrating skills, passions, talents, and practiced work in front of an audience is a mentally and physically taxing task, one that triggers performers' deepest conscious and unconscious vulnerabilities. When something profoundly personal becomes public, and when it becomes subject to fickle audience reactions, mind and body are bound to react.

Physical and cognitive arousal before performing is normal. Musicians, actors, singers, dancers, stand-up comics, and other types of performers will most likely experience some degree of performance and audition anxiety throughout their careers. Sometimes, this anxiety resolves itself after just a few minutes of being onstage, or it may disappear altogether after years of repeated exposure. Some even view this kind of arousal as beneficial when it reaches an optimal (not too high, not too low) level because it's experienced as performance excitement—which in fact is conducive to achieving task mastery and high performance quality (Kenny, 2011). However, for performers who can't bring the anxiety down, the normalcy of the preperformance jitters gets overpowered by severely compromising symptoms. Singers' voices get shaky, actors' mouths become dry, pianists' palms begin to sweat, and dancers' spatial perception gets distorted. Onstage, severely anxious performers feel removed from their bodies. They become mentally foggy. It's impossible for them to concentrate on nailing a demanding part, or to become immersed in the creative moment, when they anxiously fixate on small details, such as an audience member who looks at her phone.

Offstage, the reactions continue to be just as strong. These performers will agonize for days leading up to shows: they'll dread having to go onstage when the time comes, and even miss out on important auditions just to avoid being judged and compared to others. Sometimes performers' gastrointestinal tract gets affected, too. I once worked with a rock singer who noticed that before every performance, like clockwork, she felt irritable bowel symptoms that led to stomach pain and diarrhea. This made her more anxious about the conditions of the venues' bathrooms, which most of the time were dirty and cramped. Our work together focused on learning to anticipate these symptoms, so as not to become panic-stricken by them. We took steps to manage them, such as making small dietary adjustments and allowing for plenty of time to travel to the performance venue before shows so she could familiarize herself with the environment. Still, she was devastated with the way her anxiety was taking the joy out of performing and wanted to understand more about why she was having these feelings.

Contributing Factors: Personality Traits, Audience, Performed Work, Extraneous Variables

Roughly speaking, four factors are implicated in constructing performers' experiences as highly anxious ones. The first involves their unique personality traits and internally driven demands. Shyness, perfectionism, competitiveness, obsessiveness with approval, and low tolerance for making mistakes are high-risk factors for developing performance anxiety. The tension between the need to be positively perceived, often reinforced by formative early life experiences equating positive perception with worth, and the reality of having limitations and making mistakes gets expressed through symptoms of anxiety. Perfectionism can be experienced constructively if internally driven—that is, if it's experienced as a need to improve for the sake of improvement. However, if driven by external factors, such as parental and societal norms, it's experienced as a need to prove something to others. The need to be seen as perfect by others is likely to cause performance anxiety (Kenny, 2011), and stressful, ruminative thinking over past mistakes or future negative outcomes. My sessions with Steve revealed a need for flawlessness, reflected by latching onto an externalized object—in his case, the imaginary critic—for its fulfillment. By convincing himself that he was inadequate compared to other musicians in the audience, he was giving himself permission to judge himself harshly, all while striving for unobtainable goals: a flawless performance every time, one that would please everyone, ranging from amateur listeners to accomplished experts.

The way people think about themselves and the world around them is another personal characteristic that determines the intensity of performance anxiety. Kelly and Saveanu (2005) succinctly grouped together four pertinent cognitive distortions that occur in people with social phobia, which can also apply to performers with audition and performance anxiety. They described (a) performers' tendency to overestimate a threat (for example, thinking that one particular performance will determine overall career success or failure); (b) their tendency to underestimate their own competence by thinking about the parts they "always mess up"; (c) their tendency to selectively pay attention to their own state of anxiety or to others' negative responses (such as focusing on one person leaving during the performance or thinking that everyone can tell how nervous they are); and (d) their tendency to engage in negative and pessimistic self-talk, such as thinking that they're bound to make a mistake soon.

The second factor that makes a performance experience a highly anxious one is the projected importance of the audience and the anticipated feedback: performers will react differently, with varying degrees of anxiety, depending on how big the audience is, who composes it, the power held by casting agents, the familiarity of the audience, and so on (McGrath et al., 2017). Sometimes anxiety is induced when performers are performing in front of thousands of people, and other times simply when they're practicing while a judgmental spouse is in the other room. The audience is an integral part of the performing experience; therefore, the way performers feel about those watching it greatly affects the way they feel about doing it. Auditioning captures the subtle power interplay between auditioner and auditionee, and the former's response to authority. Many of my clients who struggle with audition anxiety more so than performance anxiety describe a similar feeling of nervousness, colored by contempt toward the perceived authority figure—the judge, the industry professional, the casting agent, and so forth. A deeply rooted feeling of defiance toward the person in the position of power ("Who do they think they are? What qualifies them to be the ones judging me?") has the potential to become a source of empowerment; however, more often than not, it results in a poorly managed preoccupation with impressing, overpowering, and proving oneself. This preoccupation, along with the uncertainty of how the performer is faring compared to other candidates, increases anxiety about auditioning.

The third factor that contributes to increased anxiety about performing or auditioning is the person's relationship to the work being presented. For example, if performers are inadequately prepared, if they struggle with *task mastery* (Wilson, 2001), if they dislike the work itself, if they view the performance as a means to an end (such as winning an award) rather than an inherently enjoyable experience, and so forth, they'll become more anxious about the quality of their performances. Similarly, a performing artist whose cultural expectation is that art is meant to be aesthetically pleasing will falter during the performance of a piece with psychologically disturbing themes, such as abuse and suicide. Prior negative experiences with the pieces being performed (having fallen during a show or having messed up an important solo section) will add to performers' fears about the outcome.

The fourth contributing factor has to do with external factors beyond one's control. A performer who's well prepared, ready to face the challenge of sharing his or her art with others, and passionate about the songs he or she is about to play will still face crippling anxiety when band members cancel at the last minute, or when sound engineers keep making mistakes. Touring often brings up these kinds of difficulties for performers who don't always sleep or eat well, and who run the risk of getting sick or having damaged equipment. Letting go of control and having to trust that collaborators and venue conditions will not disappoint can be intensely anxiety inducing.

The Role of Unconscious Emotions

Ideally, performing is an emotionally immersive experience, one that brings performers to a state of creative flow in which they're fully absorbed and rewarded by the task (Csikszentmihalyi, 1997). However, poorly managed emotions stemming from unresolved trauma and internal conflicts are likely to disrupt performers' abilities to connect with the performing experience. Unconscious ambivalence about being the center of attention will lead to discomfort in the face of standing out and excelling (Ferraro, 1999). Despite a conscious intent to succeed, unconscious perceptions of success as being inherently negative can fuel sabotaging behaviors and feelings of anxiety. For example, a child who has grown up in an environment that values passivity and submissiveness, rather than assertive self-expression, will likely develop an aversion to expressing herself passionately in the presence of others, even when she wishes for a successful performance.

Similarly, a performer might experience unconscious insecurity about the validity of his or her creative voice. A classically trained ballet performer I worked with could easily reach a calm space during her ballet performances; however, when she switched to experimental, avant-garde dance, she felt anxiously dissociated from the experience. She slowly became aware of her deep ambivalence about challenging social norms and expectations. Having internalized a conservative value system from her parents, she had unconsciously associated classical ballet with approval and acceptance, and experimental dance with rebelliousness—a trait she was far from comfortable embodying.

Regarding past trauma, performers are at risk for heightened anxiety when an easily triggered arousal response, sensitized by past traumatic events, signals the need for an anxiety response. (For more about trauma and performing artists, see chapter 5.) When trauma hasn't been effectively resolved, the psychologically arousing state of performing makes it hard for performers to separate the objective threat posed by performing from the reactivation of past threats (Swart, 2010). When this happens, people's well-established defenses, set in place to help protect the ego from painful feelings, break down during performances (Kenny et al., 2014). An example might be exposure to domestic abuse in a performer's early childhood, which led him or her to develop coping defenses, such as hiding or remaining quiet, as a way of tolerating the traumatic pain. However, such defenses become useless when faced with the vulnerability of performing, especially during solo pieces, during which performers are fully exposed. The inability of the ego's defenses to protect it from perceived threats during anxiety-inducing performances allows for stress responses (fear, shakiness, depersonalization, and so on) to surface. Being in the spotlight seems to strip performers of their ability to rely on the protective, often unconscious, defenses to which they're accustomed.

Consequences of Performance Anxiety

Left untreated, performance anxiety can affect the quality of the performance and severely limit, or even end, performers' careers. Thomson and Jaque (2017:290) point out that unmanaged "frightening thoughts and somatic reactions will continue to increase the feedback loop between the two until performance anxiety reaches the level of panic attacks." Because of the way it diminishes the ability to concentrate and causes physical tension, performance anxiety is a risk factor for sustaining injuries (Yatabe, 2014). It can lead to psychologically impairing cycles of having disappointing shows, leading to anxiety about upcoming ones, resulting in poor performances and more disappointment. Performers may begin to rely on substances and alcohol as a way of coping with the anxiety. Substance use comes with the risk of developing dependency to those substances, and it may impair the quality of performances (Kelly & Saveanu, 2005). When performers reach the point of dreading what they've passionately pursued for years, and when they struggle to manage professional demands, counseling becomes a necessity.

The Clinician's Role

Exploring Perceived Threats

As clinicians and performers work together to reduce anxiety, the clinicians' role is to uncover the thoughts clients have about performing, with the goal of discovering what about it feels threatening. To cover many possibilities, clients can engage in free-form, unstructured conversations with a wide focus, rather than narrowly emphasize the experience of anxiety. For example, a session with a musician might begin by discussing the here-and-now experience that she has onstage, go on to explore the personal meaning and significance behind the work she's presenting, analyze the interpersonal relations with her band members, and land on a conversation about early childhood performing experiences. Depending on the performer's history, themes that need to be explored are fear of rejection, perceived risks associated with failure, the performer's thought patterns, traumatic experiences off- and onstage, perfectionistic tendencies, self-esteem, familial and societal expectations, and financial pressures.

In the case of Steve, the first eight to ten sessions were primarily explorative in nature, and included discussions on the early beginnings of his perfectionistic tendencies, inheriting his mother's austere and no-nonsense attitude regarding mistakes, and earlier disappointments in his career for which he'd never fully grieved. As the sessions progressed, we gradually shifted the attention from the past to the present and from the internal to the external: after trying to understand the whys around his anxiety, we focused on helping him make peace with the performer he had become. To deepen his sense of satisfaction from his craft, we worked on empowering him through themes of artistic integrity and conscious choices. The more he faced the question of what kind of performer he wanted to be (one with the freedom to stray from mainstream musical norms), the rationale behind his artistic values (which needed to reflect his life values), and the things he'd consciously sacrificed (fitting in with other mainstream performers), the easier it was for him to become self-embracing, self-forgiving, and accepting of mistakes.

Identifying Automatic Thoughts

In line with cognitive behavioral approaches, clinicians can explore performers' automatic thoughts about mistakes, failures and rejections, and associations they've developed between success onstage and personal worth. Sessions will aim to increase awareness of harmful thought patterns, such as catastrophizing, which is linked to performance anxiety (Steptoe & Fidler, 1987), as well as the behaviors that might sustain them. For example, if a performer has the tendency to assume that the audience will dislike the performance and sustains this belief by avoiding practicing for the performance—consequently being less prepared—one of the treatment goals might be to come up with a modified practice schedule that highlights enjoyment and full immersion in the task, rather than strictly associating practicing with an upcoming performance.

Assessing Anxiety Offstage

If general traits of anxiety seem to appear in many areas of clients' lives, clinicians can explore the nature of these traits in a wider context, not just the context of performing. A guitar player I once worked with had generalized anxiety, meaning that most situations would result in a cascade of worries and negative thoughts about all the things that could go wrong. The sessions with him extended beyond his onstage experiences, given that those were reflective of overall ways of thinking.

In contrast, clinicians can investigate what performing brings up for typically nonanxious clients. One musical theater performer (a singer, dancer, and actress) I worked with had low overall anxiety and a high drive to get as many parts as she could. Yet she struggled to adjust to the demands of auditioning for parts, thinking she might not be what casting agents were looking for. Being compared to others and feeling objectified and reduced to being "just a number" among hundreds of candidates stirred up feelings of existential anxiety—she felt like she didn't matter and that she was invisible. An understanding of general trait anxiety helps clinicians target the most helpful interventions to reduce performance and audition anxiety.

Putting Physical Reactions Into Perspective

Since performance anxiety affects performers' bodies in compromising ways, treatment ought to target physical relaxation and tension release. A psychoeducational approach might help reduce the mystery around what happens to the brain and the body during moments of performance anxiety and maximize a sense of hopefulness about managing these symptoms. Clinicians can help clients understand how their bodies are giving off false signals of danger to the brain and how the brain-related experiences, both cognitive and affective, condition their bodies to react with symptoms of anxiety.

For example, at the sight of a packed house, a performer may experience a racing heart and stomach discomfort—the brain's way of communicating a perceived threat. At first, she might assume something is wrong with her body, or that these reactions will make it impossible for her to perform. Clinicians can help clients think of these symptoms as faulty anxiety alarms—instead of signs that something's wrong—and that the threat the body is responding to is most likely a projection of a negative internal state. In other words, by separating the subjective perception of anxiety from what's objectively there, the performer can begin to gain control over a strong, knee-jerk association. I've found that short reminders, such as "This anxiety is a result of my condition, not a reflection of my skills or what the audience thinks," help performers quickly draw a distinction between mental representations and external circumstances.

If the brain can communicate to the body the need to panic at the sight of an audience, causing shaking, sweating, dizziness, and dehydration, it can also communicate the need for safety-based responses like heightened focus and relaxation. Clinicians can help performers implement body relaxation techniques that help the brain reach a calmer, neutral state. Techniques, such as the Alexander technique (Connable, 1999; Woodman & Moore, 2012), which emphasizes engaging in conscious and mindful physical movements, aim to train performers to manage physical stress and increase spontaneity.

140 Performance and Audition Anxiety

Guided meditation exercises can facilitate the implementation of habits such as quieting racing thoughts, reducing physical tension, and sustaining immersion in the experience of performing for longer periods. Replacing negative thoughts with positive ones through the use of imagery—images of successfully completing a performance, of being congratulated, of accomplishing challenging situations, and so forth—can increase positive feelings and motivation associated with auditioning and performing (Monsma & Overby, 2004; MacNamara, Button, A. & Collins, D. 2010).

Discerning What the Audience Represents

Clinicians can investigate the significance of audience approval for performers, and what the need for approval—which manifests itself through anxiety—says about performers past and present relationships. For example, psychodynamic approaches that address the emotions derived from relationships with early caretakers can shed light onto what audiences represent to anxious performers. Throughout the sessions with Steve, we worked on teasing out who he saw—other than the "important critics"—when he looked at the audience. In his case, there was a strong sense of internalized duty to please his depressed mother, who seemed to feel joy only vicariously through her son's successes. Although his mother had passed away years before his performance anxiety had intensified, he was still incorporating this subconscious association between performing and the responsibility to save his mother from her depression. His anxiety was heightened by the symbolic presence of his mother in the audience.

Treatment Goals

1.	Perform with minimal impairment from physical symptoms of anxiety.
2.	Maximize enjoyment during performances.
3.	Replicate the quality of work demonstrated during practice.
4.	Remain focused and present during performances.
5.	Improve thoughts and feelings associated with being onstage.

Suggested Interventions to Achieve Goals

1. *Reframe anxiety as excitement.* Clients and clinicians can work together to think and talk about anxious experiences through the lens of feelings of excitement. Recognizing symptoms as harmless precursors to the thrill of performing can help reduce the fear that typically comes with them. This intervention, based on Brooks's research (2013), encourages performers to turn thoughts about being anxious into thoughts about being excited, instead of worrying about calming down. The idea is that the way feelings are talked about significantly influences the way they are experienced.

   > Example: When she got nervous before shows, I'd ask an opera singer to avoid pressuring herself to repeat phrases like "relax" and "calm down," and instead to think that this performance is making her feel a rush of excitement, or that she's uncomfortable because she usually doesn't feel so much excitement. Normalizing her reactions helped remove the fear attached to preperformance discomfort.

2. *Focus on breathing and posture.* Routines such as the Alexander technique (AT) bring awareness to unhealthy breathing and postural habits to help performers achieve a more natural and uninhibited performance style. The focus on breathing and posture is useful not only for the physical improvement it brings about but also for the way it bolsters the confidence of those who've mastered the technique. The effectiveness of AT is strongly supported for the relief of chronic pain and posture improvement (Woodman & Moore, 2012). The actors and performers in my practice whose professional training incorporates AT and breathing exercises tend to report higher levels of readiness and security when onstage, compared to those whose training does not.

   > Example: An actor whose audition anxiety kept him from going to auditions worked with me to manage hyperventilation and muscle tension stemming from anxiety. In our sessions, we practiced simple diaphragmatic breathing exercises, which he repeated in between sessions. I reminded him to focus his awareness on the position of his neck and shoulders, to both deepen his breathing and improve his posture. As a result, he went into auditions with less vocal tension and shakiness.

3. *Guide a visualization of the performance.* Clients can mentally recreate the experience of performing, anticipate imaginary obstacles, and visualize overcoming them. This approach borrows and modifies the fundamental principles of desensitization and exposure therapy, commonly used to reduce phobias and fears. Simulating the experience of performing—for example, by pretending to play musical instruments—helps relive the highly stressful experience under emotionally safer conditions.

Example: When I worked with a highly anxious singer, I asked her to practice closing her eyes, picturing herself preparing for a performance, walking onstage, and allowing herself to experience all the familiar symptoms of anxiety caused by a first shaky note. Then, I encouraged her to replace the image of an unsuccessful first attempt with one in which she's producing a strong, pitch-perfect note. Visualizing success despite an initial mistake helped instill confidence in her ability to do well in real life.

4. *Create safety images.* Performers and clinicians can come up with images or memories of experiences that make them feel safe, such as a heart-warming childhood moment, a serene scene, or a joyous performing experience. These images will then be used to counter the effect of anxiety-provoking thoughts. Similar to the intervention "*Guide a visualization of the performance*," clients can practice responding to anxiety-provoking thoughts (falling onstage, getting rejected, forgetting lines, and so on) with safety images that induce feelings of calm, confidence, and security. The goal is to develop the ability to retrieve safety images to reduce anxiety right before going onstage.

    Example: An orchestra musician who'd had a traumatic onstage experience (she came in too early, throwing other musicians off who then scorned her) benefited from coming up with an image of herself playing her instrument at a beach near her childhood vacation home, which induced feelings of safety and reassurance. In between shows, we'd devote part of the session to moving from the negative image to the safe one, until the negative image stopped overpowering the positive one.

5. *Challenge negative thoughts.* In line with cognitive behavioral therapy techniques applied for music performance anxiety (Kenny, 2005), this intervention targets the types of thoughts held by performers. Clients can begin by investigating how they interpret a recent mistake, what they're telling themselves about an upcoming performance, what thoughts they associate with passing or failing an audition, and so on. I sometimes ask performers to spend 10 minutes before they're about to rehearse on identifying the presence of any negative thoughts, challenging them, and replacing them with more helpful ones.

    Example: When a young singer complained of not enjoying her performances, I asked her to keep track of negative catastrophizing thoughts ("This wrong note ruined the whole performance") and all-or-nothing thinking ("Only some audience members complimented my performance; this must mean I'm horrible"). Cataloguing her thoughts helped reveal her own damaging interpretations of inconsequential events. She and I worked on developing more helpful alternatives to such interpretations.

6. *Enhance personal creative agency.* Through my discussions with performers I've noticed that they tend to become empowered when they shift the focus from audiences' expectations to the subjective importance behind each performance. Clinicians can ask clients to reflect on what performing means to them, and the ways it enriches their lives, rather than simply detailing audiences' or casting agents' reactions. Empowering clients to value their performances helps foster confidence, which can combat anxious preoccupation with what others think.

    Example: After spending a few sessions with a musician reflecting on what his performances meant to him and what he was getting from the experiences, he began to feel less pressure about pleasing and satisfying the audience. Instead of trying to prove his worth, he saw performing as a chance to improve his skills. This shift in focus helped him feel less anxious about upcoming performances.

7. *Examine the role of psychological defenses.* This intervention, based on intensive short-term dynamic psychotherapy (ISTDP) techniques and rooted in the psychodynamic appreciation of how early experiences shape our defenses against threatening situations, is effectively illustrated in a case study by Kenny and colleagues (2014). In their article, they discuss how defenses such as displacement, avoidance, confrontation, and helplessness are rendered useless in the context of a performance, during which performers are exposed and vulnerable in front of an audience. Weakened defenses during high-pressure moments like being onstage can result in significant anxiety. By examining, reflecting on, and facing their defenses in a safe, nonjudgmental space (such as the counseling room), performers can begin to build other ways to cope with anxiety without relying on defenses.

    Example: A highly anxious violinist and I explored her early attachment to primary caregivers as a way of investigating which defenses were created to cope with psychologically threatening situations. She identified a need to please and a familiar feeling of guilt, recalling moments during her childhood when she'd feel immense pressure to excel at school and make sure she never got in trouble to keep her mother happy. These defenses lost their effectiveness during performances, when she had no choice but to confront the prospect of disappointing her audiences. By tolerating the negative feelings concealed by her defenses (guilt and fear of disappointing), we were able to reduce the anxiety she felt when such feelings got triggered in the context of performing.

8. *Consider the use of beta-blockers.* James Bourgeois (1991) reviewed a series of studies that looked at the treatment of performance anxiety in performers and concluded that, after ruling out conditions such as panic disorder and social phobia, the use of beta-adrenergic blockers can be appropriate and effective. Though this type of medication, typically prescribed for high blood pressure, will not address the underlying psychological factors contributing to the experience of performance anxiety, beta-blockers can be helpful in reducing the intensity of physical symptoms, such as tachycardia and tremor, which can be debilitating during performances. Of course, as with any medication, side effects need to be considered.

   > Example: A musical theater actor I once worked with was apprehensive about taking medication for his performance anxiety. He thought it was cheating and that, by doing so, he wasn't addressing the underlying cause. Our sessions mostly involved countering the body's anxiety responses with relaxation and meditation techniques, as well as verbally articulating the joy he got out of performing. Eventually, he found that the occasional use of a beta-blocker (which he received from his prescribing doctor) was a good supplement to our in-session work, especially before a particularly important audition.

9. *Encourage physical exercise.* Exercise has well-documented benefits for reducing anxiety (Broman-Fulks et al., 2004; Byrne & Byrne, 1993; Guszkowska, 2004). Performers, who already use physical activity as a vehicle for creative expression onstage, will benefit from becoming aware of how their bodies' responses to anxiety are triggered. Dancers, whose profession entails physical movement, can try using their bodies in new ways: modern dancers can try swimming, tap dancers can try volleyball, ballet dancers can try Zumba dance, and so on.

   > Example: When I worked with an opera singer who had high anticipatory performance anxiety—sometimes starting days or even weeks before the performance date—he agreed to meet with a personal trainer with whom he developed a workout schedule that involved 30 to 45 minutes of aerobic exercise three times a week. At the end of each training session, he'd report feeling stronger and more aware of his muscles and breathing, which gave him confidence to confront the audience, knowing that his body wouldn't go straight into a panic mode.

10. *Try stress inoculation.* An analysis of 37 studies with 1,837 participants demonstrated that stress-inoculation training effectively reduced performance anxiety and enhanced stress-inducing performances (Saunders

et al., 1996). Stress inoculation involves anticipating and preparing for an upcoming performance by setting realistic expectations and becoming aware of the stress-related symptoms the performer is most likely to encounter. Performers invite, or at the very least accept, the feeling of anxiety by asserting that they're not afraid of it and that they're open to experiencing it as something normal and familiar and as an opportunity to utilize learned coping skills.

> Example: During a session with an anxious jazz saxophonist, I asked him to make a list of possible expectations associated with an important upcoming performance. He admitted to anticipating familiar negative thoughts such as "I won't be able to get in the zone" and "My shoulders will tense up." Keeping these negative outcomes in mind, we focused on rehearsing coping strategies, such as repeating helpful affirmations ("I know how to get in the zone") and moving rhythmically to relax the shoulders.

11. *Improve preparation habits.* Clinicians can ask clients to think about their practice and performance preparation habits (how often they practice, for how long, what practice methods they use, and so on), and to evaluate them in terms of helpfulness. The goal is to reinforce the ones that help performers feel more confident. Though the amount of preparation is not always predictive of the presence of performance anxiety (McGrath et al., 2017), some habits relating to how performers get ready for a show or an audition can be instrumental in managing anxiety.

> Example: When a pianist described some of his practice habits, we discovered that he was unintentionally reinforcing anxiety-inducing habits by having poor body posture while practicing and, consequently, while performing. In addition, after a small warm-up routine, he would jump straight into demanding pieces. To improve preparation habits, he worked on changing his posture to facilitate calmer breathing and doubled his warm-up time before moving on to difficult material.

12. *Try brainspotting.* This therapeutic technique, developed by David Grand (2013), is often used with athletes, artists, and performers who've gone through trauma that resurfaces during moments of performance, leading to intense anxiety. It's used when athletes and performers "choke" onstage and cannot perform well, despite high levels of preparation, skill, and dedication. The underlying idea is that severe stage fright is often associated with past traumatic experiences. This technique involves identifying the "brainspot," the eye position related to the activation of

an emotionally charged experience in the brain, and reprocessing and reconditioning the person's response to the same traumatic event.

> Example: With the help of a therapist trained in brainspotting,[1] an actor who had panic attacks right before auditions slowly moved her eyes until a spot elicited tension and shakiness associated with a painful memory of being ridiculed by her father for forgetting her lines during a childhood play. She and the brainspotting specialist reexplored the incident while maintaining the eye position on the sensitive spot.

13. *Emphasize the artistic content.* I frequently encounter clients whose tension is visibly reduced when they talk about the meaning and message behind each performance, instead of the high stakes associated with doing well. Performers' anxiety is relieved by focusing on the lyrics, the story, and the overall creative vision being expressed. Thinking of oneself as a vehicle and a communicator of an artistic message helps reduce the anxiety that comes from associating a performance strictly with the performer's merit.

> Example: One of my singer-songwriter-actor clients ruminated over what audiences would think right before every performance. To help shift the focus of her thoughts, I asked her to identify and verbalize what she hoped to communicate through the performance. She thought about the emotional impact of the lyrics she sang, the powerful messages of the characters she embodied, and the immersive musical experience of her melodies. Going onstage with the intention of communicating a message to the audience helped tame her anxiety.

Additional Interventions

14.
15.
16.

Takeaways

* Performance anxiety is a common experience reflecting performers' state of arousal while onstage. It can severely limit, or even end, a career due to its strong physical, mental, and emotional effects.

- Factors that heighten the intensity of performance anxiety include a performer's need for perfection or rigid, all-or-nothing, ways of thinking; the perception of the audience's importance; the way the performer feels about the work he or she presents; and performing conditions.
- Counseling can help performers understand the conscious and unconscious meaning assigned to the experience of performing.
- Clinicians and clients can work on managing the body's reactions and on minimizing the impact of harmful thoughts. This will help clients see performances as chances to foster and demonstrate their enjoyment of the performing experience.
- By increasing confidence, improving preparation habits, and embracing the vulnerability associated with being onstage, counseling increases performers' comfort with the idea of being evaluated.

Note

1 For information on trainings, you can visit https://brainspotting.pro/panel/information-trainings.

References

Bourgeois, J. (1991). Management of performance anxiety with beta-adrenergic blockers. *Jefferson Journal of Psychiatry*, *9*(2), 13–28.

Broman-Fulks, J. J., Berman, M. E., Rabian, B., & Webster, M. J. (2004). Effects of aerobic exercise on anxiety sensitivity. *Behavior Research and Therapy*, *42*(2), 125–136.

Brooks, A. W. (2013). Get excited: Reappraising pre-performance anxiety as excitement. *Journal of Experimental Psychology: General*, *143*(3), 1144–1158.

Byrne, A., & Byrne, D. G. (1993). The effect of exercise on depression, anxiety and other mood states: A review. *Journal of Psychosomatic Research*, *37*, 565–574.

Csikszentmihalyi, M. (1997). *Creativity. The flow and the psychology of discovery of invention.* New York, NY: HarperCollins Publishers.

Ferraro, T. (1999). A psychoanalytic perspective on anxiety in athletes. *Online Journal of Sport Psychology*, *1*(2), 15–21.

Grand, D. (2013). *Brainspotting: The revolutionary new therapy for rapid and effective change.* Boulder, CO: Sounds True.

Guszkowska, M, (2004). Effects of exercise on anxiety, depression and mood. *Psychiatria polska. 38.* 611–20.

Kelly, V. C., & Saveanu, R. (2005). Performance anxiety: How to ease stage fright. *Current Psychiatry*, *4*(6), 25–34.

Kenny, D. (2005). A systematic review of treatments for music performance anxiety. *Anxiety, Stress, and Coping*, *18*(3), 183–208.

Kenny, D. (2011). *The psychology of music performance anxiety*. Oxford: Oxford University Press.

Kenny, D. T., Arthey, S., & Abbass, A. (2014). Intensive short-term dynamic psychotherapy for severe music performance anxiety. *Medical Problems of Performing Artists*, *29*(1), 3–7.

MacNamara, A., Button, A., & Collins, D. (2010). The role of psychological characteristics in facilitating the pathway to elite performance part 1: Identifying mental skills and behaviors. *The Sport Psychologist, 24*, 52–73.

McGrath, C., Hendricks, K. S., & Smith, T. D. (2017). *Performance anxiety strategies: A musician's guide to managing stage fright*. Lanham, MD: Rowman & Littlefield.

Parker, W. D., & Adkins, K. K. (1995). Perfectionism and the gifted. *Roeper Review, 17*(3), 173–176.

Saunders, T., Driskell, J. E., Johnston, J. H., & Salas, E. (1996). The effect of stress inoculation training on anxiety and performance. *Journal of Occupational Health Psychology, 1*(2), 170–186.

Steptoe, A., & Fidler, H. (1987). Stage fright in orchestral musicians: A study of cognitive and behavioral strategies in performance anxiety. *British Journal of Psychology, 78*, 241–249. doi:10.1111/j.2044-8295.1987.tb02243.x

Swart I. (2010). *The influence of trauma on musicians* (Unpublished doctoral dissertation). University of Pretoria, Pretoria, South Africa.

Thomson, P., & Jaque, S. V. (2017). *Creativity and the performing artist: Behind the mask*. London, UK: Academic Press.

Valentine, E. (2002). *The fear of performance*. In J. Rinkey (Ed.), *Musical performance: A guide to understanding*. Cambridge: Cambridge University Press.

Wilson, G. D. (2001). *Psychology for performing artists: Butterflies and Bouquets* (2nd ed.). Hoboken, NJ: Wiley.

Woodman, J. P., & Moore, N. R. (2012). Evidence for the effectiveness of Alexander Technique lessons in medical and health-related conditions: A systematic review. *International Journal of Clinical Practice, 66*(1), 98–112.

Yatabe, K., Yui, N., Kasuya, S., Fujia, H., Tateishi, K., Terawaki, F., & Musha, H. (2014). Anxiety and mood among ballet dancers: A pilot study on effects of a medical approach invoking periodic intervention. *Annals of Sports Medicine and Research, 1*(1), 1002.

Chapter 8

Artists' and Performers' Bodies

When I worked with a 25-year-old dancer and actress, I was struck by a noticeable contrast: on one side was a highly confident woman who performed in front of hundreds of people many times a month; intensely goal oriented, she managed to set up one performing gig after the other. The other side revealed a vulnerable, self-doubting woman racked with insomnia-inducing anxiety over whether she'd get hired. She got depressed when she disappointed peers and directors, and she worried constantly about how she looked. In particular, she worried that she wouldn't get parts because, in her eyes, she didn't have a "celebrity body." To maximize her chances of getting hired, she'd developed habits that put her physical health at risk: she'd go hours without eating, especially before auditions, and she'd practice without breaks, ignoring sensations of fatigue, pain, and hunger. When she wanted to celebrate a good show, she'd eat large amounts of food, rich in sugar and carbs, but would make up for it the next day by not eating at all. Her successes proved she could handle many aspects of her career. She set goals, networked with industry professionals, and knew her strengths as a performer. However, she was mistreating the one thing she needed to ensure long-term career success: her body.

The body—a tool for creative expression, an object to be "consumed" by spectators, and a vehicle for demonstrating skills and talents—is an indispensable part of artists' and performers' careers. It needs to be nurtured and protected to achieve career longevity and overall wellness. However, artists and performers often throw self-care to the bottom of the list when demands for excellence kick in. Preoccupied with perfect results or the right "look," artists and performers place great stress on their bodies. I've worked with musicians who go home after an MRI exam for pain in their hand only to practice for hours on end, fighting through the pain. I've had sessions with actors who've repeatedly binged and purged to stay at a desired weight, ignoring the health risks. Like the singer and actress discussed previously, many artists and performers are subject to demands (both internally and externally driven) placed on their bodies. Two ways in which such demands affect their physical health are the development of disordered eating and the incurrence of injuries. This chapter is divided into two parts that explore each of these topic areas. Through the lenses of eating disorders and injuries, we'll look at how the body sometimes suffers in the name of creative excellence.

Clearly, the psychological experience of having an eating disorder is vastly different from that of an injury. Eating disorders—a diagnosable psychiatric condition specifically addressed in the Diagnostic and Statistical Manual (DSM), characterized by a range of emotional and behavioral symptoms around food and body image—seep into broader areas of psychological functioning. They cause a distorted self-image, intrusive obsessions about calorie intake, and low self-esteem. Injuries, on the other hand, are just that: physical harm or damage. They cause physical discomfort, which in turn interferes with the ability to achieve desired results. They might lead artists with repetitive strain injury (RSI) to disregard their bodies' warning signs, to self-medicate to dull the pain, and to hide all evidence of the injury to protect their reputations. In light of such differences, the two topics, along with suggestions for treatment interventions, are addressed separately.

Despite the differences, however, certain similarities tie these two topics together. The most obvious connection is that both eating disorders and injuries speak to the damage caused by high expectations around artists' and performers' bodies. Eating disorders and injuries are different expressions of the pressure to demonstrate flawlessness in looks and physical mastery. Injuries resulting from poor practice and performing habits and disordered eating among performing artists often reflect similar rigid thinking (a performance is either horrible or perfect; one is either adored or hated). When artists and performers think this way, they'll go to great lengths to ensure positive outcomes, even if that means health problems later on. Another pertinent connection is that performers with eating disorders and preoccupations with the body are likelier to exercise excessively, adding to the risk of strain or injury (Thomson & Jaque, 2017). Last, injuries—whether single incidents or repetitive—and eating disorders can have similar effects on livelihoods and mental health: they can trigger depressive episodes, impair the quality of creative work, and prematurely end careers (Hamilton, 1998).

This chapter explores the shared themes of the role of body as an instrument for creative expression and for professional success. It investigates what makes artists and performers both objectify and neglect this sacred vessel. It provides guidance on treatment that prioritizes physical health, yet honors the daily sacrifices performers have to make to pursue their creative dreams.

Part I: Eating Disorders

The physical aesthetic ideals that permeate the dance, acting, music, and other performing-arts industries can't be ignored. Performers trying to land lead parts tell of being scrutinized for excess weight, of being compared to thinner candidates, and of being asked to follow strict diet and exercise regimens. A musical theater performer once told me she'd been highly praised at her audition, but had been warned she wouldn't get the role unless she lost 15 pounds. This might have been less devastating had she not heard similar comments throughout her career—from her teenage years well into adulthood. A seemingly confident, outspoken person, she changed completely as she spoke to me about her embarrassment over the size of her legs and stomach. She averted her eyes and lowered her voice as she described what she'd felt when, as a child, she'd discovered how good she was at singing and dancing, yet, simultaneously, how she wouldn't get cast because of the shape of her body. To cope, she took turns between crash dieting, binge eating followed by excessive exercising, and simply taking long breaks from auditioning to avoid confronting her feelings about her weight—which, of course, drastically decreased her career prospects. Most importantly, her response to the message that she didn't look right cultivated a deep sense of well-concealed, yet profoundly impactful, self-rejection. She had constant feelings of body dissatisfaction and turned her body into an enemy that deserved to be punished for not cooperating. Unfortunately, similar experiences ring true for many performers.

Prevalence and Performing-Arts Culture

The performing genre, the culture around one's training, professional demands, and each performer's unique psychological traits all affect the extent to which eating disorders abound in the performing arts. Based on the analysis of 33 relevant studies by Arcelus and his colleagues (2014), ballet dancers were found to have a documented overall eating disorder prevalence of 16.4 percent, a prevalence of 4 percent for anorexia nervosa (the obsessive preoccupation with weight loss), and a prevalence of 14.9 percent for eating disorders not otherwise specified.[1] The risk of developing an eating disorder, according to the study's conclusion, is three times higher for ballet dancers than it is for the general population. Another study showed that 55 percent of ballet dancers had symptoms of eating disorders not otherwise specified, 6.9 percent had symptoms of anorexia nervosa, and 10.3 had symptoms of bulimia nervosa (binge eating and purging) (Ringham et al., 2006). In 1998, Linda Hamilton found that "as many as 46 percent of dancers report eating problems," although in a survey study she did for *Dance Magazine*, 4 percent of dancers met the clinical criteria for a diagnosis of an eating disorder. In another study, eating disorders, as well as other disordered eating habits that don't meet criteria for diagnoses, were higher in dancers than nondancers (Friesen et al., 2011). It's important to remember that disordered eating in dancers goes beyond what one might typically expect, such as refusal to eat. It includes harmful food-related habits like all-day food restriction followed by binge eating at night, use of laxatives to lose weight, purging without binge eating, and excessive dieting after meals.

Eating disorders tend to emerge at a young age. When activities that value appearance begin at an early age, preoccupation with thinness tends to increase (Thomson & Jaque, 2017). A study of ballet students with a mean age of 15 showed high scores in eating disorder inventory scales (Thomas et al., 2005). For young dancers who are beginning to consider a career in dancing, the messages about the importance of thinness that come from trainers and coaches are crucial (Penniment & Egan, 2012). A supportive space that acknowledges the impact of unrealistic demands, educates dancers and other performers on the dangers of eating disorders, and promotes dancers based on merit rather than physical appearance is much less likely to communicate the implicit value of extreme weight loss; therefore, it's less likely to contribute to the development of an eating disorder.

It's not just the culture in ballet that leads dancers to be preoccupied with their bodies: modern dancers, too, want to maintain a lean body and experience anxiety around their shape, though eating disorder rates tend to be lower than those in ballet dancers (Reel, 2003). The pressure to be thin isn't exclusive to dancers. Actors and singers are subject to the same expectations that trigger weight-related obsessions. In the competitive world of the performing arts, where industry hopefuls compete fiercely for a limited number of sought-after opportunities, having a body that's different from those represented in film and onstage is perceived as undesirable and a disadvantage. Whereas a ballet dancer might try to live up to the image of the long, slender ballerina, other performing artists often aspire to physical ideals of thinness promoted by the media and pop culture, resulting in what Thomson and Jaque (2017) describe as the objectification of their bodies. To achieve the idealized physique of a movie star or a chart-topping artist, performers frequently turn to extreme dieting, binge eating and purging, excessive exercising, and obsessive calorie counting. An actor, who'd already achieved moderate success with small roles in sitcoms, was so concerned with being called "fat" online that he'd go on extreme diets for the duration of the shoots (by eating only a bowl of yogurt, a piece of toast, and a piece of fruit all day), and then binge eat when he was done filming.

These weight-loss methods can provide temporary feelings of satisfaction with performers' abilities to assert control over their bodies, which can be mistaken for confidence—a necessary and highly desirable trait in order to muster the courage to audition for role after role. However, the false sense of confidence is temporary and superficial, and it quickly wears off. It reveals a self-rejecting attitude and a conditional sense of self-love ("I love myself only when I weigh a specific amount"). This feeling intensifies after rejections or critiques from powerful people in the industry. Vulnerable performers, upon hearing they aren't good enough, develop an even more hostile response toward their bodies. Along with hostility come feelings of isolation, depression, anxiety, shame, and obsessive rumination about food.

Not all performers develop eating disorders even though they're all exposed to similar pressure. What sets apart those who do from those who don't? As is the case for eating disorders in the general population, this is not a single-answer question. As discussed previously, for performers it's a combination of the culture's aesthetic ideals, the pressure experienced on an interpersonal level (criticism from coaches, rigid weight criteria in order to be considered for parts), and the personal psychological traits unique to each person (a high need for control, self-aggressive tendencies, and perfectionism).

Perfectionism

Obsessive tendencies and perfectionist personality traits have long been linked to eating disorders (Bastiani et al., 1995; Bulik et al., 2003; Thomson & Jaque, 2017). Performers, especially those in highly competitive fields, such as classical ballet, where discipline and self-sacrifice are highly valued (Hamilton, 1997; Thomson & Jaque, 2017), rely on their perfectionism to train hard and to persevere when things get tough. A fictionalized, and surely exaggerated, representation of these dynamics is captured in Darren Aronofsky's 2010 movie, *Black Swan*, in which the lead performer's obsession with becoming the perfect prima ballerina leads to a spiraling of psychological disturbances.

Performers with certain physical and psychological attributes might still have developed eating disorders had they not become performers: however, the performing-arts world is a highly triggering environment that enables preexisting tendencies. One dancer I worked with identified perfectionism in herself from a very young age. As a 5-year-old, she'd had her first exposure to feelings of perfectionistic anxiety during a casual and fun school activity. At the teacher's suggestion, students tried to draw a picture of their favorite animals. Most students drew an indeterminate and ambiguous mass with four legs and two eyes. My client, however, aware of how the creature she was drawing looked nothing like her pet cat, felt a rush of compelling persistence to keep trying until she got it right. Ignoring her teacher's reassurance that what she'd done was fine, she was taken over by an obsessive energy to strive for perfection. A few years later, when she discovered her passion for creative expression through dance, she entered into a setting that, unfortunately, allowed her to project her perceived inadequacies ("My technique is never good enough," "I don't look graceful and thin enough"). Through dance training she could set her controlling perfectionism in motion ("I can't control every aspect of my career, but I can control how many hours I practice, and I can control my body by exercising more and eating less"). Being praised by her instructors and peers for her self-discipline and sacrifices, my client never got the chance to practice tolerating mistakes and imperfection. Her psychological and personality traits, combined with her love for dance as an art medium and the environment's perpetuation of a narrow body-type ideal, all contributed to her abusing her body as a means of satisfying these demands.

Health Effects of Disordered Eating

The psychological effects of eating disorders in performers include depression, low energy, and anxiety from the constant scrutiny of one's body and appearance. Eating disorders can cause decreased empathy and emotion-recognition skills, which are particularly important for actors whose onstage presentation of characters relies on the sophisticated use of emotions (Kucharska-Pietura et al., 2004). A performer with a reduced ability to empathize and recognize emotions in others will have a hard time identifying, developing, and portraying a character successfully, and will likely struggle to develop meaningful personal relationships with collaborators and peers. Furthermore, the medical complications associated with anorexia, bulimia, and other types of disordered eating can be extremely serious and damaging to performers' health and careers. Ranging from cardiovascular anomalies and gastrointestinal problems to excessive fatigue and dental problems, eating disorders are extremely harmful (Casiero, 2006; James, 2006). Excessive exercising and poor nutritional habits increase the likelihood that performers will sustain injuries (Thomson & Jaque, 2017). Without prevention and early detection, eating disorders can get in the way of career longevity and satisfaction, and in severe cases become life threatening.

The Clinician's Role

Appreciating Performers' Conflicts

Working with performing artists with eating disorders is a challenge because it requires fully grasping the conflicts around issues of health, both physical and emotional, and career-imposed body ideals. Sure, a clinician could propose to an actor with disordered eating that he leave the industry altogether, or suggest to a dancer that she embrace her full figure. But these interventions wouldn't speak to the person's deep commitment to his or her craft, nor to the realities of the pressures to maintain a certain size. In addition, clinicians and clients alone cannot change systemic aesthetic and physical demands in performing-arts careers. They are caught in a delicate balancing act between the choice to be healthy and constraints about extreme body ideals—between self-acceptance and conformity.

The first objective is to demonstrate empathy by gaining insight into what messages the performing artist has internalized. For men, such messages might be less about thinness and more about muscle mass and definition. For actors, they might be about fitting the body type of the lead role. For dancers, they might be about the value placed on self-sacrificing behaviors for the sake of a "dancer's body." Carefully listening to the client's experience is essential to make the client feel safe, understood, and valued.

Clinicians may wish to do their own independent research, to ask questions, and to read relevant literature to understand the conditions faced by performing artists. This will help them develop a more nuanced perspective on the pressures around eating. For example, when Joe, a singer I worked with, presented with many textbook symptoms of an eating disorder (obsessive thinking about calories and food choices, going extremely long periods without eating, and weight loss) my initial thought was that the disordered eating had to do with maintaining a thin appearance for his shows. However, the nature of the obsessions revealed preoccupations and extreme rigidity around healthy eating habits in order to prevent any damage to his voice. He opened up about the pressures of having to sing demanding roles in front of large audiences, and the ways in which eliminating all spicy food, junk food, dairy products, caffeine, and alcohol helped him feel more in control over the sound of his voice. To maintain the quality of his singing, he refused to eat in restaurants with friends, spent hours worrying about what to eat, and felt tremendous guilt for every lapse. After looking into more information on similar concerns, I realized that Joe was not alone in these behaviors. What he described—documented as *orthorexia*,[2] the pathological focus on health and nutrition (Koven & Abry, 2015)—abounds in performing artists according to a 2009 study (Aksoydan & Camci, 2009). Singers' anxieties about protecting their voices and the disordered eating habits they develop to sound perfect offer insight into a different kind of manifestation of the demands placed on performers' bodies. Clinicians who work with this population must make sure that they leave no stone unturned to understand all the connecting parts.

Using Psychoeducation

Upon developing a thorough understanding of the circumstances around the person's eating disorder, clinicians can incorporate psychoeducation regarding food and diet. For example, a dancer with anorexia nervosa may express satisfaction in how calorie restriction helps her look thinner onstage, fit into costumes better, and get parts more easily; however, she may not have fully considered the long-term risks associated with food deprivation, such as fatigue, dehydration, and proneness to injury (Liederbach & Campagno, 2001).

Often a performer intellectually knows this information but still struggles with making healthy choices when caught in emotionally triggering moments, such as learning that one didn't get a part because of one's size. In line with motivational interviewing approaches, it's important for clinicians to use each session to articulate and reinforce the dangers of eating disorders and the negative impact they can have on health and career longevity, while acknowledging the pressures performers face around excessive thinness.

Empowering Vulnerable Clients

Eating disorders can become all-consuming conditions that diminish a person's sense of autonomy and self-esteem. It's important for counseling sessions to help empower clients by strengthening their personal agency and confidence in their choices. This kind of work requires moving well past the bounds of the most recent symptoms and experiences that initially bring clients to the office. Clinicians may want to look into incidents that have weakened their clients' sense of autonomy, such as having been harshly reprimanded by early caretakers and authority figures. Empowering clients involves improving their interpersonal skills so that they're better at setting boundaries and seeking out supportive figures that help them feel safe enough to make healthy choices.

Freedom to make choices is important because it allows performers to embrace a wider range of body-type representations in performances, seek out like-minded collaborators, and value diversity. Joe, the singer with symptoms of orthorexia, started to look for role models that challenged notions of generic, cookie-cutter singing voices and became more comfortable with the idea that a slight rasp or hoarseness in his voice might shift his singing-career options, but would not end them. Sure, he remained vigilant about overall health and nutrition, but we worked on incorporating flexible attitudes. Luckily, despite the cognitive rigidity that characterizes many people with eating disorders, creative people are, by and large, at an advantage when it comes to the ability to demonstrate flexibility and fluidity in thinking styles. This means that, perhaps, they could be open to changing some of their perspectives on expectations related to their bodies and appearance.

Increasing Assertiveness

In line with the idea of empowerment and cultivating a sense of agency, clinicians can encourage their clients to practice speaking up and, when possible, to act as their own advocates. Though the focus is on clients' well-being rather than on bearing the responsibility of changing the status quo, I've worked with clients who've benefited from pointing out discrimination based on size and asking their professional dance schools to provide eating disorder treatment resources. Some have gone on to establish dance and theater companies that cultivate a culture of body positivity and that don't exert the same type of size-related pressures.

Balancing the Need to Be Healthy With Industry Standards

Clinicians can help clients develop their own perspectives regarding which industry norms they choose to adhere to. It's important to focus on protecting clients' identities as performers while ensuring that their health is prioritized. When weight loss is necessary, clinicians can express recognition of the real pressures that their clients are experiencing and open up a discussion on healthy ways to do so. Other times, striking a balance might mean having to turn down a part, audition for a different role, or take time off to focus on other things. Attempts toward establishing a balance might include involving outside resources such as the help of a nutritionist, family, friends, coaches, and trainers. Turning to others can create a supportive safety net that helps vulnerable clients maintain perspective on their priorities.

Treatment Goals

1.   Reduce preoccupations with food and weight.
2.   Improve body satisfaction.
3.   Identify and confront environmental pressures to be thin.
4.   Develop healthy eating and exercise habits.
5.   Balance career- and health-related needs.

Suggested Interventions to Achieve Goals

1. *Substitute emphasis on size with emphasis on health.* Performing artists frequently hold onto harmful beliefs such as that shape is more important than stamina (Hamilton, 1998), or that thinness is aesthetically preferable to a fuller body type. Emphasis placed on size not only promotes disordered eating but also undervalues other qualities that are essential for a successful and fulfilling career, such as physical strength, overall health, talent, and unique skills. Clinicians can work with their clients to uncover harmful beliefs associated with the significance of body shape, and underscore the role that other characteristics have played for creative and professional satisfaction.

   Example: I once asked a dancer to discuss ways in which her strong and healthy body has helped her complete difficult dance routines or stay up for many hours practicing. She initially focused on results that related to her appearance ("People said I looked beautiful during my jump") but I urged her to think about words related to how she felt ("I felt competent and powerful"). Once she got used to valuing strength and stamina, she noticed she was making more associations between meals and health, rather than weight.

2. *"Negotiate" with industry's standards.* Artists who are evaluated on the basis of their appearance (whether they "look" the part), and who rely on such evaluations to move ahead, usually think they have no choice but to adhere to such norms. A part that calls for a lead in her 20s invites comparisons to other such characters, among whom there tends to be little variation in body types. In dance, a similar idea is that a dancer's body must be long, lean, and thin. Although it's true that restrictive industry standards about artists' bodies often come into play, relinquishing all power and personal accountability causes additional psychological damage. Clinicians can work with their clients to challenge rigid weight standards by encouraging them to connect with like-minded performers, casting agents, production managers, and coaches. In addition, even when roles seem to be out of reach because they're traditionally given to thin candidates, clinicians can encourage their clients to continue to seek them out so that they demonstrate other ways they're right for the part.

   > Example: An actress I worked with, who struggled with a thyroid condition that made it difficult for her to lose weight, continued to try out for leading parts until she found a production team that held similar values on the qualities that make for exceptional acting: instead of paying attention to a candidate's size, casting agents, directors, and producers prioritized the actors' ability to bring their characters to life.

3. *Encourage conversations on eating habits.* Despite the prevalence of eating disorders in the performing arts, one's peers, coaches, and colleagues might be inclined to look the other way. This inclination reflects the systemic perception of eating disorders as an inevitable extension of the field's body-consciousness, resulting in a don't-ask-don't-tell mentality. It's important for clinicians to resist falling into the same trap by assuming that their clients' excessive dieting and exercising are normal reactions to career norms. Clinicians must follow clients' lead, as they may not always volunteer details around disordered eating. But when an opening presents itself, clinicians ought to pursue it, rather than assume that weight-related concerns are inevitable among performers.

   > Example: A recent acting-school graduate, thin but not underweight, sought out treatment for generalized anxiety and depression. She occasionally hinted at weight-related anxiety, jokingly stating that she'd better keep the weight off to get cast, but she never shared more. After yet another casual mention of how she mustn't gain weight before her next audition, I asked her if it'd be alright to talk more about her weight concerns. When she responded that it would, I gently inquired about the pressure she felt to keep weight

off. This simple question led to an outpouring of revelations about her efforts to lose weight, including her habit of purging.

4. *Promote art-body synergy.* Performing artists' bodies become the site and vehicle for expressing their art. Art and body coexist in a relationship that requires physical health in order to realize artistic potential. Sessions can focus on empowering the integrity of clients' artistic visions by highlighting how a healthy body that's well taken care of can ensure a long and creatively fulfilling career, and thus opportunities for creative expression. This intervention also applies to injured artists and performers who push themselves to achieve flawless, machine-like results. In such cases sessions can emphasize proper physical care as a means to achieving creative goals (see part II of this chapter on injuries).

> Example: I once asked a dancer with bulimia to talk about what artistic message she tried to communicate through her dancing. Combined with a guided relaxation exercise to help her connect to her body's physical sensations, we worked on highlighting how her body acted as an instrument for expressing her feelings. Her strong legs could perform high kicks that could show anger; her core, supported and sustained by muscles that depend on the intake of necessary carbohydrates and proteins, could facilitate a dynamic posture to communicate pride and power.

5. *Suggest practicing mindful eating.* Arthur-Cameselle (2017) makes a case for the helpfulness of *mindful eating*, meaning the conscious, nonjudgmental, attentive awareness of everything involved during one's meal, including the origins of the ingredients, the colors of the food, the duration of the meal, and the way it satisfies hunger. Performers and artists whose size is an important factor for their professional success can become mindful of how food stimulates the senses and evokes emotions. Clinicians can focus on helping their clients develop a constructive relationship with food—eating to be healthy, and stopping when they've had enough.

> Example: Instead of dissociating from his hunger and fullness cues, a singer and dancer I recently worked with practiced eating mindfully by taking breaks throughout the day to check in with his body's needs, and by noticing the nutritious value of the food he chose to eat. Doing so weakened some of his unhealthy automatic eating habits, such as skipping meals or eating mindlessly when bored or stressed.

6. *Manage perfectionism.* Obsession with perfection is prevalent in eating-disordered clients (Egan et al., 2014), as well as in certain types of performing arts, such as ballet, which has rigid ideals of what a perfect ballerina must look like. To reduce the frequency and intensity of food

and weight preoccupations, treatment can begin by targeting the perfectionistic tendencies that sustain them. Examples of habits clinicians can inculcate to minimize the impact of perfectionistic thinking patterns are practicing self-compassion during internal dialogues, tolerating mistakes, and evaluating the real (as opposed to the feared) consequences associated with imperfection.

> Example: A contemporary dancer who was a self-described perfectionist approached me to "improve her relationship to food." After a few sessions, she identified the all-or-nothing rules she tended to follow—that is, she could be either fat or thin, she could either monitor every calorie or lose self-control, and she could be either adored or ridiculed for her body. We worked on relabeling "rules" as gentle guides, merely pointing in the right direction, which allowed room for less-than-perfect results.

7. *Encourage experimentation with roles.* Recommending that a performer choose different roles—perhaps ones that have flexible size requirements and therefore don't exacerbate disordered eating—may seem like giving up. It may feel like telling clients to abandon their dreams because of how they look. However, flexibility in the types of parts one tries out for conveys an empowering message: that performers have choices, creativity lies in more than one performance style, and the problem isn't with the person's appearance but with rigid industry traditions.

> Example: A college dance student who'd spent most of her life training in ballet had been accustomed to hearing that she had the "wrong body for ballet." Sometimes she was told she was too muscular, or that her arms and legs weren't long enough. Initially, she took these remarks as a challenge to work hard and mold her body into a stereotypical ballerina's body. However, our work together revealed the damaging psychological impact that continuously rejecting her body was having on her self-worth. With the same enthusiasm, now hoping that her natural body type would find more acceptance, she decided to take modern dance and jazz dance classes.

8. *Refer to a nutritionist.* Coordinated care by nutritionists and medical and mental health professionals is particularly effective for treating eating disorders. A nutritionist who understands the physical needs of the performer-athlete, along with the aesthetic needs of the performer-artist, will be able to guide clients around proper nutrition and fueling before and after training. Major concerns will be how to eat leading up to performances, how to eat to prevent fatigue and soreness, when to hydrate to avoid bloating (which interferes with costume fitting), and so forth.

> Example: A dancer who had made great progress in understanding the roots of her anorexia, her beliefs about industry demands, and

the interpersonal relationship patterns that sustained it was ready to make changes in her approach to eating. The steps she took were small but noticeable. With the help of a specialized dietician, she became better educated about which foods gave her energy, the kinds of snacks that have nutritional value, and nutritional habits that help sustain lean body mass.

9. *Distinguish between self-referenced and interpersonal comparisons.* In a 2009 study by de Bruin and colleagues, gymnasts' and dancers' tendencies to compare themselves to others was a risk factor for developing disordered eating; however, those who were motivated by task mastery and improvement for improvement's sake didn't indicate higher incidence of eating-disorder symptoms. A shift in comparison targets gradually diminishes competitive attitudes (such as focusing on who's thinner or who gets more callbacks) that tend to reinforce disordered eating.

Example: During my work with a highly competitive singer and dancer, I asked him to come up with small weekly goals to demonstrate progress in something he found challenging in his craft. Examples of the goals he came up with were to achieve better balance during a leg extension, or to improve breathing in passages involving long notes. As we compared notes on his weekly performances, he focused less on what others were doing and more on becoming better in his own eyes. When the pressure of outperforming others decreased, his restrictive eating habits became less prominent.

Additional Interventions

10.
11.
12.

Part II: Injuries

Stephanie, an opera singer I once worked with, suffered from discomfort in her vocal chords that persisted for months. She could sing beautifully up to a certain note of the scale. Above that point, she'd feel a strain, the accumulation of phlegm, and a distortion in her tone. Because of this, she'd cancel her voice coaching lessons, hoping that her coaches wouldn't notice. She hesitated to ask for help, fearing that her "vocal issue" would indicate bad technique, and that word would spread making her less hireable. She was caught between downplaying her discomfort, both to others and to herself, and becoming increasingly aware of the limitations imposed by it. Unfortunately, when she did finally get help, she was diagnosed with vocal polyps, which required her to take time off from singing. She blamed herself for not having sought help earlier, yet the no-pain-no-gain attitude she'd cultivated throughout her career made her think that admitting injury meant admitting defeat.

Despite the high risk of injuries in professional artists, especially performers, this kind of attitude is common. Surveys of artists who've experienced, or performed under, physical distress document proportions as high as 79 percent of musicians having pain from playing (Brandfonbrener, 2009), 55 percent of Broadway actors and dancers sustaining injuries from performing (Evans et al., 1996), and 82 percent of modern dancers performing while injured (Shah et al., 2012). Injuries are sometimes acute and sudden, such as when falling during a performance or pulling a muscle while carrying instruments and other equipment (Klickstein, 2009). More commonly, they result from repetitive and chronic strain placed on the body from overtraining (Thomson & Jaque, 2017). Repetitive movements in physically demanding or contortionist positions increase the risk for knee and ankle injuries in young dancers (Steinberg et al., 2013); prolonged loud music damages musicians' hearing; and the chronic use of certain chemicals leads to respiratory problems and dermatological injuries for printmakers, painters, and sculptors (Zuskin et al., 2007). In a way that echoes the harsh realities discussed in the section on eating disorders, physical injuries reflect an attitude pervasive in the performing arts: striving for perfection, trying to be tough, and having to make sacrifices for one's art.

The Need for Specialized Care

Though artists' injuries are common, treatment warrants a specialized approach—one that may be inadequately addressed by physicians who treat the general population. It wasn't until 1989 that a group of physicians specializing in the health of performing artists formed the Performing Arts Medicine Association to take performing artists' unique physical and psychological needs into consideration. Examples of these needs are the small impairments that result from specific movements associated with playing an instrument, which may go unnoticed or be underestimated by professionals who don't specialize in these types of concerns (Rozmaryn, 1993).

In addition, specialized care ensures that the psychological and environmental factors that affect injured artists and performers are being addressed. For example, regarding psychological factors, performers and artists who are prone to injuries caused by overuse often display traits such as perfectionistic tendencies (Thomson & Jaque, 2017) and a strong desire to please others. They may ignore early signs of physical discomfort, or hesitate to speak up, fearing that they'll be labeled complainers or that they'll miss out on an opportunity. Low self-efficacy, which is associated with the fear of injury in athletes (Chase et al., 2005), was found to increase chances of injuries in circus artists (Shrier & Halle, 2011). Those who doubt their abilities are likely to be less relaxed, risking injuries associated with physical tension and nervousness.

When it comes to environmental factors, performers often endure long practice hours, multiple performances in a single day, poor sleeping conditions on tour, exposure to loud music, and pressure from peers and coaches that the "show must go on." Visual artists spend many hours engrossed in creative work that can't always be left unfinished, while exposed to toxic chemicals and without proper ventilation, eyewash stations, masks, and other precautions (Hamilton, 2000). It's important for treating professionals to understand the attitudes toward tolerating pain in the arts-and-entertainment world (Mainwaring et al., 2001), and the psychological and environmental forces that make artists and performers susceptible to adopting them.

The Psychological Effects of Injuries

Injured artists, by virtue of how devastating serious injuries can be to their careers, experience severe psychological stress. Aside from sudden and acute injury, most injuries result from gradual microtraumas that become increasingly problematic. When artists do notice a problem and take steps to address it, they often feel tremendous anxiety about what it could mean for their ability to work. This anxiety might exacerbate the initial problem or create new ones. Dina, a ceramic artist who worked long hours preparing for a show, was in denial about the symptoms of carpal tunnel syndrome (CTS) that were coming on. She felt numbness and tingling but continued to work on the potter's wheel without taking breaks. When she visited a doctor, who gave her the diagnosis of CTS, she became overwhelmed with paralyzing anxiety about her health, her upcoming show, and her career overall. She obsessively spent hours on online forums reading about other artists' similar stories and prognoses, and stayed up at night assessing every physical sensation she felt in her arm. Paradoxically, however, she continued to work many hours each day to finish what she was planning to exhibit.

The preoccupation over her health combined with the pressure to keep working gave rise to an extremely challenging inner tension. On the one hand, without the ability to work on her art and without the show, Dina risked becoming depressed, as she'd be creatively compromised and without a sense of daily purpose structured around her show. On the other hand, without the break that was necessary for a full recovery, following a possible surgery, she risked long-term and recurrent pain that would remove the joy from making art in the future. Rationally, she knew that career longevity was a priority; however, she found having to redirect her life, which was centered on making art, emotionally challenging. Linda Hamilton (1997), a psychologist who specializes in the mental health of dancers, refers to this kind of emotional pain as the *injured psyche*—the psychological distress that comes from not being able to engage in creative work because of a physical injury.

Mild and moderate injuries trigger intense emotional reactions in artists. They cause anxiety about when and how to seek help, and about having to reveal the injuries to peers and other professionals. A pianist I worked with had to take a few weeks off from practicing as a result of tendon pain. He worried about how the injury would make him "lose his technique," and about the possibility of a future reinjury. Being forced to abstain from the activity that offered him creative fulfillment brought up immediate concerns ("I don't know what to do with my free time" and "I haven't been able to make money from teaching piano"), as well as some big-picture existential worries ("What's my purpose if I can't play?" and "My primary means of expressing myself is in jeopardy"). Missing out on important professional opportunities, especially while peers are getting ahead, spurs anger and frustration. Dancers who had to observe class rather than participate because of mild injuries reported feeling guilt and anger (Mainwaring et al., 2001). Fortunately, however, as psychologically challenging as mild and moderate injuries can be, depending on various internal and external circumstances (resilience, commitment to rehabilitation, access to care, social support, and so forth), artists and performers can develop and maintain an outlook optimistic enough to help them return to their creative work with minimal long-term damage.

Severe injuries, which require prolonged breaks for recovery, put artists at a greater risk for long-term psychological distress. The psychological effects of severe injury on artists involve a wide range of cognitive, emotional, and behavioral responses (Mainwaring et al., 2001). Artists might go through periods of shock or denial about the severity of their injury, engage in cognitive appraisal of the implications of the injury, experience fluctuations between optimism and pessimism about their prognosis, develop a terrifying sense of lack of control or anger about the circumstances that led to the injury, and worry about others' reactions to the injury (Mainwaring et al., 2001). Hamilton (1997) describes three recovery stages: the first one involves denial, both in a protective way, which ensures that artists remain hopeful, and in a harmful way, which interferes with the motivation to get adequate help. The second stage involves commitment to the recovery process by understanding that it's a journey, by anticipating setbacks, and by recognizing small improvements. The third stage, for non-career-ending severe injuries, involves resuming creative work while remaining focused on treatment, accepting limitations, and coming to terms with having to reject opportunities that are too demanding.

Career-ending injuries bring up a different set of psychological challenges. In addition to feelings of shock and disbelief about the nature and extent of the injury, artists and performers must process the dramatic changes in their postinjury lives. A changing identity, from the identity of an active talent to that of an inactive one, introduces a sense of painful self-alienation, and grief over unrealized creative potential. It can also lead to social isolation. Performing artists see their relationships drastically change as they spend less time with peers, coaches, and teachers and miss out on bond-forming trips and performances. Frequently, they're perceived differently by those still involved in the creative work. A hip injury forced a dancer with whom I once worked to drop out of a dance company to which she'd belonged for 15 years. She was surprised at how alienated she'd become from her close circle of friends. She thought that her friends were hesitating to reach out because they feared they'd be reminding her of what she was missing out on and make her sad. She, too, was struggling to relate to the same people she'd once shared so much with—exchanging frustrations about their exhausting schedules, commiserating about teacher demands, and sharing creative ideas about how to approach a dance piece.

Depending on the circumstances of the injury, the impact of such a life-altering shock can introduce posttraumatic stress. Hamilton (1997) points out that every performer's reaction will vary based on unique psychological traits, but she outlines three mourning stages that might apply to performers who've been forced to end their careers. The first one involves looking back on their careers and having to come to terms with ambitions that won't be realized. The second stage involves leaving the performing past behind. The third stage involves moving toward a new career identity. Career-ending injuries require artists and performers to face the daunting task of transitioning to a different kind of work. Unfortunately, many of the skills that artists use aren't transferrable to other professional settings (Rozmaryn, 1993); however, with the right kind of coaching, artists and performers can identify and develop the ones that are transferrable. This will help them develop a more positive outlook on the future. For example, Hamilton (1997) points out that actors have good communication skills, dancers are good at setting goals, and performers in general tend to have good work ethics. Furthermore, no physical injury can take away a person's innermost creativity—and creativity itself is invaluable for a wide range of professions. A glimmer of hope following debilitating injuries comes from redirecting one's creative energy to a different path—one that could perhaps turn into a new profession.

The Clinician's Role

Supporting Clients' Worries

Though clinicians can't do anything about the injury itself, they can play a supportive role in providing a space for clients to express their most disturbing fears and worries. Stephanie, the opera singer, knew that I lacked the medical expertise to identify the cause of her vocal problems, but she benefited from knowing that I offered a place to discuss her concerns openly without fear of being criticized for her technique or scared into believing she wouldn't get future roles. During the recovery phase, clinicians can support their clients by helping them prepare for and anticipate the worsening of symptoms, which can be typical during treatment. It's helpful for clinicians to contain their clients' frustrations and feelings of hopelessness that come from not being able to control the speed with which the body recovers.

Exploring How Clients Think About Their Injuries

Clinicians can explore the attitudes and beliefs that have sustained artists' and performers' harmful habits, or have even prevented them from receiving treatment. For example, a dancer might come to believe that an ankle injury is the beginning of the end of her career and perceive any kind of help as pointless. Or, conversely, the shock immediately after an injury might be so strong that she is in denial about the need to receive treatment right away. Other performing artists might think that seeking help will raise flags, making an artistic director of a dance or theater company think twice before offering an opportunity. Stephanie was tremendously ashamed of her diagnosis of polyps and assumed that others would reject her because of it, even after being reassured by those around her.

It's important to explore the circumstances leading up to an injury, the way artists and performers internalize the experience, and their outlooks on getting help. Clinicians can shed light on all the factors that contributed to getting injured, such as harsh practice conditions, anatomical concerns (playing an instrument that's not ideal for the person's body), personality tendencies (persisting despite pain), and interpersonal factors (hesitating to speak up on account of social pressure). This part of the counseling relationship might reveal the presence of performance anxiety linked to proneness to injury. Performers' tendencies to practice excessively to compensate for perceived inadequacies that make them anxious (Klickstein, 2009) increases the likelihood of straining or injuring their bodies.

Guiding Clients Throughout Treatment for Their Injuries

The period during and after an injury poses significant psychological challenges for artists and performers. The clinicians' role is to help clients navigate the difficult waters of dealing with life as injured performers. Doing so involves gently inviting clients to confront the reality of the limitations posed by their injuries. Sometimes this means encouraging clients to seek medical help, helping them decide the best time to do so, and encouraging them to implement a consistent physical therapy routine (Hamilton,

1997). Stephanie felt isolated after receiving her diagnosis. She believed that a good singer would never have developed such a problem, so she hesitated to set up restorative vocal coaching sessions. Our sessions acted as a reality check, helping her put the diagnosis into perspective. We worked together to develop the necessary momentum to keep her treatment going without her feeling ashamed. Other times, the clinicians' role involves instilling a hopeful outlook and managing the anxiety or depression triggered by taking time off from making art or performing.

Coming to Terms With Life Changes

Unfortunately, some injuries do force artists and performers to take time off from their creative and professional lives, sometimes permanently. The clinicians' role is to help them grieve the loss of their past selves, to make sense of their future options, and to remain open to the possibilities of using their talents in new ways. For example, a singer who had an operation that caused permanent voice damage felt ready to move on from the stress and depression caused by her inability to sing the way she used to. She wanted to prevent unfulfilled dreams from haunting her, and she wanted help figuring out her next steps. Instead of singing, she knew that she could compose music; instead of performing, she knew that she could write blog reviews for others' performances. In our sessions, I gave her space to tame her destructive impulse to give up the music world altogether and to maintain a clear path for where she wanted to go next. The goal is to capture the core elements of a person's artistry, while applying them to new areas of his or her life.

When clients enter new careers that are far removed from what they used to do, clinicians can work with them to ensure that they maintain healthy relationship with their pasts: they can emphasize the pride and satisfaction derived from old accomplishments and can create a thread of continuity between their past and present identities. For example, a musician who was forced to become a real-estate agent when a shoulder injury ended his music career eventually managed to stomach watching old videos of his performances without feeling grief, and continue to call himself a musician, albeit not a practicing one, despite being away from the music world.

Managing the Pace of Return to Creative Activity

Clinicians can guide clients fortunate to return to their craft after a recovery by discussing if and when clients fall into old, harmful habits that pose the threat of reinjury. Injured artists and performers eager to get back to their art might think they're in the clear. They may rush into overpracticing, overcompensating for lost time by setting too many and too difficult goals and saying yes to every opportunity. The clinicians' role is to help such clients stay focused on the goal of reintegration into their performing or artistic

168 Artists' and Performers' Bodies

lives, while paying attention to any discomfort, and to remind clients that they owe it to themselves to slow down.

Treatment Goals

1. Cope emotionally with injury-related stress.
2. Reduce the influence of the pain-tolerance culture.
3. Establish healthy art-making and performing practices.
4. Take steps to begin rehabilitative treatment.
5. Work through the challenges of career transitions.

Suggested Interventions to Achieve Goals

1. *Manage life stress.* Research conducted with athletes and dancers demonstrates that the presence of stress affects the onset and duration of injuries (Mainwaring et al., 2001). Being preoccupied with worries about a recent argument with a coworker or family member, financial concerns, and other stressors can make concentrating on safety practices more challenging, increasing the chances of injury. Clients and clinicians can work together to identify sources of stress and manage its impact.

   > Example: To get a better sense of the kind of stress he was under, I asked a dance student I worked with to identify the distressing thoughts that popped in his head while he was performing, practicing, or working on his craft. Apart from thoughts about the quality of his dancing, he mentioned conflicts with his dance instructor and a general feeling of pressure about doing well in school. Then, to minimize the impact of his stressors, he and I implemented stress-management activities, such as making sure he was communicating effectively, taking frequent relaxation breaks, asserting his needs, and reaching out to classmates for support.

2. *Refer to osteopathic physicians, physical therapists, and other health professionals.* Rehabilitative professionals that specialize in the treatment of artists' and

performers' injuries are familiar with industry-specific pressure placed on the body.[3] They understand the need for endurance, flexibility, and range of motion and are aware of the obstacles to recovery, such as not being able to wear protective gear onstage or having to postpone a training season. Getting the right guidance on injury treatment and prevention, as well as advice on proper posture and the use of tools and instruments, encourages clients and helps them gain the confidence needed to set and meet recovery goals.

> Example: When a guitarist noticed pain in her arm, we discussed whether she'd rather rely on advice from coaches and peers, wait it out, or visit a trained specialist who could observe her in action and evaluate both injury and technique. She decided that the last option would lead her to a more accurate diagnosis and treatment plan, and a faster recovery. The specialist gave her useful tools on how to keep practicing for an upcoming performance while minimizing the risk of long-term damage.

3. *Reconsider habits and technique.* A positive outcome that comes from sustaining an injury is that it's an opportunity for clients to reevaluate their approaches to art making and performing. Clients often ignore their bodies' mild warning signs and focus on doing what they can to get by; sometimes they identify a problem, but instead of treating it they use poor techniques that help them compensate. It's when severe injuries occur that they decide to confront poor habits and take on the task of correcting them.

> Example: A pianist I worked with for a few months had frequent pain during his practices. This made him worry about his ability to play well during his performances. In one of our sessions, he surprised me by proclaiming that the injury was one of the best things that happened to him. It forced him to rethink the way he plays, how he sits, and the tension in his wrists and finger. He was convinced that, had it not been for the time he took to recover, he wouldn't have thought to reevaluate his playing habits, which would then compromise the overall quality of his playing. I encouraged him to maintain this positive attitude and to continue evaluating the habits and techniques that help.

4. *Emphasize other identities.* Injuries sometimes force clients to take time off from their art—or even worse, to stop altogether. Those who identify entirely with their roles as artists and performers will feel the disruption to their identities more deeply than those who have maintained other sources of creative and professional fulfillment. This is challenging for professional artists, who have spent most of their lives developing and perfecting their crafts, and whose social circles involve people in their

field. However, it's never too late to think about expanding and going outside one's niche. Doing so helps protect clients from the devastating loss of their abilities to be fully invested in their art.

> Example: A folk singer–songwriter developed a voice disorder that caused her to take a break from singing. We tried to access other parts of her identity by recalling old interests or activities in which she excelled, aside from singing, such as yoga and blogging. I encouraged her to take steps to spend more time on those activities, to reflect on why they matter to her, as well as to strengthen relationships with people who weren't part of the performing world.

5. *Encourage assertiveness.* People in the performing-arts world generally accept that enduring pain, like having a battle scar, is an inevitable part of true dedication—that suffering is preferable to disrupting a production by canceling shows or looking for understudies (Klickstein, 2009). As a result, artists and performers hesitate to speak up and thus put themselves at risk for serious injuries. Assertiveness skills make it possible for performers to say something when they aren't feeling well, to seek help without the fear of being stigmatized, to become involved in the process of finding replacements, and to negotiate the terms of their returns to their roles.

> Example: A client who was terrified of confrontation practiced role-playing with me. We rehearsed ways to decline terms that she wasn't comfortable with, and to say no to additional rehearsal after she'd announced her injury concerns to teachers, coaches, and musical directors. Once she overcame her initial reluctance, she found that people were more understanding than she'd anticipated.

6. *Build self-efficacy skills.* A principle of sports psychology (Chase et al., 2005; McCaffrey et al., 2014) that can be applied to the performing-arts fields is that fear of injury or reinjury, and lack of belief in one's ability to perform certain tasks, increase the chances of sustaining an injury. This could be because feelings of low competence change performers' and athletes' perceptions of their abilities and lead to physiological changes that impair concentration and other skills necessary for peak performance (Heil, 1993). Clinicians can focus on strengthening their clients' feelings of self-efficacy so that they trust their abilities to use their bodies appropriately. This will make resorting to physically damaging shortcuts less likely.

> Example: To help improve feelings of self-efficacy, I invited a guitarist to describe times when he executed a guitar solo well, and a ballet dancer to bring videos demonstrating a quadruple pirouette. I encouraged them both to model the achievements of role models

Artists' and Performers' Bodies 171

who've inspired them, and to set their eyes on high goals. When these clients began to feel more confident in their techniques and abilities, they reported sometimes feeling that their bodies seemed to cooperate by executing tasks safely.

7. *Engage in guided-imagery and relaxation exercises.* Injured performers, such as dancers, who must display a great deal of athleticism benefit from mental preparation in which they visualize their performances (Chase et al., 2005; Reese et al., 2012). They can imagine moving their bodies in the ways they did before their injuries, and they can mentally rehearse performing difficult parts. Doing so increases confidence as it allows performers to "see" themselves doing something well, even in the presence of an injury's limitations (Hare et al., 2008). In addition, imagining the healing process—for example, that the pain in one's elbow is disappearing, or that the knee feels more stable—helps performing artists access the calm of a hopeful outcome regarding their bodies' progress.

> Example: An injured dancer and I practiced imagining what it would feel like for her to be onstage again. I encouraged her to visualize a state of physical calm: to imagine that her muscles are relaxed, and that she's safe. She described images of the tissue around her knee repairing, and imagined putting weight on her leg again. This exercise motivated her to continue with her physical therapy sessions, and helped her remember what it felt like to do the thing she loves the most.

Additional Interventions

8.
9.
10.

Takeaways

- Artists and performers rely on their bodies for creative fulfillment and for their professional and artistic success.
- The pressure that artists and performers feel to ensure that their bodies look right and perform well, combined with preexisting psychological vulnerabilities, puts them at risk for neglecting their physical health.
- For performers who face impossible standards of aesthetic ideals, physical self-neglect manifests in disordered eating, such as starvation, purging, and excessive exercise.

- For artists and performers who have learned to disregard their bodies' needs for breaks and proper care, physical self-neglect results in repetitive strain and chronic injuries.
- The high expectations set in place by the arts-and-entertainment industry, combined with artists' and performers' desires to please and strive for perfection, often get in the way of seeking help.
- Counseling can help artists and performers listen to their bodies' needs and to become their own advocates for proper care. Clinicians can work with clients to help them strike a balance between the need to adhere to industry expectations and the need to ensure a healthy and long career.
- Counseling can alleviate the anxiety and depression triggered during career breaks or transitions caused by severe injuries.
- Counseling can help performers with eating disorders improve their relationship to food so they can enjoy a long and healthy creative career.

Notes

1 An *eating disorder not otherwise specified* (EDNOS) diagnosis is given for disordered eating that causes significant psychological distress but does not fit the criteria for anorexia or bulimia nervosa. In the DSM-V, two new categories, *other specified feeding or eating disorder* (OSFED) and *unspecified feeding or eating disorder* (UFED), were introduced to reflect the many variations of types of eating disorders.
2 Orthorexia is not an official DSM diagnosis. It's a term developed by doctor Steven Bratman in 1996 to describe a pathological fixation with eating healthily.
3 The Performing Arts Medicine Association provides access to information for professionals who specialize in performance-related injuries; www.artsmed.org/referrals.

References

Aksoydan, E., & Camci, N. (2009). Prevalence of orthorexia nervosa among Turkish performance artists. *Eating Weight Disorder*, *14*(1), 33–37.

Arcelus, J., Witcomb, G. L., & Mitcell, A. (2014). Prevalence of eating disorders amongst dancers: a systemic review and meta-analysis. *European Eating Disorder Review*, *22*(2), 92–101.

Arthur-Cameselle, J. (2017). Mindfulness, eating, body and performance. In A. L. Baltzell (Ed.), *Mindfulness and performance (current perspectives in social and behavioral sciences)*. Cambridge: Cambridge University Press.

Bastiani, A. M., Rao, R., Weltzin, T., & Kaye, W. H. (1995). Perfectionism in anorexia nervosa. *International. Journal of Eating Disorders*, *17*, 147–152. doi:10.1002/1098-108X (199503)17:2<147::AID-EAT2260170207>3.0.CO;2-X

Brandfonbrener, A. G. (2009). History of playing-related pain in 330 university freshman music students. *Medical Problems of Performing Artists*, *24*(1), 30–36.

Bulik, C. M., Tozzi, F., Anderson, C., Mazzeo, S. E., Aggen, S., & Sullivan, P. F. (2003). *American Journal of Psychiatry*, *160*(2), 366–368.

Casiero, D., & Frishman, W.H. (2006). Cardiovascular Complications of Eating Disorders. *Cardiology in Review*, *14*(5), 227-31. doi:10.1097/01.crd.0000216745.96062.7c

Chase, M. A., Magyar, M., & Drake, B. M. (2005). Fear of injury in gymnastics: Self-efficacy and psychological strategies to keep on tumbling. *Journal of Sports Sciences, 23*(5), 465–475.

De Bruin, A. P., Bakker, F. C., & Oudejans, R. R. D. (2009). Achievement goal theory and disordered eating: Relationships of disordered eating with goal orientations and motivational climate in female gymnasts and dancers. *Psychology of Sport and Exercise, 10*(1), 72–77.

Egan, S. J., Wade, T. D., Shafran, R., & Antony, M. M. (2014). *Cognitive-behavioral treatment of perfectionism*. New York, NY: Guilford Publications.

Evans, R. W., Evans, R. I., Carvajal, S., & Perry, S. (1996). A survey of injuries among Broadway performers. *American Journal of Public Health, 86*(1), 77–80.

Friesen, K. J., Rozenek, R., Clippinger, K., Gunter, K., Russo, A. C., & Sklar, S. E. (2011). Bone mineral density and body composition of collegiate modern dancers. *Journal of Dance Medical Science, 15*(1), 31–36.

Hamilton, L. (1997). *Behind the mask: A guide to performing arts psychology*. Greenwich, CT: Ablex Publishing Corporation.

Hamilton, L. H. (1998). *Advice for dancers: Emotional counsel and practical strategies*. San Francisco, CA: Jossey-Bass.

Hamilton, S. (2000). *Health hazards and safety tips for artists*. Retrieved from www.carfac.sk.ca/rsu_docs/advisorynotes59-05e173dcf572e91ecfcc1f130e2e4103.pdf

Hare, R., Evans, L., & Callow, N. (2008). Imagery use during rehabilitation from injury: A case study of an elite athlete. *The Sport Psychologist, 22*, 405–422.

Heil, J. (1993). *Psychology of sport injury*. Champaign, IL: Human Kinetics.

Klickstein, G. (2009). *The musician's way: A guide to practice, performance, and wellness*. Oxford: Oxford University Press.

Koven, N. S., & Abry, A. W. (2015). The clinical basis of orthorexia nervosa: emerging perspectives. *Neuropsychiatric Disease and Treatment, 11*, 385–394. http://doi.org/10.2147/NDT.S61665

Krasnow, D., Kerr, G., & Mainwaring, L. (2004). Psychology of dealing with the injured dancer. *Medical Problems of Performing Artists, 9*, 7–9.

Kucharska-Pietura, K., Nikolaou, V., Masiak, M., & Treasure, J. (2004). The recognition of emotion in the faces and voice of anorexia nervosa. *International Journal of Eating Disorders, 35*, 42–47. doi:10.1002/eat.10219

Liederbach, M., & Campagno, J. (2001). Psychological aspects of fatigue-related injuries in dancers. *Journal of Dance Medicine & Science, 5*(4), 116–120.

Mainwaring, L. M., Krasnow, D., & Kerr, G. (2001). And the dance goes on: Psychological impact of injury. *Journal of Dance Medicine & Science, 5*(4), 105–115.

McCaffrey, A., Mrazik, M., & Klassen, R. (2014). The relation between self-efficacy, injury and fear of injury among elite athletes. *British Journal of Sports Medicine, 48*, 636.

Mitchell, J. E. & Crow, S. (2006). Medical complications of anorexia nervosa and bulimia nervosa. *Current Opinion in Psychiatry, 19*(4), 438–443

Penniment, K. J., & Egan, S. J. (2012). Perfectionism and learning experiences in dance class as risk factors for eating disorders in dancers. *European Eating Disorders Review, 20*, 13–22. doi:10.1002/erv.1089

Reel, J. J. (2003). *Eating disorders: An encyclopedia of causes, treatment, and prevention*. Santa Barbara, CA: Greenwood.

Reese, L. M., Pittsinger, R., & Yang, J. (2012). Effectiveness of psychological intervention following sport injury. *Journal of Sport and Health Science, 1*(2), 71–79.

Ringham, R., Klump, K., Kaye, W., Stone, D., Libman, S., Stowe, S., & Marcus, M. (2006). Eating disorder symptomatology among ballet dancers. *International Journal of Eating Disorders, 39*, 503–508. doi:10.1002/eat.20299

Rozmaryn, L. M. (1993). Upper extremity disorders in performing artists. *Maryland Medical Journal, 42*(3), 255–260.

Shah, S., Weiss, D. S., & Burchette, R. J. (2012). Injuries in professional modern dancers: Incidence, risk factors, and management. *Journal of Dance Medicine Science, 16*(1), 17–25.

Shrier, I., & Halle, M. (2011). Psychological predictors of injuries in circus artists: an exploratory study. *British Journal of Sports Medicine, 45*, 433–436.

Steinberg, N., Siev-Ner, I., Peleg, S., Dar, G., Masharawi, Y., Zeev, A., & Hershkovitz, I. (2013). Injuries in female dancers aged 8 to 16 Years. *Journal of Athletic Training, 48*(1), 118–123. http://doi.org/10.4085/1062-6050-48.1.06

Thomas, J. J., Keel, P. K., & Heatherton, T. F. (2005). Disordered eating attitudes and behaviors in ballet students: examination of environmental and individual risk factors. *International Journal of Eating Disorders, 38*(3), 263–268.

Thomson, P., & Jaque, S.V. (2017). *Creativity and the performing artist: Behind the mask*. London, UK: Academic Press.

Zuskin, E., Schachter, E. N., Mustajbegovic, J., Pucarin-Cvetkovic, J., & Lipozencic, J. (2007). Occupational health hazards of artists. *Acta Dermatovenerologica Croatica, 15*(3), 167–177.

Chapter 9

Stress in the Arts-and-Entertainment World

The similarities in the frustrations that professionals in the arts-and-entertainment world describe are remarkable.[1] Disappointed photographers, musicians, dancers, writers, visual artists, and other clients from various creative domains share with me their predicaments about their unshakable desire to move their careers forward while somehow being trapped in professional limbo. Perhaps their sales aren't high enough, the critical reviews are lukewarm, the calls from collaborators are infrequent, or the views and hits from their online content remain stagnant. Hearing repeated variations of the same story was an early indication that my work with creative clients would be incomplete if it didn't consider the unpredictable and unforgiving nature of the arts-and-entertainment industry. Not knowing if and when success will come can be agonizing.

Disillusioned by New York's competitive music world, Nick, a musician who moved to the city from a suburban area, contacted me to help him understand why he couldn't catch a break. He wanted to know how to stay motivated despite not having attained the success he'd hoped for. After 3 years of knocking on doors, getting bands together, sending out press kits, promoting his music online, and developing relationships with people in the music scene, he'd made little progress. He felt as if he'd been spinning his wheels—which was making him run out of hope. An "office job," as he put it, was out of the question. Still, he could see that he was becoming irritable, depressed, and angry. He asked me to help him manage his daily stress and hoped to make sense of his conflicting feelings toward his career.

One of the challenging realities that Nick and other artists face is the need always to be vigilant about the psychological and environmental obstacles that threaten their career longevity. Having to continuously juggle many stressors makes it difficult for professional artists to remain focused, hopeful, and fulfilled by their creative pursuits. In this chapter, I identify common sources of stress in the lives of arts-and-entertainment professionals, primarily artists and performers. Cataloguing these concerns puts a name to clients' experiences and points in the direction of suitable responses and solutions.

Wearing Many Hats

A few years into their careers, arts-and-entertainment professionals realize that their work entails more than just excelling at their craft: they must become self-sufficient in handling career-related demands. Technological advances enable them to have control over their online presence and social media representation, to create marketing and promotional material, and to produce and distribute the creative content themselves. On the one hand, this kind of control opens up invaluable creative opportunities for self-expression; on the other hand, it compels artists and performers, especially those who can't afford hired help, to take on many roles, some of which can be particularly stressful. They must become administrators who send hundreds of e-mails, make calls, and manage spreadsheets with potential press contacts. They often have to design press kits and put them in the mail, organize band members' schedules, and so forth. They must act as public-relations representatives who go to social events, approach potential collaborators, follow up on conversations electronically, and engage audiences on social media. Artists often need to make their own websites, learn audio-engineering skills, and design their album covers and flyers advertising their shows. These roles are, of course, additional to their primary one: practicing their crafts.

Transitioning from one role to another can be overwhelming and, more importantly, can lead artists and performers to feel insecure about their creative and artistic identities. A painter I once worked with complained that he didn't feel like an artist because he'd spent most of his week calling people to promote his show. Many artists dread the noncreative parts of their work. They'd rather be in the studio playing music instead of calling venues to set up shows; they'd rather be out taking pictures instead of editing e-mails to send to potential clients; they'd rather be onstage instead of following social media accounts to increase traffic on their pages. Nevertheless, they have little choice but to take on these tasks, and wear multiple hats, in the hope that their chances for success will be maximized.

Financial Stress

Artists are generally well educated. According to an American Community Survey conducted by the US Census Bureau with data for 2005–2009 and 2010–2014, 59 percent of artists have a bachelor's degree or higher, compared to 31 percent in the rest of the population; however, their income doesn't reflect their education: on the contrary, they tend to earn less than people with the same level of education in other fields (Center for Cultural Innovation, 2016; National Endowment for the Arts, 2011). Many artists and performers work on a gig basis, meaning that their relationships with employers is inconsistent and they're not employed full time (Jackson et al.,

2003). Consequently, they may be unsure about when and how they'll get their next paychecks. Often, they must pay large amounts before seeing any of it again (to produce records, buy art supplies, take acting lessons, and so on), with the hope that these investments will kick-start an income stream. Artists without a steady salary (from teaching or working for a company or a nonprofit organization) are highly anxious about their financial statuses.

Instability in employment and income may result in difficulties accessing adequate health insurance. Health coverage can be a problem for many artists and performers who don't receive health insurance benefits from their employers, and thus they must pay for it themselves (Hamilton, 1998; Jackson et al., 2003). General medical care, mental health care, and recovery from performance-related injuries can't be properly taken care of without access to health care or the money to pay for treatment. People who aren't offered health insurance by their jobs and can't afford to get insurance face additional stress that stems from worrying about their mental and physical well-being.

Financial insecurity can make it difficult to focus on creative pursuits. I once worked with a visual artist who wanted to talk about his upcoming art installation project, but couldn't focus on anything other than getting the funds to pay the rent. His financial strain took precedence over his creative ambitions. The stress was so severe that it took time away from working on the artwork he hoped one day would make him money. Artists who share similar experiences usually try to solve such problems in two ways: the first one is moonlighting—working multiple jobs unrelated to one's artistic profession (Alper & Wassall, 2000). A 2015 Strategic National Arts Alumni Project survey of 140,000 art-and-design school graduates showed that half of them earned more than 60% of their living from their artistic profession (Center for Cultural Innovation, 2016). The second way to solve the problem of financial uncertainty is producing creative work for the purpose of selling it, even when it's not creatively fulfilling (for example, making work that sells during the holiday season, singing for money in cover bands, and so on). These solutions to the problem of low income are frustrating both in terms of impracticality—as it can be hard to strike a balance between time to create and time to make money—and in terms of artistic integrity. A musical theater actor I worked with, who moonlighted as a bartender, struggled to wake up early enough to audition. But his most hindering challenge was maintaining the self-perception of an actor when most of his time was spent waiting on customers. Not making enough money from acting hurt his bank account, but spending time making drinks instead of acting hurt his confidence even more.

Competition

Performers waiting for their turns to audition are surrounded by hundreds of other performers with the same goal—to get the part. Musicians followed by other acts on the same night have to make a lasting impression on jaded audiences. Likewise, photographers sending out e-mails to potential clients have to make a case about why their services are better than those of others. People in the arts live in cutthroat world, and they undergo the emotionally charged experiences that come with it. Having to compete to get ahead is hardly unique to the arts-and-entertainment world, as it's not unusual to have to work hard to rise above competitors. However, there are two significant challenges that make competitiveness in the arts-and-entertainment world highly troublesome. The first challenge is that in artistic domains, especially the performing arts (Gaylin, 2015), there are far fewer opportunities than there are interested parties. This increases artists' and performers' urgency to demonstrate their superiority, reinforcing feelings of competitiveness. The second challenge is that people in such industries are often competing on the basis of who they are, rather than, say, a service or product that's separate from their core personal traits. A person's looks, voice, creative choices, talent, aesthetic vision, creative expression, and so on are integral parts of one's sense of self, yet they become dispensable commodities when repeatedly put up against those of others. This sentiment was captured effectively by a dancer I once worked with. After every audition, she felt exhausted by the pressure of having to summon the grace to persuade judges that she was worthier than the other candidates. In the end, she wasn't sure which was worse: the feeling of having to "sell herself" or the reality of not having many "buyers." The harsh reality of a cutthroat industry adds to artists' day-to-day stress.

Slow-Moving Careers

Artists and performers who hope for career longevity must find the courage to continue despite not achieving desired results quickly enough. Sometimes their attempts at garnering interest in their work fail, or they're simply going through periods where things are moving slowly. They might be setting up fewer shows, getting hired and selling less, or having low creative output. These fluctuations, normal and expected as they are, often catch professional artists like Nick by surprise, and worry and discourage them. In such cases, artists must manage their disappointment and persevere.

One possible explanation why interest in artists' and performers' work sometimes fails to pick up is the subjectivity and ambiguity involved in how their work is evaluated. Gatekeepers, reviewers, critics, and audiences can be cruelly fickle. As discussed in chapter 3, on self-doubts, in an empirical exploration of the factors that influence art appreciation, Lauring and his colleagues (2016) found that consumers' evaluations of paintings was influenced by how expensive the artwork was and whether peers and experts had reacted positively or negatively to it. Other factors such as luck and financial resources might be involved. Sometimes the difference between getting a positive or a negative review, or even no press coverage at all, can amount to nothing more than a chance encounter with a reviewer at a show or the funds to hire a public-relations service.

Nevertheless, even when their careers are moving slowly and the impulse to flee is strong, time and time again, my creative clients proclaim that there's nothing else they'd rather be doing. When a TV network was interested in my client's comedy series, she was ecstatic because her hard work had finally paid off. Unfortunately, a few months later, she found out that the network had decided not to air the show. She felt as if the rug had been pulled out from under her feet, and that years into her career, she was back where she was when she first started. Despite the disappointment that had completely derailed her focus and creative motivation, she couldn't fathom switching to another career because it'd feel like giving up part of her identity.

Erratic Schedules and Traveling

Another common stressor among professional artists involves their erratic schedules and employment patterns (Hamilton & Kella, 1992; Jackson et al., 2003). A 2016 study found that there's an association between artists' well-being and whether they work regular hours with consistent workload and employment (Tuisku et al., 2016). However, achieving regularity is hard because last-minute gigs come up unexpectedly, the hours artists and performers have to work change on a weekly or even daily basis, and they freelance and are hired on a short-term basis. In addition, press reviews will accelerate demand for work that will only slow back down when the hype is over. These facts mean that industry professionals must get used to a start-and-stop, hurry-up-and-wait routine and be prepared for the unexpected. Having a flexible schedule can be appealing, but it often makes artists and performers anxious. I once worked with an actress who always had to leave her schedule open in case she got cast in a role. She wanted to do many other things, including taking yoga classes and committing to weekly counseling appointments, but knowing that she'd have to cancel plans if she got an e-mail for a shoot, she could only make plans a day or two ahead. Being out of work for some time can be especially hard for those who struggle with self-discipline (Hill, 2001). For example, performers who've come to plan their days based on call-time, soundcheck, and rehearsal schedules may feel lost when, after the show's over, they must manage their own time.

Similarly, touring artists' routines are constantly fluctuating. Their show times may be fairly predictable, since they're booked in advance, but most things leading up to the shows are uncertain—and beyond artists' control. When it comes to locations, people, venue conditions, sleep schedules, food options, exposure to substances, commuting, and so forth, most touring artists are unsure what to expect. In addition, once touring season is done, artists must go back to a lifestyle that moves at a different pace. This sudden change in pace may not be a problem for all touring artists, but those who are already prone to anxiety and depression will find it stressful, and they might even be affected by postperformance depression—the feelings of emptiness and sadness that follow the intensity of an exciting performance.

Aging

Physical attributes associated with youth are highly valued in the arts-and-entertainment world. Actors with a young look are in demand, and dancers need to be in peak physical condition. Physical changes associated with aging, such as a deeper sounding voice and decreased physical agility (Thomson & Jaque, 2017), can change the quality of performances. Ballet dancers will be considered for fewer roles by the time they are in their mid-20s, unless they've already reached moderate success (Hamilton, 1998). People in the entertainment field care about looking young even when they're behind the camera and offstage because they're still expected to look as if they have their careers ahead of them. A common question my clients often ponder is whether to lie about their ages when they meet potential agents, promoters, and managers: they worry that revealing their real ages will make them less marketable. Age-sensitive careers preoccupy artists and performers with age-defying creative goals and ambitions.

Rejections

Getting a rejection or no response at all is par for the course in this industry. Many stories of famous and influential artists tell the tale of hearing no along the path to success. Sylvia Plath's poems were rejected by the *New Yorker*, Andy Warhol's work was rejected by the Museum of Modern Art in New York, and, more recently, J. K. Rowling's *Harry Potter*, a best-selling series of fantasy novels, was rejected 12 times before it became a multibillion-dollar brand. Most people consciously understand that rejections are common in one's path toward success, but still struggle with the emotions that they bring up. A jazz composer I worked with feared rejection even though she tried not to let her fear stop her. After applying for a residency, she commented that she knew she had no chance of getting it but that she wanted to apply "just because." When she received a rejection letter, she became severely depressed, and reported that she had regretted applying. Rejections feel deeply personal to artists who are emotionally invested in the work they submit for consideration. Those who aren't psychologically prepared to tolerate rejections and the uncertainty that comes with maybes suffer a drop in their confidence and in their motivation to seek out more opportunities.

Despite all the pain they cause, rejections can have a positive side to them. Kim and colleagues (2012) found that being rejected from a group reinforced creative people's desire to uphold their status as being unconventional and unique, thereby making them more creative. However, this happened only with people who had an independent self-concept to begin with. For those whose self-concept was more reliant on others, rejection didn't have the same positive effect. This caveat can inform clinicians who work with clients whose self-concept is tied to, and threatened by, rejection.

Burnout

More so a result of industry-related stress than a source of it, "burning out" refers to the extreme emotional and physical exhaustion associated with chronic stress. Often mistaken for procrastination, creativity blocks, and low motivation, it differs by reflecting a general sense of detachment and non-caring, and a perception of having lost the stamina to keep going. It's the feeling of being incapable of continuing to work—of the "smothering of a fire that was once burning" (Schaufeli et al., 2009:205). It results from long working hours, high expectations, unrealistic goals, and neglect of self-caring practices, such as taking vacations and meeting with friends. The risk for burning out is especially high in the arts-and-entertainment industry, where the lines between professional and personal life can be blurry, where artists and performers are required to be constantly alert to new opportunities and make the most of them when they come along, and where the financial rewards are disproportionate to the time and dedication put into the work.

Substance Abuse

Though there are many factors implicated in the development of substance-use habits, their high incidence in the arts-and-entertainment world suggests that, at the very least, this world exacerbates preexisting risk factors. A 2015 Substance Abuse and Mental Health Services Administration national survey on drug use and health looked at substance-abuse disorder among adults aged 18–64 between the years 2008 and 2012 across various industries. The arts, entertainment, and recreation industry had the third-highest number of substance-abuse incidence (Bush & Lipari, 2015). Musicians and writers have frequently been targeted as groups of artists with severe substance-use habits. One-third of the musicians who took part in a survey ($N = 3,278$) said drug use (marijuana, cocaine, and amphetamines) was prevalent in their field (Chesky & Hipple, 1999). According to Wolkewitz and his colleagues (2011), habits associated with rock 'n' roll lifestyles increase exposure to alcohol and other substances. Eminent writers have often been linked to alcohol consumption (Pritzker, 1999).

One of the reasons hypothesized for the increased prevalence of substance use in these professions is the perception that drugs and alcohol enhance creativity by reducing cognitive control. Some studies have debunked this perception, attributing any connection between substances and heightened creativity to expectancy effects or placebo (Hicks et al., 2011; Lapp et al., 1994). Beyond the placebo effect, other studies have found that any enhanced creativity associated with substance consumption, in particular alcohol (Benedek et al., 2017), is as a result of how drinking weakens inhibitions, leading to fewer cognitive constraints and, perhaps, fewer creativity-hindering self-doubts.

The other explanation for why substances are frequently used in the entertainment world looks at the impact of a stressful environment. The stressors addressed in the other sections of this chapter (juggling multiple roles, the pressure to succeed, erratic schedules, and so on) all contribute to the need to look for relief. Artists and performers might consider drugs and alcohol for help with sleep, to calm their nerves, or to enhance focus and concentration. Performers who experience performance anxiety may seek out alcohol or other anxiety-reducing substances to cope with their discomfort. In addition, frequent exposure to alcohol and drugs can make people likelier to turn to them. Although artists' "hang-out culture"—staying out late after shows to network and support other artists—can be a breeding ground for creative ideas and collaborations, it frequently involves alcohol and other substances making artists, performers, and others vulnerable to using and abusing them.

The Clinician's Role

Maintaining a Hopeful Outlook for Success

Like sports coaches who push and challenge their athletes to get up after a fall and try again, I often find myself coaxing my clients into holding onto their goals for as long as they can. I try to help them solve problems along the way, and I make practical suggestions for resources they might find useful. I remind them that even when some opportunities are long gone, it's only by setting eyes on the next one that they increase their chances for success. Clients who are fed up with how their careers are going are often driven and talented, but they've become frustrated and resentful toward the industry's state of affairs and lose the conviction that it'll improve. It's important for clinicians to instill hope and an optimistic outlook so that clients don't get overwhelmed by negative thinking. Then, client and clinicians can explore the kind of success that clients envision and tackle obstacles that get in their way.

It's helpful when clinicians look at clients' varying measures of success. Some define success based on the size of the audience, others based on their income, and others based on their personal attachment to the creative content they produce. Being clear on what success means makes it easier for clients to make specific action plans to achieve it.

Managing the Stress of the "Hustle"

Clinicians' can't get someone discovered. As much as I root for my clients— I'll admit to wishing for them to have a chance encounter with an agent

Stress in the Arts-and-Entertainment World   183

that'll skyrocket their careers—I know that focusing on creating these kinds of results is beyond my remit. The reality is that artists and performers must put in a lot of work to bring about desired results. Clinicians don't have control over what happens to their clients outside the office. They can, however, help them respond effectively to the stresses involved; they can help clients come up with plans and strategies and encourage them to take breaks when they're overworked and overwhelmed, manage success when it comes, and maintain momentum despite disappointments.

Taking a Look at the Creative Work

Sometimes it's helpful for a clinician to glimpse the artist's work itself. Though this might make some clinicians uncomfortable, as it makes them feel they must review the quality of the content, looking at the work can lead to important insights. When a rock guitarist I worked with was at his wit's end with garnering attention for his band, a chance to listen to his music (with him in the room) led to an illuminating discussion about his choices in melody, tempo, style, and instrumentation. Our conversation revealed that he kept leaning toward avant-garde, minimalist, and experimental music even though he was trying to attract mainstream pop and rock audiences. Listening to his music helped us work through this conflict together.

In addition, looking at clients' work reveals how they react to and talk about their work when it's right there in front of them. A frustrated photographer who was annoyed at how little attention he was getting from galleries seemed passionless when he showed me his images. Acknowledging this helped us uncover his own feelings about the direction he'd taken and to engage in a conversation on what kind of work would inspire him.

Recognizing the Need to Step Away

Sometimes the high levels of stress in the arts-and-entertainment world causes creative clients to begin contemplating other career options. Upon confronting their limitations, whether these are limitations in their skills and abilities, or in their psychological resilience to persevere, clients may need support as they make decisions about whether to stay in their creative fields. Though the primary role of clinicians is to help creative clients build the skills to handle occupational stress, ensuring their psychological well-being—by taking time away from their creative goals or switching careers altogether—may take precedence. For example, if regular working hours or full-time employment seem to minimize a photographer's episodes of depression, transitioning from a freelance artist to company employee might be a good idea. Similarly, if a burned-out writer is struggling to support her family because of low sales, she may wish to think about using her talents differently. Clinicians can help their clients voice their concerns and come up with ideas for alternative yet, hopefully, fulfilling career ideas.

Addressing Factors for Career Success

Clinicians can help their clients build the necessary psychological tools to survive industry-related stress. They can provide a roadmap for potential areas for exploration by addressing the following factors:

- *Creative content.* How do clients feel about what they do? Are they passionately engaged in their creative pursuits? What are their practice and preparation habits?
- *Marketing and business plans.* How do clients let the world know about their work? Do they have actionable plans to advertise and engage audiences?
- *Networking.* How do clients feel about establishing relationships with others in their field? Do they put time into creating contacts?
- *Persistence.* Do clients give up after one or two attempts toward achieving their goals? Do they persevere despite obstacles?
- *Chance.* Are clients prepared for chance factors to affect their likelihood of success? Are they comfortable with random and unpredictable occurrences leading to both positive and negative outcomes?
- *Patience.* Do clients allow time for their efforts to pay off? Do they wait for the seeds they plant to grow?

Treatment Goals

1. Seek out career-advancing opportunities proactively.
2. Anticipate and manage the industry's challenges.
3. Maximize creative fulfillment by managing occupational stress.
4. Learn to persevere in the face of obstacles.
5. Improve the overall balance between a career and personal life.

Suggested Interventions to Achieve Goals

1. *Provide resources.* Navigating the world of the arts-and-entertainment industry can be overwhelming. The lack of structure and the absence of tried and true career paths make it so professional artists have to figure things out for themselves. Clinicians who've accumulated knowledge on resources that can ease some of their clients' anxieties can direct clients on how to access information on acquiring health insurance, becoming a business owner, filing tax forms, getting union representation, applying for grants, and so forth. Other resources might include additional support for medical problems associated with injuries, eating disorders, and substance abuse.

   > Example: A 26-year-old painter I worked had just given up her teaching job to become a full-time artist. She became increasingly anxious as tax season was approaching. She was worrying about accurately representing how much she'd made and was terrified at the idea of owing money. I suggested that she look into the New York Foundation for the Arts[2] to access financial-planning resources. Knowing that there were resources she could take advantage of alleviated much of her stress.

2. *Set career goals.* Setting career goals is a great way to clarify which opportunities clients think are worth pursuing. Clinicians and clients can spend time articulating what clients hope to achieve. They can begin by clarifying their definitions of success and by establishing long-term and short-term goals. Doing so will give clients a sense of direction, reinforcing the idea that their actions are part of a purposeful plan.

   > Example: A photographer I worked with felt unsure as to what career steps to take next. Years of commercial photography had left her feeling discouraged and uninspired, yet worries about finances kept her there. When she decided to make an important career change by specializing in maternity portraits, we worked on setting specific goals and taking concrete steps to achieve them. She began by contacting others with similar expertise, doing some shoots for free to gain relevant experience, and giving out at least five business cards a week to start building a reputation.

3. *Separate the person from the career.* Clients' creative and self-identities are inevitably interconnected. Because of this, building a career around their creative identities makes it dangerously easy for artists and performers to equate professional success with personal worth. To prevent burnout from rejections and emotional exhaustion, it's important to draw a distinction between how clients fare in their careers and how they fare in life. Though it can be tempting for clients to seek validation about

personal worth through their number of gigs and sales, it's emotionally refreshing to recognize that they're more than their careers.

> Example: I once asked a jazz percussionist, who was discouraged by the number of gigs he had booked recently, to list activities and interactions that didn't center on professional success yet he found to be meaningful. He came up with spending time with his pet, volunteering for an environmental group, and reaching out to friends. He then identified personal traits not typically associated with his career, such as leadership skills and compassion. Doing so helped him see himself as more than a jazz musician who wasn't getting gigs.

4. *Cultivate an independent self-concept.* The study by Kim and colleagues (2012) included in this chapter describes how an independent self-concept turns social rejection into an impetus for creative thinking. Clinicians can work with clients on fostering their unconventionality and independence by discussing unique qualities, creative quirks, and prior achievements. Doing so can help reframe rejection as a validation of what sets them apart rather than as a reason to abandon their creative ideas.

> Example: An off-Broadway actress and I spent time discussing what sets her apart from other actors. After being rejected from an audition that was important to her, I asked her to think about her unique qualities—she came up with her distinct voice, her petite stature, and the expressive use of her body. Securing an independent self-concept increased her drive to find suitable roles that would represent her individuality and creative values.

5. *Identify occupational perks.* When clients feel disillusioned with their chosen careers, ask them to articulate the appeal of being part of the arts-and-entertainment industry. Some people might find the inherent creativity of a creative field to be overwhelmingly rewarding; others might emphasize the flexibility in work hours or the opportunities for collaborative work and travel.

> Example: A freelance saxophonist once complained of never having a reliable schedule and of never having predictable sleeping patterns. He then wondered how people with "normal jobs" do things such as go to the post office or the bank. I asked him to weigh the pros and cons of the two lifestyles. He acknowledged that the flip side of not having a set schedule was that he could do whatever he wanted almost whenever he wanted to.

6. *Reduce ambivalence about selling art.* Internal conflicts about profiting off art is a perpetual dilemma in the world of artists (Michels, 2009). Many hard-working creative individuals hesitate to promote their work, to

put a price on it, and to part with what they've created. They have the deeply rooted belief that selling art indicates lack of artistic identity, that making money from artwork automatically makes the art less authentic, or that commodifying their creativity diminishes its value. The problem with such beliefs is that they limit potential opportunities for financial and professional growth, and generate feelings of low self-worth by communicating the message that artists aren't worthy of being rewarded. Sessions can help clients make peace with the idea that they deserve to be compensated for their work.

> Example: A painter I once worked with was anxious about having to price her paintings. When I asked her to explore her thoughts about making money, she revealed attachment to the myth of the starving artist. She reported feeling that turning her art into a sellable product makes it less valuable. Our discussions focused on reframing the nature of the transaction: instead of being a dry exchange of art for money, the transaction ensured the buyer's aesthetic satisfaction and the artist's peace of mind that she'd have the funds to keep making art.

7. *Clarify the motivation behind choices.* It's easy to feel lost when confronted with all the possibilities for courses of action. To advance their careers, professional artists have a wide range of possible options: they can audition, set up meetings, go to others' shows, engage in social media, send newsletters, practice, create new content, and so forth. A discussion on why clients do what they do (whether, for example, it is for money, for improvement, or for social network expansion) helps them maintain focus and put more effort in their actions.

> Example: A professional drummer I worked with chose to spend a week creating short clips of himself playing complicated drum beats. At the end of each day, he posted one clip on his social media pages. I asked him to discuss what motivated him to do so. He responded that he wanted to pop up in followers' feeds in order to remain relevant. Clarifying the motivation behind his choice—in this case, to stay on followers' minds—helped him attach purpose to his actions.

8. *Encourage involvement in artistic communities.* Making connections with other artists, dealers, promoters, reviewers, and curators establishes one's place in the community and opens up opportunities. It creates a space for sharing similar experiences and provides access to social support. Clinicians can encourage their clients to think about ways to become involved in communities of like-minded creative people.

> Example: A young painter and part-time graduate student volunteered at a local collectively run art space. Initially doubtful about having what it takes to be around more accomplished artists,

188 Stress in the Arts-and-Entertainment World

I encouraged her to become a bigger part of the community by showing up to more meetings and hosting open mics. This increased her confidence and eased her transition from graduate school to the New York City art world.

9. *Build time-management skills.* Most professional artists' day-to-day life is unstructured. Unless they're working on a show or a project that has a set schedule, they'll likely find themselves wondering how to spend their days. This increases the risk of poor time management habits, such as sleeping at different times each day, multitasking, putting tasks off, and focusing on too many goals at once. Although it's important to maintain a reasonably flexible schedule, one that encourages the spontaneous pursuit of creative work, it's also important to set some time-management guidelines. Doing so helps artists develop expectations about how they want to spend their days.

> Example: One choreographer I worked with discovered that to make daily progress with his dance piece, he needed to have many things planned during the first part of the day. If he had no morning plans, he found himself waking up later, taking longer to warm up and start, and becoming more critical of his work. He and I brainstormed ways to commit to morning activities that would get him out of the house earlier in the day so that he'd be more inclined to work on the dance piece.

10. *Build money-management skills.* Professional artists often have mixed feelings about the role of money in their lives. How should they price their work? When should they stop spending money on art supplies or music gear? Does struggling financially mean they're making the wrong choices? Is it OK to spend the royalty check on celebrating? Clinicians can help their clients identify their spending patterns and the beliefs and habits that sustain them. Sessions can set expectations around money-related behaviors that align with clients' goals.

> Example: A socially anxious musician would spend a significant amount of money on drinks after shows to loosen up and talk to people. We worked on setting a budget for how much he wanted to spend on postshow drinks and how much to use for creative and professional development purposes. He decided to spend most of it on advertising and on a new guitar amplifier.

11. *Separate feelings from actions.* Creative professionals must approach tasks with an action-oriented mind-set. They must send out electronic press kits, call venues, send mass invites, apply to many opportunities, and so forth, without focusing on the negative feelings that might arise should things go poorly. Sessions can work on confronting the fears that take

away momentum from necessary tasks and, when possible, separating the negative feelings from the actions. Doing so helps them see such tasks as part of the job instead of an emotional minefield ready to explode with each disappointment.

> Example: Even though his budget was limited, a photographer I worked with agreed to hire a part-time assistant to do what he had labeled "the emotionally draining work." The assistant spoke to people on the phone and sent out hundreds of e-mails. Being less emotionally invested made these tasks easier for her, while my client felt satisfied that the work was getting done. He reported being glad that he wasn't "checking his e-mail account every 5 minutes."

Additional Interventions

12.
13.
14.

Takeaways

- A career in the arts-and-entertainment industry exposes creative professionals to erratic schedules, fluctuating income, success uncertainty, fierce competition, and other occupational stressors.
- Such stressors put clients at risk for burnout, discouragement, anxiety, and substance abuse.
- Counseling can help clients manage the negative consequences resulting from industry-related stress. It can investigate clients' efforts for success and identify psychological obstacles that hold them back.
- Clinicians and clients can work on strengthening psychological coping tools so that clients keep pursuing career-advancing opportunities.
- Sessions can instill hopefulness, clarify goals, and develop actionable plans so that clients can maintain the energy and optimism needed to achieve their creative and professional goals.

Notes

1 The descriptions of the arts-and-entertainment industry and statistical information presented in this chapter reflect the conditions in the United States. They may not accurately represent conditions in other countries.
2 NYFA is a resource that aims to help and empower artists; see www.nyfa.com.

References

Alper, N. O., & Wassall, G. H. (2000). *More than once in a blue moon: Multiple jobholdings by American artists.* Santa Ana, CA: National Endowment for the Arts. Retrieved from www.arts.gov/sites/default/files/BlueMoon.pdf

Benedek, M., Panzierer, L., Jauk, E., & Neubauer, A. C. (2017). Creativity on tap? Effects of alcohol intoxication on creative cognition. *Consciousness and Cognition, 56,* 128–134.

Bush, D. M., & Lipari, R. N. (2015). *The CBHSQ report: Substance use and substance use disorder, by industry.* Rockville, MD: Substance Abuse and Mental Health Services Administration, Center for Behavioral Health Statistics and Quality. Retrieved from www.samhsa.gov/data/sites/default/files/report_1959/ShortReport-1959.pdf

Center for Cultural Innovation. (2016). *Creativity connects: Trends and conditions affecting U.S. artists.* Washington, DC: National Endowment for the Arts. Retrieved from www.arts.gov/sites/default/files/Creativity-Connects-Final-Report.pdf

Chesky, K. S., & Hipple, J. (1999). Musicians' perceptions of widespread drug use among musicians. *Medical Problems of Performing Artists, 14*(4), 187–195. Retrieved from www.bls.gov/careeroutlook/2015/article/creative-careers.htm

Gaylin, D. H. (2015). *A profile of the performing arts industry: Culture and commerce.* New York, NY: Business Expert Press.

Hamilton, L. H. (1998). *Advice for dancers: Emotional counsel and practical strategies.* San Francisco, CA: Jossey-Bass.

Hamilton, L. H., & Kella, J. J. (1992). *Personality and occupational stress in elite performers.* Paper presented at the Centennial Annual Convention of the American Psychological Association, Washington, DC.

Hicks, J. A., Pedersen, S. L., Friedman, R. S., & McCarthy, D. M. (2011). Expecting innovation: psychoactive drug primes and the generation of creative solutions. *Experimental and Clinical Psychopharmacology, 19*(4) 314–320.

Hill, A. (2001). *Making it in the business: Overcoming obstacles and achieving your goals in the entertainment industry.* Berkeley, CA: Center Press.

Jackson, M. R., Kabwasa-Green, F., Swenson, D., Herranz, J. Jr., Ferryman, K., Atlas, C., & Rosenstein, C. (2003). *Investing in creativity: A study of the support structure for U.S. artists.* Culture, Creativity, and Communities Program, Urban Institute. Retrieved from http://webarchive.urban.org/UploadedPDF/411311_investing_in_creativity.pdf

Kim, S. H., Vincent, L. C., & Goncalo, J. (2012). *Outside advantage: Can social rejection fuel creative thought?* Retrieved from http://digitalcommons.ilr.cornell.edu/articles/613

Lapp, W. M., Collins, R. L., & Izzo, C. V. (1994). On the enhancement of creativity by alcohol: Pharmacology or expectation? *American Journal of Psychiatry, 107*(2), 173–206.

Lauring, J. O., Pelowski, M., Forster, M., Gondan, M., Ptito, M., & Kupers, R. (2016). Well, if they like it. . . . Effects of social groups' ratings and price information on the appreciation of art. *Psychology of Aesthetics, Creativity, and the Arts, 10*(3), 344–359.

Michels, C. (2009). *How to survive and prosper as an artist: Selling yourself without selling your soul.* New York, NY: Holt Paperbacks.

National Endowment for the Arts. (2011). *Artists and arts workers in the United States.* NEA research note #105. Retrieved from www.arts.gov/sites/default/files/105.pdf

Pritzker, S. (1999). Writing and creativity. In M. A. Runco & S. R. Pritzker (Eds.), *Encyclopedia of creativity* (Vol. 2, pp. 727–735). London, UK: Academic Press.

Schaufeli, W. B., Leiter, M. P., & Maslach, C. (2009). Burnout: 35 years of research and practice. *Career Development International, 14*(3), 204–220.

Strategic National Arts Alumni Project. (2015). *Annual report*. Retrieved from http://snaap.indiana.edu/pdf/2015/2015_Sample_SNAAP_Institutional_Report.pdf

Thomson, P., & Jaque, S.V. (2017). *Creativity and the performing artist: Behind the mask*. London, UK: Academic Press.

Tuisku, K., Houni, P., Seppanen, J., & Virtanen, M. (2016). Association between unstable work and occupational wellbeing among artists in Finland: Results of a psychosocial survey. *Medical Problems of Performing Artists, 31*(2), 104–109.

Wolkewitz, M., Allignol, A., Graves, N., & Barnett, A. G. (2011). Is 27 really a dangerous age for famous musicians? Retrospective cohort study. *The BMJ, 343*, d7799. Retrieved from http://doi.org/10.1136/bmj.d7799

Index

Abraham, Anna 93
absorb state 37
ADHD *see* attention deficit hyperactivity disorder (ADHD)
aging 180
aha moments 27
Alexander technique 139, 141
Amabile, T. M. 13
American Community Survey 176
anxiety 17, 60; eye-movement desensitization reprocessing (EMDR) for 86; offstage 138–139; performance and audition (*see* performance and audition anxiety); reframed as excitement 141; trusting the 87
Arcelus, J. 151
Aronofsky, Darren 153
art-body synergy 159
Arthur-Cameselle, J. 159
Artist's Way, The 43
assertiveness 69–70, 156, 170
attention, sustained 98
attention deficit hyperactivity disorder (ADHD) 90, 92–94; brain-activation patterns in 95–96; clinician's role in addressing 94–97; dialectical behavioral therapy for 99–100; establishing an accurate diagnosis of 95; improving social functioning with 96–97; maximizing benefits, minimizing impairment with 94–95; social skills with 96–97, 99; strengthening self-esteem in 96; suggested interventions to achieve goals with 97–100; treatment goals 97; understanding brain-activation patterns in 95–96; working with symptoms of 100
audience in performance and audition anxiety 134–136

audition stress 177–178; *see also* performance and audition anxiety
authenticity 72
automatic thoughts 138
autonomy 16

Baas, M. 18
balance, sense of 14
Bandura, Albert 46
Batey, M. 124
Bergman, Ingmar 61
beta-blockers 144
bipolar disorder 90, 92, 110–112; addressing how symptoms help the creative process in 112–113; addressing stigma associated with 116; assessing the interaction of bipolar traits in 113–114; clinician's role in addressing 112–114; dispelling myths surrounding 118; distinguishing between confident and delusional thinking in 114–115; medication management of 117; mood journals for 115–116; overall lifestyle changes for 118–119; preparing for mood volatility in 113; protecting creativity during treatment for 114; reflecting during depression in 117–118; stabilizing mood in 116–117; suggested interventions to achieve goals for 115–119; treatment goals 115; using hypomania as a creative tool in 115
Black Swan 153
blocks, creativity 25–26; causes of 29–31; clinician's role in addressing 31–34; context of 31–34; identifying stage in 32; identifying strategies to overcome 33–34; low motivation and 28–29; trauma role in blocking 82; types of 26–27

194 Index

bodies, artists' and performers' 149–150; eating disorders and 150–161; injuries to 161–171
Bourgeois, James 144
Bowie, David 47
brain-activation patterns in ADHD 95–96
brainspotting 145–146
breathing and posture 139, 141
brooding 105–106
Brooks, A. W. 141
Brown, Thomas 98
burnout 181
busy schedules 21

Cameron, Julia 43
carpal tunnel syndrome (CTS) 163
Carson, Shelly 30, 37, 111, 121
Chang, W. 11
chasing the flow 36–37
Claridge, G. 123
clinicians: creativity-sensitive treatment by 1; role in addressing stress 182–184; role with ADHD 94–97; role with bipolar disorder 112–114; role with creative motivation issues 14–17; role with creativity blocks 31–34; role with depression 103–106; role with eating disorders 154–157; role with injuries 165–168; role with performance and audition anxiety 137–140; role with personal and professional relationships 65–67; role with psychotic disorders 122–123; role with self-doubts 47–50; role with trauma and creativity 80–83; variety of clients seen by 1; see also treatment interventions
close loved ones, relationships with 64–65, 68–69
Cobain, Kurt 64
cognitive defusion 51
cognitive skills and trauma 85–86
Colbert, Stephen 10
collaborations, creative 20–21, 60–62
competence, building of 53
competition stress 177–178
competitors and gatekeepers, relationships with 62–63
concentrative meditation 37–38
confidence 69–70, 114
conflict resolution 21
confrontation of criticism 19
Consensual Assessment Technique 43

context of creativity blocks 31–34
counseling see treatment interventions
creating in the middle of things 35
creative clients 1–2; bodies of (see bodies, artists' and performers'); creative blocks in (see blocks, creativity); eating disorders in (see eating disorders); income of 11, 176–177, 188; injuries in (see injuries); lifestyle differences among 2–3; motivation in 18; need to be different 11; with performance and audition anxiety (see performance and audition anxiety); personal and professional relationships of (see relationships, personal and professional); with psychiatric disorders (see psychiatric disorders); psychiatric disorders in (see psychiatric disorders); right to create 49; self-doubts in (see self-doubts); trauma in (see trauma, psychological)
creative identity 10, 54, 169–170, 185–186
creative motivation see motivation, creative
creative process, understanding the 31–32; trauma effects and 77–79
creative thinkers 1
creativity 2; blocks in (see blocks, creativity); emphasizing the value of creating and 16; many forms of 8–9; stages of 27–28, 32; trauma and (see trauma, psychological); unlearning harmful lessons about 33
Creativity and Madness: Psychological Studies of Art and Artists 75
Creativity in Science: Chance, Logic, Genius, and Zeitgeist 30
creativity-sensitive treatment 1
criticism, confronting 19
Csikszentmihalyi, M. 32–33, 65

Dance Magazine 151
Deci, Edward 11
deciding to matter 16
decreased latent inhibition 120
defusion, cognitive 51
delusional thinking 114
depression 90, 92, 100–103; clinician's role in addressing 103–106; distinguishing between ruminating and brooding in 105–106; encouraging art

activities for 106–107; encouraging creative habits in 105; encouraging persistence through rumination in 108–109; establishing the right work pace for 108; exploring the interaction between creativity and 103–104; identifying challenges with 107–108; interpreting feelings of 104; listening to clients' inner voices and 107; managing occupational triggers for 109–110; recognizing accomplishments and 109; reflecting during 117–118; suggested interventions to achieve goals for 106–110; treatment goals 106; triggered by occupational stress 105

desensitization through creativity 84

Diagnostic and Statistical Manual (DSM) 150

dialectical behavioral therapy (DBT) 99–100

Dickinson, Emily 61, 110

Dijksterhuis, A. 27

distracting environment as creative block 29–30

divergent thinking 93, 94, 111

Djikic, Maja 102

domain-specific knowledge 25

Dylan, Bob 47

eating disorders 150–151; appreciating performers' conflicts with 154–155; balancing the need to be healthy with industry standards in 156–157; clinician's role in addressing 154–157; distinguishing between self-referenced and interpersonal comparisons with 161; empowering vulnerable clients to avoid 155–156; encouraging conversations about eating habits and 158–159; encouraging experimentation with roles and 160; health effects of 154; increasing assertiveness to avoid 156; mindful eating for 159; "negotiating" with industry standards and 158; perfectionism and 153, 159–160; prevalence and performing-arts culture 151–153; promoting art-body synergy and 159; referral to nutritionists for 160–161; substituting emphasis on size with emphasis on health for 157; suggested interventions to achieve goals 157–161; treatment

goals 157; using psychoeducation with 155

Eat Pray Love 52

Eisenberg, J. 63

entitlement, sense of 52

environment, considering the 38

Erez, M. 38

erratic schedules and traveling, stress of 179–180

excitement, reframing anxiety as 141

expertise as creative block 29

expressive therapies, benefits of 77, 85

extraneous variables in performance and audition anxiety 134–136

extrinsic motivation 12–13

eye-movement desensitization reprocessing (EMDR) 86

Eysenck Personality Questionnaire 120

failure, permission for 52

fans, followers, and students, relationships with 64

Farmer, Steven 46

financial stress 176–177, 188

flow, chasing the 36–37

followers, relationships with 64

Forgeard, Marie 79

Furnham, A. 111, 124

gatekeepers and competitors, relationships with 62–63

giftedness 65

Gilbert, Elizabeth 52

goals, treatment: ADHD 97; bipolar disorder 115; creative blocks 34; creative motivation 17; depression 106; eating disorders 157; helping clients with setting of specific 19–20; injuries 168; performance and audition anxiety 140; personal and professional relationships 68; psychotic disorders 123; self-doubts 50; stress 184; trauma and creativity 83

Grand, David 145

Gregoire, C. 45, 61

groups and collaborations 60–62

guided-imagery 171

guided meditation 140

habits 15–16; for addressing creative blocks 32–33; after injuries 169; encouraging conversations about

eating 158–159; implementing healthy competitive practices and 70–71; preparation 145; social skills and 67; that foster creative self-efficacy 53–54
Hamilton, Linda 151, 163–164, 165
Harry Potter series 180
Heilman, Kenneth 31, 103
hyperreflexivity 126
hypomania 111–112, 114, 115

identity, creative 10, 54, 169–170, 185–186
improvisation 35–36
income in creative careers 11, 176–177, 188
incubation 27, 36
injured psyche 164
injuries 150, 161–162; building self-efficacy after 170–171; career-ending 164–165, 167; clinician's role in addressing 165–168; coming to terms with life changes due to 167; emphasizing other identities after 169–170; encouraging assertiveness after 170; exploring how clients think about their 166; guided-imagery and relaxation exercises after 171; guiding clients throughout treatment for their 166–167; managing life stress and 168; managing the pace of return to creative activity after 167–168; need for specialized care for 162–163; psychological effects of 163–165; reconsidering habits and technique after 169; referral to rehabilitative professionals for 168–169; suggested interventions to achieve goals 168–171; supporting clients' worries about 165–166; treatment goals 168
inner voices 107
inoculation, stress 144–145
intensive short-term dynamic psychotherapy (ISTDP) 143
interventions *see* treatment interventions
interviewing, motivational 17–18
intrinsic motivation 12–13, 20
introversion 59–60
inverted-U hypothesis 101, 122–123

Jamison, Kay Redfield 110
Jaque, S.V. 63–64, 77, 137, 152
Jarman, Matthew 26

Johnson, S. L. 113
Jones, M. 102
journals: mood 115–116; motivation 18

Kaufman, S. B. 45, 61
Kaufmann, A. 103
Kaufmann, G. 103
"keep at it" strategy 34
Kelly, V. C. 135
Kendall, J. 80
Kenny, D. 143
Kim, S. H. 180, 186
Kinney, D. 112
Kluger, A. N. 19
Kyaga, S. 110–111, 120

Lauring, J. O. 43, 178
leaky attention 94
lifestyle changes for bipolar disorder 118–119
low motivation 28–29

mad artist archetype 91
magical and unusual experiences 120
Maisel, Eric 16, 35, 71, 102
Making Your Creative Mark 71
mantras, motivation 20
Marshall, Barry 58
Martin, Demetri 10
meaningful messages, finding 19
medication management: of ADHD 99; of bipolar disorder 117; for performance and audition anxiety 144; of psychotic disorders 123, 127
meditation: concentrative 37–38; guided 140
mental illness *see* psychiatric disorders
mental itches 26
mentors and teachers, relationships with 63–64, 70
messages, meaningful 19
Michels, Caroll 62
Miller, R. W. 17
mindful concentration 38
mindful eating 159
mindfulness 38, 98, 159
Misdiagnosis and Dual Diagnoses of Gifted Children and Adults: ADHD, Bipolar, OCD, Asperger's, Depression, and Other Disorders 94
Mitchell, J. T. 98
Mohr, C. 123

Index   197

money-management skills 188
mood, improvement of 18–19
mood elevation 111–112
mood journals 115–116
mood stabilization 116–117
mood volatility 113
motivation, creative 8–9; clinician's
    role in addressing 14–17; conflicting
    goals and 13; creativity blocks and
    low 28–29; intrinsic versus extrinsic
    rewards and 12–13, 20; patterns of
    14–15; in professional artists 10–11;
    psychological well-being and 9–10;
    reasons for faltering of 12–17; thoughts
    of unworthiness and 14
motivational interviewing 17–18
motivational synergy, model of 13
motivation journals 18
motivation mantras 20
Mozart, Wolfgang Amadeus 75
Museum of Modern Art, New York 180

naming the rewards 15
natural curiosity 37
need to be different 11
negative thoughts and feelings 17, 37;
    about self-perception 47–48; in
    anxiety 17; automatic 138; challenging
    142–143; in depression 104, 109;
    encouraging optimism to counter
    52–53; fostering a sense of entitlement
    to counter 52; guided meditation for
    140; separating actions from 188–189
networking 70
New Yorker 180
nonconformity 58–59
Nouri, R. 38
nutritionists 160–161

Oatley, Keith 102
occupational stress 105, 109–110
O'Keeffe, Georgia 61
optimism 52–53
orthorexia 155
osteopathic physicians 168–169
outcome blocks 26–27, 30
overinclusive thoughts 120

Pearl Jam 64
Pennebaker, James 77
perceived threats 137–138
perfectionism 153, 159–160

performance and audition anxiety
    133–134; assessing anxiety offstage
    and 138–139; beta-blockers for 144;
    brainspotting for 145–146; challenging
    negative thoughts and 142–143;
    clinician's role in addressing 137–140;
    consequences of 137; contributing
    factors to 134–136; creating safety
    images for 142; discerning what
    the audience represents in 140;
    emphasizing the artistic content for
    145; enhancing personal creative
    agency for 143; exploring perceived
    threats in 137–138; focus on breathing
    and posture for 139, 141; identifying
    automatic thoughts in 138; physical
    exercise for 144; preparation habits for
    145; putting physical reactions into
    perspective in 139–140; reframing
    anxiety as excitement for 141; role of
    psychological defenses against 143; role
    of unconscious emotions in 136–137;
    stress inoculation for 144–145;
    suggested interventions to achieve
    goals 141–146; treatment goals 140;
    visualization for 141–142
performed work in performance and
    audition anxiety 134–136
performing-arts culture and eating
    disorders 151–153
personal creative agency 143
personality traits in performance and
    audition anxiety 134–136
physical exercise for performance and
    audience anxiety 144
physical therapists 168–169
Picasso, Pablo 75
Plath, Sylvia 110, 180
positive psychology 54–55
posttraumatic growth 79–80
posttraumatic stress disorder (PTSD) 80
preparation habits 145
prioritizing 98
process blocks 26–27
professional artists, creative motivation in
    10–11
Proust, Marcel 61
psychiatric disorders 90–92; attention
    deficit hyperactivity disorder 90,
    92–100; bipolar disorder 90, 92,
    110–119; depression 90, 92, 100–110;
    psychotic disorders 90, 92, 119–128

psychoeducation 155
psychological characteristics in creative blocks 32–33
psychotic disorders 90, 92, 119–121; building social skills for those with 125; clinician's role in addressing 122–123; connecting psychotic symptoms to the right 124; creative impacts of symptoms of 122–123; evaluating substance abuse comorbidity with 125; identifying role played by schizotypal traits in 124–125; including the family in interventions for 126; medication management of 123, 127; suggested interventions to achieve goals for 124–127; treatment goals 123; understanding clients' needs in 122; using art to communicate in 126–127

recently activated knowledge task 94
reconnecting clients with their creative drive 14
reflection: during depression 117–118; on successes 51
rehabilitative professionals 168–169
rejections, stress of 180–181
relationships, personal and professional 57–58; clinician's role in addressing 65–67; with close loved ones 64–65; with competitors and gatekeepers 62–63; with fans, followers, and students 64; groups and collaborations and 60–62; introversion and 59–60; managing demands placed by close 68–69; nonconformity and 58–59; nurturing 71; suggested interventions to achieve goals with 68–72; with teachers and mentors 63–64
relaxation exercises 171
repetitive strain injury (RSI) 150, 162; *see also* injuries
Richards, R. 112
right to create, validating the client's 49
risk taking, fostering of 34–35
Riter, S. M. 27
Robinson, Ken 92–93
Rollnick, S. 17
Rothenberg, Albert 114
Rowling, J. K. 180
Roy, M. 102
RSI *see* repetitive strain injury (RSI)
rumination 102–103, 105–106, 108–109
Ryan, Richard 11

safety images 142
Saltz, Gail 102, 112
Sass, Louis 126
Saveanu, R. 135
Sawyer, K. 65
schizotypal traits 111, 120, 124–125
Schumann, Robert 110
self-acceptance 49–50, 104
self-blame 86–87
self-concept, cultivation of independent 186
self-defeating attitudes 109
self-determination theory 11
self-doubts 42–43; causes of 43–45; clinician's role in addressing 47–50; creative self-efficacy and 46–50; suggested interventions to achieve goals with 51–55; treatment goals 50
self-efficacy, creative 46–50, 53–54, 170–171
self-esteem and ADHD 96
self-identity 10
self-motivated creative activity 11
self-perception, attachment to negative 47–48
sense of entitlement 52
Shah, Prit 94
shared vulnerability model 111
Shelley, Mary 75
Silverman, L. K. 45
Simonton, Dean 30, 34
Slate 58
"sleeping on it" strategy 36
slow-moving careers 178–179
social skills 67; with ADHD 96–97, 99; in psychotic disorders 125
social stigma 116
stages of creativity 27–28, 32
Sternberg, R. J. 35
Stien, P. T. 80
stigma, social 116
Strategic National Arts Alumni Project 177
strengths-based therapy 54–55
stress 175; addressing factors for career success and 184; of aging 180; burnout 181; clarifying motivation behind choices and 187; clinician's role in addressing 182–184; competition 177–178; cultivating an independent self-concept for 186; encouraging involvement in artistic communities and 187–188; of erratic schedules and

traveling 179–180; financial 176–177, 188; identifying occupational perks and 186; inoculation against 144–145; life 168; maintaining a hopeful outlook for success and 182; managing the "hustle" 182–183; providing resources for 185; recognizing the need to step away and 183–184; reducing ambivalence about selling art and 186–187; of rejections 180–181; separating feelings from actions and 188–189; separating the person from the career and 185–186; setting career goals and 185; of slow-moving careers 178–179; substance abuse and 181–182; suggested interventions to achieve goals 185–189; taking a look at the creative work and 183; time-management skills and 188; treatment goals 184; of wearing many hats 176

students, relationships with 64

Stumpf, H. 13

substance abuse 125, 181–182

Substance Abuse and Mental Health Services Administration 181

successes, reflecting on 51

sustained attention 98

talking about the work 69

task mastery 135–136

teachers and mentors, relationships with 63–64, 70

Thompson, W. F. 63

Thomson, P. 63–64, 77, 137, 152

Tierney, Pamela 46

time-management skills 38–39, 97–98, 188

Tortured Artists 75

Touched with Fire 110

touring artists 179–180

trauma, psychological 75–76; awakening the need for creativity 76; benefits of expressive therapies for 77; clinician's role in addressing 80–83; effects on the creative process 77–79; posttraumatic growth and posttraumatic stress after 79–80; suggested interventions to achieve goals with 83–87; treatment goals for creativity and 83

traveling, stress of 179–180

treatment interventions: addressing attachment to negative self-perception 47–48; addressing habits

and psychological characteristics 32–33; addressing self-blame 86–87; approaching trauma with caution in 81–82; assessing openness to incorporating creativity after trauma 80–81; for attention deficit hyperactivity disorders 94–100; beta-blockers 144; bipolar disorder 115–119; for bipolar disorder 112–119; brainspotting 145–146; building cognitive skills related to trauma 85–86; building confidence and assertiveness in clients 69–70; building money-management skills 188; building self-efficacy 170–171; building social skills for those with psychotic disorders 125; building time-management skills 38–39, 97–98, 188; challenging negative thoughts 142–143; clarifying motivation behind choices 187; creative blocks 34–39; creative motivation problems 17–21; cultivating independent self-concept 186; densensitization 84; for depression 103–110; determining the root of the conflict 66–67; dispelling myths where they exist 118; distinguishing between self-referenced and interpersonal comparisons 161; for eating disorders 157–161; emphasizing other identities after injury 169–170; emphasizing the artistic content 145; emphasizing the value of creating 16; encouraging art activities 106–107; encouraging assertiveness 69–70, 156, 170; encouraging conversations about eating habits 158–159; encouraging experimentation with roles 160; encouraging involvement in artistic communities 187–188; encouraging networking and the search for a mentor 70; encouraging persistence through rumination 108–109; encouraging self-acceptance 49–50; enhancing feelings of autonomy 16; enhancing personal creative agency 143; establishing an accurate diagnosis of ADHD and 95; establishing the right work pace 108; evaluating substance abuse comorbidity with psychotic disorders 125; examining anxiety and other negative feelings 17; exploring helpful habits 15–16; family inclusion in psychotic disorders' 126; focus on breathing and

200 Index

posture 139, 141; guided-imagery and relaxational exercises 171; helping build social skills 67; identifying challenges with depression 107–108; identifying occupational perks 186; identifying problematic relationships 65–66; identifying strategies to overcome blocks 33–34; identifying the blocked stage 32; improving social functioning with ADHD 96–97; including others in 68; for injuries 168–171; integrating trauma responses 83; listening to clients' inner voices 107; looking at clients' work 48–49; looking for clues to trauma in creative work 84–85; looking for what feels authentic 72; looking into clients' motivation patterns 14–15; managing life stress 168; managing occupational triggers for depression 109–110; managing perfectionism 159–160; mindful eating 159; naming the rewards 15; "negotiating" with industry standards 158; nurturing relationships 71; overall lifestyle changes 118–119; performance and audition anxiety 141–146; physical exercise 144; practicing talking about the work with clients 69; preparation habits 145; promoting art-body synergy 159; psychological defenses 143; psychotic disorders 124–128; recognizing accomplishments 109; reconnecting clients with their creative drive 14; reconsidering habits and technique after injuries 169; reducing ambivalence about selling art 186–187; referral to nutritionists 160–161; referral to rehabilitative professionals 168–169; reflecting during depression 117–118; reframing anxiety as excitement 141; relationship issues 68–72; role in addressing relationship issues 65–67; role in addressing self-doubt 47–50; role in helping with creative motivation 14–17; role in understanding the creative process 31–32; role in unlearning harmful lessons about creativity 33; safety images 142; seeing the good in others 71–72; self-doubts 50–55; separating feelings from actions 188–189; separating the person from the career 185–186; setting career goals 185; stabilizing mood 116–117; strengthening self-esteem with ADHD 96; stress 144–145, 185–189; stress inoculation 144–145; substituting emphasis on size with emphasis on health 157; suggested interventions to achieve goals 17–21; trauma and creativity 80–87; trusting the anxiety 87; for understanding how trauma affects performers 82, 83–84; for understanding how trauma blocks creativity 82; for understanding the person's disposition 66; using art to communicate 126–127; utilizing expressive therapy methods in 85; validating clients' right to create 49; visualization 141–142

unconscious emotions in performance and audition anxiety 136–137
unworthiness, thoughts of 14

value of creating 16
Van Dijk, D. 19
Van Gogh, Vincent 110
Vedder, Eddie 64
Verhaeghen, P. 102
Verkuillen, J. 102
visualization 141–142

Warhol, Andy 31, 180
Warren, Robin 58–59
Webb, J. T. 94
White, Holly 94
Williams, Hank 47
Winner, E. 45
Wolkewitz, M. 181
Wyszormirski, M. J. 11

Young, L. N. 103, 106

Zabelina, D. 12, 94, 100
Zampetakis, L. A. 38
Zara, Christopher 75